ARTHUR F. BUEHLER is Senior Lecturer in Religious Studies Emeritus at Victoria University of Wellington and Senior Editor of the *Journal of the History of Sufism*. He is the author of several books, including *Sufi Heirs of the Prophet: The Indian Naqshbandiyya and the Rise of the Mediating Sufi Shaykh* and *Revealed Grace: The Juristic Sufism of Ahmad Sirhindi, 1564–1624*.

'All too often students complain, after reading an introduction to Sufism, that they have learned about historical developments and some major Sufi figures and yet still know very little about what it truly means to be a seeker on the Sufi path. Arthur F. Buehler's new introduction offers astute guidance for the reader embarking on a study of Islam's major contemplative tradition.'

ELIZABETH SIRRIYEH, Senior Lecturer Emerita in
Islamic Studies, University of Leeds

'This readable survey places contemplation and transformation at the heart of Sufism, past and present. Based on deep familiarity with texts and practices, *Recognizing Sufism* covers doctrines, teaching methods, pilgrimages and politics, with an emphasis on the spiritual purpose of the Sufi path. Erudite and engaging, Buehler's book blends the scholarly and personal with rare poise.'

NILE GREEN, Professor of History, UCLA, author of
Sufism: A Global History

Recognizing Sufism

Contemplation in the Islamic Tradition

Arthur F. Buehler

I.B. TAURIS
LONDON · NEW YORK

In memory of
Annemarie Schimmel
(1922–2003)

Scholar of heart

Published in 2016 by
I.B.Tauris & Co. Ltd
London • New York
www.ibtauris.com

ISBN: 978 1 84885 789 6 (HB)
       978 1 84885 790 2 (PB)
eISBN: 978 0 85772 981 1
ePDF: 978 0 85772 783 1

A full CIP record for this book is available from the British Library
A full CIP record is available from the Library of Congress

Library of Congress Catalog Card Number: available

Typeset by Fakenham Prepress Solutions, Fakenham NR21 8NN
Printed and bound in Great Britain by T.J. International, Padstow, Cornwall

MIX
Paper from
responsible sources
FSC
www.fsc.org   FSC® C013056

CONTENTS

ILLUSTRATIONS

PREFACE

BOOKS INTRODUCING THE subject of sufism would benefit from having detailed labels, just like processed food. A reader has the right to understand the background of the author, whether academic or sufi. The first step in this direction is authorial transparency. The second is for the author to be sceptical about what he thinks he knows. This writer is not a sufi, yet is writing about sufis after working with sufis and reading hundreds of books on sufism over the past 25 years. This is akin to someone who sits with people drinking wine in taverns all over the world and who has read hundreds of catalogues and descriptions of wine, but who has never really tasted wine except accidentally a few drops here and there.

It is only recently that I have begun to realize the importance of self-disclosure. My first book, *Sufi Heirs of the Prophet*, written as a pre-tenured assistant professor, deliberately omitted some background details, both for personal reasons and for the safety of readers, because it was (and still is) physically dangerous, especially for foreigners, to visit those discussed in the text. Often there are other good reasons for not revealing one's collaborators because sufi activity is more than frowned upon in some countries and may even result in jail sentences. In my last book, *Revealed Grace*, I became over-zealous about self-disclosure and was kindly reminded by Professor Chodkiewicz that his reference to the initiatory robe of Ibn al-'Arabi was necessarily non-specific in order to protect one of his colleagues.

This is a good reminder for me not to take what I think I know too seriously. The following is a short synopsis of my involvement with sufism. It is a sufi story because most of the people in it are sufi teachers. How did I come to know about sufism? I first studied with the late and great Annemarie Schimmel (d. 2003).[1] In Pakistan the late Sayfurrahman Sahib (d. 2010) taught me a repertoire of the Naqshbandi contemplative practices. (Naqshbandi is the name of a sufi lineage/set of practices named after Baha'uddin Naqshband, d. 1389 in Bukhara, Uzbekistan). Sayfurrahman Sahib was a grandshaykh, with hundreds of visitors each day coming from all over the eastern Islamic world and beyond. In my case, there did not seem to be any significant ego transformation or ethical improvement from this 'assembly line approach' of sufi transmission. This type of teaching is common elsewhere and, as a result, teaching certificates often have nothing to do with progress on the sufi path.

The transformative sufi learning that I encountered while I was seeing Sayfurrahman Sahib was achieved in such a skilful manner that I did not realize my actual sufi teacher had been the late Hakim Muhammad Musa Amritsari (d. 1999). Hakim Sahib, as his name indicates, was a Greek medical doctor based in Lahore, Pakistan. He was also a sufi practitioner in the Chishti sufi lineage (named after Mu'inuddin Chishti, d. 1236, Ajmer, Rajasthan, India) and a recognized scholar of sufism. Hakim Sahib was the person, more than anyone else, who was able to help me search for important texts that could be discovered scattered around Pakistan.

Walking through a room with pots of boiling herbs, I would enter the small room where people in the neighbourhood came for medical treatment and where scholars and writers came to talk to Hakim Sahib. He carried on a two- or three-way conversation with the scholars. When the line of patients on his left reached three individuals, he would pause and take care of them, examining their pulses and looking at their tongues. I went there about twice a week. Hakim Sahib, knowing my fixation on gathering texts, gave me seven or eight tasks that held out a promise of finding some books. He sent me to all kinds of places – Qur'an schools, mosques, shops and offices. After completing these errands I reported back to him. Sometimes, when the search was unsuccessful, he would smile, reach down and hand me the book I had been looking for.

This went on for about a year before Hakim Sahib sent me out to sufi lodges in the Panjab and the Northwest Frontier Province (now called Khyber Pakhtunkhwa). This latter task was Hakim Sahib's way of introducing me to a common ongoing phenomenon (globally as I later discovered from my colleagues) of what people perceived as 'sufi activity'. Having visited a couple of dozen Naqshbandi sufi lodges in those provinces, it was very unexpected for me to observe that they had dispensed with transformative Naqshbandi practices and formal ethical guidance. After six months I returned, depressed and disillusioned, to Lahore, hoping that I had missed something. Instead Hakim Sahib, with a laugh, said that they were just going through the motions and that it had been this way for at least two generations.

It was not until I arrived back in the US and started reading the hundreds of texts gathered in the previous two years that I realized how much I had learned about Indo-Muslim culture and sufi practice as a direct result of Hakim Sahib's errands. I also experienced a sudden and intimate awareness about Hakim Sahib. It became clear that he had given me a most precious gift: his example. All I had ever seen him do was give freely to others. He showed me that which can never be communicated in words and this has left a very lasting impression on my heart: a poignant example of how sufi teaching can happen without the banner of sufism.

Another source of my sufi learning has been through the privilege of meeting sufis from all over the world at an annual conference organized by Drs Nahid Angha and Ali Kianfar under the auspices of the International Association of Sufism. Over the years I have come to develop many friendships with people I have met at these gatherings. Translating the sufi letters of Ahmad Sirhindi (d. 1624), I had the privilege of working with the late Shaykh Ma'sum Naqshbandi (d. 2007) from Biyara, Iraq, whom I met through Dr. Ahmed Mirza, head of the Naqshbandi Foundation for Islamic Education. Since 2009 I have had the great honour of a gifted teacher, a student of the late Hazrat Azad Rasool Sahib (d. 2006), finding me and giving me an opportunity to learn about myself.

When people ask me what I study, the invariable follow-up question is, 'What is sufism?' I reply, 'Islamic mysticism.' This is a conventional answer, reinforced by Annemarie Schimmel's classic *Mystical Dimensions of Islam*.

Literally no one ever asks the follow-up question of what mysticism is. I suspect that it is not because mysticism is a clear term. Quite the contrary. It is a mystifyingly vague term. But it is a *commonly known* vague term that allows people to put sufism in a mental box. Ideally this book will help the reader to recycle such boxes and/or to have an expanded and open-ended conceptual box.

Recognizing Sufism is written for those who know little or nothing about sufism but want a *serious* introduction. In some respects this book delves deeper than many advanced academic books written on sufism, because it questions the pre-suppositions that those text-centred authors take for granted. It is another perspective, one that attempts to bridge both the academic study of sufism and the practice of sufism. For those new to the subject, the book's message is that there are well-trodden pathways to support us in transforming the ego-ridden suffering that we inflict on ourselves every day.[2]

The process of sufism is a radical transformation, equivalent to the transition between a caterpillar and a butterfly. For sufi aspirants, this book serves as a window on sufism across lineages, cultures and time – an incredibly diverse and contradictory set of phenomena. The reader who prefers simplicity and apparent closure on subjects will experience forays into complexity and paradox. Sufism is a controversial (sometimes), globally vast and unusual subject – and warrants patience. The consensus of scholars studying sufism is that more than half of the 1.7+ billion Muslims on the planet are associated in some way with sufism.[3] Something is definitely going on – more than you can imagine.

My main qualification for writing this book is having spent almost all of my adult life in sufi kindergarten, repeating and repeating and repeating, reading and reading and reading. It makes no difference if you have just walked in – we may very well be sitting in the same classroom. Let me show you around.

ACKNOWLEDGEMENTS

WITHOUT AN INVITATION from Alex Wright, the executive editor at I.B.Tauris, I would have never considered writing an introductory book on sufism. Thank you, Alex, for being a pleasure to work with. At the time of his request one unfilled niche for introductions to sufism was an integrative focus on the transformative aspects of sufi practice. Another gaping lacuna was communicating the global, multicultural diversity of sufism. I intended to fill both of these large gaps with my to-be-written book. Soon after signing the book contract, Nile Green's global history of sufism appeared, allowing me to focus on one theme. I thank the 'Green man' for his useful work, thereby rescuing me from the difficult task of covering two themes within one book. Shamim Humayun graciously drew the Nasruddin diagram and gave me much valuable feedback on preliminary drafts. Along the way, Nurhan Atasoy, Irfan Basik, Marianne Buehler, Ibrahim Gamard, Kabir Helminski, Ekrem Işın, Shabda Kahn, Michael Kemper, Al and Polly Roberts, Alexandre Sawczuk da Silva and Thierry Zarcone have assisted me in certain important details (see endnotes and photo credits). The research for the book was finished in late 2013 and the sources after that date have not been consulted systematically. Bridget Lely has marvellously copy-edited the book manuscript with a follow-up by Kim Storry.

It is likely that readers will enjoy the chapter of interviews with Camalnur Sargut and Nahid Angha. Often when my students were asked in teacher evaluations about what they liked best about my classes, they would comment positively on the guest speakers. So know, Camalnur and Nahid, that your presence in this short book is much appreciated. My wife Josemi has been a constant support in all my endeavours, more than I realize. It is a great blessing for me that she is in my life.

INTRODUCTION:
SUFISM, SUFIS AND
TRANSFORMATION

*It shall take a long-term, keenly processed, whole-world paradigm shift in
our consciousness to perceive, acknowledge, and accept that all that we see,
hear, smell, touch and taste are but five tiny shells on one small dune on
the cosmic beachhead of Everywhere Else.*

BARRY WINDSOR-SMITH, *OPUS, VOLUME TWO*[1]

NASRUDDIN IS A well-known wise-fool character in many parts of the
world. One evening, Nasruddin's neighbour saw him under the oil light
in front of his house, searching for something on the ground. Intending
to help, the neighbour asked Nasruddin what he was doing. Nasruddin
replied that he was looking for the key to his house. The neighbour asked
where he had last seen it and Nasruddin said that he had lost it inside
the house. 'Then why aren't you looking for it in the house?' asked the
bemused neighbour. Nasruddin replied, 'It's dark in there.'

At this point in the story people usually laugh, because Nasruddin is doing
something completely counter-intuitive. But from a sufi perspective, this is
no laughing matter. Most people are indeed looking outside their own house
for the key to who they really are – and for good reason. Who wants to deal
with the darkness and cobwebs of one's ego-self? It is much easier and more

comfortable to look outside the self. Sufi practice metaphorically moves us upstream, against the habitual denial of who we really are. It is a process of going inside the house and staying there for extended periods. Those who do go inside their houses soon discover that a little bit of light dispels much of the darkness.

The same story could be related in modern parlance. Long before the internet, the American novelist Walter Percy asked, 'Why is it possible to learn more in ten minutes about the Crab Nebula in Taurus, which is 6,000 light years away, than you presently know about yourself, even though you have been stuck with yourself all your life?'[2] In contemporary modern societies, it is unlikely that any of our primary, secondary or university education is focused on self-learning, so any self-knowledge we have usually comes about accidentally, over time. Conscious exploration of inner being takes time and dedication, and for most people this is hard to achieve without support. One path to exploring one's inner being in a conscious way, however, is through the experience of sufi transformative practice. In modern terms, this kind of learning is called subjective knowledge, but it quickly becomes more than this, as succinctly summarized in one of the Prophet Muhammad's sayings, 'A person who knows one's self knows God.'[3]

To put this inner-focused sufi realm of subjective knowledge into relief, consider that the vast majority of knowledge in the modern world, and therefore almost all of our learning, is focused on objects, as discussed in Alan Watts's book, *On the Taboo Against Knowing Who You Are*.[4] Like most taboos, it is only when someone transgresses this taboo in the contemporary globalized emphasis on *object*-ive learning and knowledge, by asking embarrassing *subjective* questions, that the taboo becomes apparent. If a level playing field existed between objective and subjective knowing, every child would be educated in some of the technologies of self-awareness before graduating from secondary school. Instead, children learn about some combination of modern science, the 'social sciences', and one or more disciplines in the so-called 'humanities', or something else. These disciplines, almost without exception, all focus on the dualistic enterprise of an unexamined subject and the 'objective' researcher, who is studying people, cultures or physical phenomena as objects.

One of the results of this preoccupation with the objective world out there under the street light is the exponentially expanding technological cornucopia and its dizzying rate of change. The other tangible result is a populace with a collective lack of awareness about the possibility for deep, insightful self-knowledge. Sufi transformative practices and other methodologies that increase self-awareness and wisdom threaten this status quo, whether religious or secular, in that they open up the mind to new realms of being that are difficult to explain in objective terms. Post-rational experience, for example, is passing beyond our everyday dualistic rational world to experience the unity of the universe, beyond the space–time–ego constructs that frame our lives. A post-rational experience also propels one beyond the normal everyday experience of being a separate egoic entity (I), dissolving ego boundaries and revealing the transpersonal. Selfless unconditional love is a perfect example of this process and is very different from the romantic, egoic view of love portrayed in the cinema.

Few churches, mosques and synagogues are places for sharing these types of experiences. As Sam Lewis (d. 1971), commonly known as Sufi Sam, said, 'If you believe in angels you are in, but if you see them you're out.'[5] In a secular working environment, who would tell his colleagues that he had just become initiated into a sufi group and was expected to do hours of practice a day? Inner knowledge is taboo. Transformation, fundamental life-changing transformation, not only disturbs the status quo of the person himself, but also disrupts the 'comfortable' unquestioned everyday consensus reality of those around him. No wonder most people prefer to be outside, milling about under the street lights, rather than looking inside, to sit in the true comfort of their homes. In a very real sense, sufi contemplative practice is a process of returning home. After all, home is where the heart is – and the practice of sufism is most definitely a cultivation of the heart.

What is sufism?

As Carl Ernst says, 'The subject of Sufism is difficult to approach.'[6] Part of the reason for this situation is intrinsic to the sufi experience itself, because it goes beyond the very narrow confines of rationality. Most people reading and writing about sufism are not even aware that this vast universe beyond the dualistic mind even exists, except perhaps as a vague concept. Whether one uses the term post-rational, transrational, or supra-rational, these are markers that point to a non-linear realm where subject–object distinctions collapse in direct experience. Chapter 6 explains more about other realms, including this contemplative, transrational domain. Unitary experiences are, of course, difficult to express in words, like many other experiences in life. It is very hard, for example, to describe precisely what a strawberry tastes like.

The origin of the English word 'sufi-ism' can be traced back to the late eighteenth-century British Orientalists working in India.[7] Their ideas about sufi-ism were largely a projection of their partial understanding of texts and their nineteenth-century Christian-based misconceptions of Islam. In lexical terms, 'sufism' is the English translation of the Arabic term *tasawwuf,* the fifth-form verbal noun, meaning 'the process of becoming a sufi'. This linguistic insight demonstrates that sufism, with its lower case initial to remind people of its verbal quality, is more than a static noun. With the realization that sufism involves a dynamic *process*, we are pointed towards transformative processes resulting from sufi practice. Indeed, sufism is a difficult subject to approach, because so few people have any experience or knowledge of these kinds of transformative processes. One goal in writing this book is to make the subject of sufism more approachable.

In the modern, individualistic West there also has been an emphasis on sufism's role in facilitating an individual's becoming close to God in a process of spiritual transformation. However, if we look at the long history of sufi literature and at actual sufi practice, these notions ignore the equally, if not greater, social dimension of sufi teaching as a radical ethical transformation also. This is the *inter-subjective* transformation that is also associated with sufi practice. Sufism is not just about an individual's transrational experiences and transformation, but includes interpersonal interactions within a person's socio-cultural environment.

Who is a sufi?

If sufism is the process of becoming a sufi, then who exactly is a sufi? Historically, the word *sufi* was first used in eighth-century Islamic texts to describe ascetics, wearing coarse scratchy woollen robes, starting with Abu Hashim (d. 768, Kufa, Iraq) because *suf* is the Arabic for 'wool'.[8] The wearing of coarse wool paralleled the practices of Christian ascetics in the deserts of the Near East. Generally, sufis did not often use the term 'sufi' to describe themselves or others, because it was pretentious to claim that one had 'arrived' and had realized an exalted spiritual status through transforming one's ego and achieving great intimacy with God. Instead, 'sufi aspirant' (*mutasawwif*) was a more common term, because it reminded everyone that a person was still on the path. One of the first Europeans to notice sufis *as sufis* was Georges de Hongrie, who spent 20 years as a prisoner of the Ottomans in the mid-fifteenth century. He notes that sufis (*ezofilar*) were 'involved with meditation and spiritual exercises and are considered to be the heirs of the prophets'. In his Latin memoirs, he distinguished sufis from another group, dervishes, whom he defines as those who did not practice the ritual precepts of Islam.[9]

I have arbitrarily formulated seven categories of sufis that cover a broad, but not complete, spectrum of sufi identity and characteristics.

Sufis as dissident ascetics

The term 'sufi' has a broad range of meanings, not only historically, but also geographically and culturally. The history of the term, in some respects, parallels the early history of sufism, which will be discussed in the next chapter. In the first historical stage of sufism, beginning in Baghdad at the end of the eighth century, there were many types of individuals who renounced the sudden worldly materialistic turn of Baghdad Muslim society during the first century of Abbasid rule (*c.*745–845). Baghdad had become the economic centre of the world, following the most extensive conquest in human history, stretching from Spain to Central Asia. Those who reacted against the societal effects of this sudden influx of wealth were called ascetics or obedient worshippers of God. Some groups of unconventional renunciants, wearing woollen robes as an outward marker of their religio-moral protest, were called sufis (sometimes as a pejorative). Here is a poignant reminder that renunciation in that context also included a religio-ethical stance of criticizing the government by advocating what was religiously enjoined and forbidding the unlawful.

Outside Baghdad there were many similar pious individuals. In Basra, Iraq, we find Abu Hatim al-'Attar ('the druggist', d. *c*.880) and many others. In Nishapur, located in northwest Iran, there were the Blameworthy (*malamatiya*), who protested against religious pretentions and outward shows of renunciation by keeping a very low profile and blending into society. In Central Asia, where the term 'sufi' had not yet arrived, the counterparts to sufis were called sages, the most famous of whom is Hakim al-Tirmidhi (d. *c*.910), whose name indicates his hometown of Tirmidh in what is today's Uzbekistan. By the middle of the tenth century, sufism started to embrace a set of recognizable family resemblances, pointing to the performance of transformative practice. Abu Bakr b. Yazdanyar (d. 945) notes, 'Sufism of Khurasan is practice and no talk; sufism of Baghdad is talk and no practice; sufism in Basra is talk as well as practice; and sufism of Egypt is no talk and no practice.'[10] By the end of the tenth century, these disparate renunciants (who probably were not regular wearers of woollen clothing), whether in Baghdad, Persia or Central Asia, began to be identified collectively as sufis.

Sufis heading institutions

The next major stage in sufism was the development of sufi lineages, the subject of Chapter 2. Sufism began to become a mainstream activity from the twelfth century onward, as powerful sufi lineages developed, each stemming from a eponymous founder-figure, such as 'Abdulqadir al-Jilani, d. 1166, Baghdad, or Baha'uddin Naqshband, d. 1389, Bukhara. Prominent sufi leaders (shaykhs) were found in sufi lodges, funded by the elite, influential members of society. This institutionalized sufism depended on large amounts of funding, which often entailed an overlap of interests between sufi shaykhs and the ruling elites. It also was in the interest of sufis to keep the sufi lodge complex in the family. Consequently when the shaykh died, instead of the most spiritually qualified person taking his place, it was often the shaykh's eldest son. Institutionalized sufi groups cut across social divisions, socially integrating Islamicate societies ('Islamicate' is a term that honours the non-Muslims who contributed to majority-Muslim societies), sometimes with political implications (discussed in Chapter 4).

Sufis as transgressive ascetics

Radical ascetic individuals dropped out of mainstream Muslim society in response to this institutionalization, which continues today in parts of the Islamic world, particularly in South Asia. These wandering ascetics were called qalandars, haydaris, malangs or simply dervishes. It was a radical departure from the early sufis because they consciously transgressed societal norms. However, one principle of all these wandering ascetics was radical poverty, which meant itinerant begging, sometimes done aggressively, and celibacy. Self-mortification and wearing iron garments and large rings in their ears and around their necks made the formerly smelly and ragged woollen sufi robe almost the medieval equivalent of a Brooks Brothers suit in comparison (see fig. 0.1). These individuals were the antinomian (more correctly, paranomian) fringes of sufi communities, in that they did not pray and fast, nor did they behave according to the norms of the Islamic societies at that time. In a radical departure from the early sufis, many drank and smoked intoxicants openly. Some even used a haydari cover for criminal behaviour – in 1492, a haydari reportedly tried to assassinate the Ottoman ruler Bayazit II. There were sufi-transformative justifications for this unconventional outward appearance. For example, twisted locks of hair symbolized controlling the ego-self; wearing collars and chains among the haydaris was a mark of being 'Ali's servant ('Ali was the cousin and son-in-law of the Prophet Muhammad); earrings symbolized hearing only that which brought one closer to God; and bracelets were to avoid touching illicit items. There is no way of knowing to what extent these 'left-handed paths' facilitated the transformation of the egoic self.

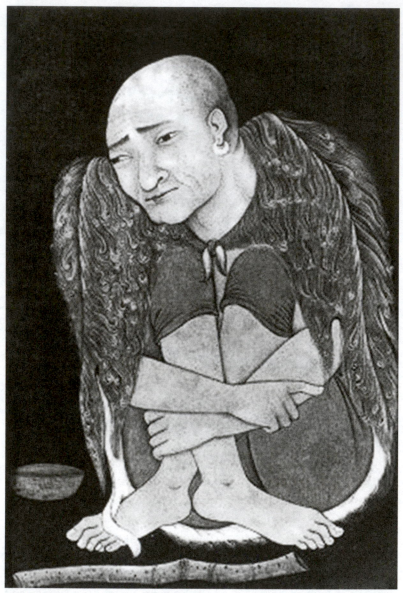

FIGURE 0.1 Portrait of a qalandar, Timurid, late ninth/fifteenth century.

Sufis as mediators, both dead and alive

Living sufi shaykhs, with their perceived intimacy with God, have long been mediators between God and humans, while also functioning as mediators between the rulers and ordinary people (e.g. as tax collectors in Mughal and British India), and between individuals and factions. This mediating function was one reason why the ruling elite funded sufi lodges. It also drew sufis into politics. Just as Muhammad is assumed by Muslims to intercede for them after his death, deceased sufi shaykhs, as heirs of the Prophet, are also believed by many Muslims to mediate for people – although this is a controversial topic for some Muslims.

From the eleventh century (if not earlier), people have been visiting deceased sufis' tombs, some of which became elaborate shrine complexes over time. These tomb-shrines, with caretakers overseeing them, became potent places to visit. (One *visits* deceased sufis, because 'pilgrimage' in an Islamic context is only to Mecca.) Many of these tomb-shrines developed into elaborate architectural complexes that now have libraries, mosques and hospitals. Radiating the blessings and spiritual power of (*baraka*) of the deceased shaykhs, these sufi tombs expanded the scope of sufi activity to the general population, both Muslim and non-Muslim, who continue to visit and ask deceased sufi shaykhs for blessings to satisfy their material and spiritual needs. Chapter 3 will explain this aspect of sufi activity in greater detail.

Sufis as those with unitary knowledge

Now we move to inner sufi characteristics. Dhu'l-Nun (d. 859), a pivotal sufi figure from Upper Egypt, articulated a sufi way of knowing based on direct experiential knowledge (*ma'rifa*) to differentiate it from the everyday linear knowledge (*'ilm*) of jurists. Many sufis have had both types of knowledge. In these two ways of knowing, there is another way of exploring the difference between the rational and the transrational.

Rational, mental knowledge gets communicated through words, written or oral – it is book and classroom knowledge, generally taught in modern education. This is the knowledge concerned with the attributes of something, a transmitted knowledge that is 'knowledge-about'. From the previous discussion, we know that it is *object*-ive knowledge – knowing things as objects out there, versus knowing subjectively within. We acquire this knowledge through the process of thinking about things, comparing propositions through internal dialogue or contrasting images via internal vision. It is conceptual, dualistic and representational.

Sufis have written about their experiences of oneness and unity, so that others after them would be able to discern between unitary experience and delusion. However, people who try to read sufi texts recounting transrational experience, without having gone through these experiences themselves, often have little idea what they mean. Sufis are not trying to keep secrets or code 'esoteric' knowledge, any more than a quantum physicist or a computer programmer. Sufi practice has its own technical vocabulary and experimental/experiential procedures. Those who do the lab procedures/contemplative practices, test the results with qualified people and gain mastery of the discipline are following the appropriate path to actualize any kind of knowledge.

Sufis as ethical exemplars

As we will see below, in Gabriel's Hadith, one Islamic textual justification of sufism is cultivating beautiful outward behaviour and sincere inward character. Muhammad Qassab (d. 888, Baghdad) declared sufism to be exemplary behaviour; and his student, Junayd (d. 910, Baghdad), underlined this notion by saying that sufism is substituting poor character traits with noble ones.[11] Arguably, the ethos of Islamic societies is a cumulative result of the ethical teachings exemplified by Muhammad's example (the sunna). In many Islamic religious schools (madrasas), learning beautiful behaviour is a part of the juristic and theological learning process. Sufis have never had a monopoly, in an Islamic context, on facilitating transformative experiences or on teaching the highest ethical behaviour.

Sufis as those having altered states of consciousness

One outcome of sufi practice is the experience of ecstasy or some other altered state of consciousness. Sufi literature is replete with ecstatic utterances, often overtly at odds with Islamic theological norms. The most famous is that of Mansur al-Hallaj (martyred 922) saying, 'I am God.' Then there is Bayazid Bistami (d. 874) saying, 'Glory be to me' (instead of the acceptable 'Glory be to God'); and Junayd saying, 'In my robe there is nothing but God.' These expressions have come from the intensity of what they have experienced in altered states of consciousness (which sufis call a *hal*) in ecstatic attraction to God and overflowing love. Sufis explain these experiences as a temporary ego annihilation, where nothing remains except the Beloved. Their overflowing and overpowering love often includes a great feeling of love for their spiritual preceptor (the shaykh) and the Prophet Muhammad. From these types of experiences, and the resultant poetry, sufis are often known as lovers of God (sing. *'ashiq* or *muhibb*).

'Altered states' is the current cognocentric English term for such phenomena. What we call altered states, people in a vast array of other cultures call reality. There is disagreement among sufis as to whether these altered states of consciousness are the *goal* of sufi practice or simply elementary way stations on the sufi path. Sufis who focus on transforming aspirants' egoic natures do not usually associate most ecstatic states with spiritual attainment. From their perspective, fostering altered states of consciousness among seekers, and thus avoiding the necessary hard work needed to deal with out-of-control egos, is not upright sufi practice. This has been a long-standing situation in the history of sufism, not just contemporary New Age versions of sufism. It is much more exhilarating to lose oneself in the ocean of Oneness than to deal with the ego-self. That being said, the experience of altered states can motivate one to do what is necessary, so that a temporary altered state can become a transformed human being. The sufi consensus is that the goal of sufi practice is to transform in stations that are progressively closer to God, while becoming a better human being in everyday life – not to get high on an altered state.

Those who are not qualified specialists in the supra-rational contemplative realms can only rely on the external data of their outer senses. This means that the awe and bewilderment of a very advanced seeker appears to be the same as the ecstasy of a beginner. Asking each of these sufi aspirants about their experiences has them describe their experiences in very similar terms. The all-important difference between the beginner and the realized seeker is that the latter is experiencing bewilderment and love *after* the cleansing and taming of the ego-self. Ahmad Sirhindi, one of the rare sufis who apologized for his ecstatic utterances, said that anyone who really gets close to God is quite humble and does not dare to utter any kind of ecstatic utterance or to talk about union or oneness.[12]

Contemporary sufis

The entire spectrum of sufi activity outlined above can be found today in its modern form. There are even small numbers of transgressive ascetics still walking around as qalandars or malangs, smoking hashish, in South Asia and probably other places. The dissident sufis in wool would be those in woollen business suits, applying their sufi principles in white-collar environments, subtly protesting the scientific-materialistic premises of many modern societies through their extraordinary being. The handful of sufis I know (there could be tens of thousands more doing this worldwide) who do these kinds of activities around the world do not do so under the banner of sufism. These 'modern sufis in wool' are renunciants, not because of the coarse wool worn against the skin, but because they renounce being a separate egoic self in order to live up to the highest ethical ideals. They strive through their example and application of their wisdom to enhance ethical behaviour with whomever they come in contact. Note also that in countries where institutional sufism is banned, whether legally or in a de facto manner, anyone transforming the egos and hearts of others is going against the grain of either a nationalistic-inspired militant secularism (Turkey) or a government-enforced militantly narrow interpretation of religious practice and freedom (Saudi Arabia and Iran). Whether the sufis in these latter three countries consider themselves to be dissidents or not, many in positions of power consider them to be engaging in religiously illegal behaviour and punish them accordingly.

As in any sphere of activity, one finds frauds and charlatans who are playing subtle and not-so-subtle ego games in the name of sufism. Last, but surely not least, there are those in the sufi community who represent some of the most exquisite examples of what it is to be human. One of the recurring themes of this book is that appearances are deceptive. Many are quick to judge contemporary forms of sufism, because they do not conform to their fixed idea of what sufism is or was. The profile looks different in many ways over the centuries, but the dynamics of sufi activity in the shaykh–seeker relationship retain similar contours over time, if for no other reason that the human ego has remained a constant challenge to those who seek to tame it and thus to become closer to God. Note this dialogue between Abu'l-Hasan Farghani and Abu Bakr al-Shibli (d. 945) about who is a sufi. Abu'l-Hasan asked:

> ['W]hat is Sufism?' [Shibli] said, 'Being in harmony [with others], detachment and avoidance of excess [...] submitting to the purification of the hearts at the hands of the All Knowing of the Unseen [...] exalting God's command and compassion towards God's creatures.' Then [Abu'l-Hasan] asked, 'And better than this what is a Sufi?' (Shibli) said, 'One who is clear of impurity, free of defilement, occupied with reflection; one for whom gold and clay are equal.'[13]

What is transformative-contemplative practice?

Transformative-contemplative practice is directly related to human development and if done properly, over time, these practices appear to enhance human development. There have been very few people in any time period who have grown beyond the everyday conventional and rational cognitive world space into stabilized experiences in transrational and transpersonal domains. Therefore, there are severe restrictions on studying this group of people, because they are rare. If we look at the aggregate of contemplatives in any religious tradition, they comprise a minuscule percentage of the population and not all contemplatives can be assumed to have transformed themselves. Sometimes the works of contemplatives become translated down to the masses, but their message will be adapted to the needs and level of understanding of the average person.

For this discussion, one operating principle is that adult human beings have different levels of awareness that allow those with more awareness to see life's events in a larger and larger context. This was brought home to me very tangibly. Every Tuesday evening, the local sufi shaykh would be at his favourite teashop, ready for spiritual conversation with anyone who turned up. One evening, I was among those listening to him – but that day it seemed very ordinary to me, nothing special or 'profound'. About eight years later, I happened to accompany a friend, one of that same sufi's long-time students, to visit the shaykh again. This time I found that I was hanging on the shaykh's every word – it felt as though he was talking to me personally. So I explained to my friend what had happened and asked him whether the shaykh had modified his teachings in the intervening eight years. He laughed and said that he had had the same experience – and that he could verify that the shaykh's teachings were consistent, because he had taken notes from the beginning. My friend had evidence that his own awareness had changed over time. So had mine.

We can see in our own lives how awareness increases. Would you have picked up a book on sufism ten years ago? People do have different levels of awareness, so it is not surprising that the majority have no idea that there are limitless domains of transrational and transpersonal experience. William James explained it in another way:

> I think it may be asserted that there are religious experiences of a specific nature, not deducible by analogy or psychological reasoning from our other sorts of experience. I think that they point with reasonable probability to the continuity of our consciousness with a wider spiritual environment from which the ordinary prudential man [...] is shut off.[14]

Sufis often express unitary experience as an expansion of the heart to include more and more. In the beginning one loves one's parents, then later other family members and friends. Others are outsiders, excluded from love. This is one level of heart limitation. As the heart expands, it includes more and more, and love becomes unconditional. Nothing or no one is excluded. This is an open heart, the fruit of a transformed human being. Here we are in the world with fellow humans of all different degrees of open hearts. When I am asked to give a community talk on sufism and recite Rumi's poetry I can see the twinkling eyes and smiles of some, and the blank stares of others.

Transformative practice is a gateway to beyond-the-rational-mind ways of knowing that sufis experience. It is seeing, or more properly, witnessing with the eye of the heart instead of with one's physical eyes. This witnessing is done contemplatively in the heart and sometimes experienced in an altered state of consciousness. In Shabda Kahn's words, 'The inner eye is closed to [ego] separation.'[15] It is like stilling the ever-breaking waves of the mind and being able to perceive what is in the depths of the ocean below the surface stillness.

There are many varieties of witnessing, but *contemplative* witnessing is a methodology that allows human beings to find out who they are beyond the ego-created surface-level stories of everyday life. Contemplation is investigating what *is*, with the mind stopped. It is the gateway to go beyond the mind (hence *post*-rational or *supra*-rational) to what is considered to be a universe that is incomparably vast when compared to the expanding physical universe. Remember that a mind cannot look at itself. Contemplative witnessing is the methodology that allows every normally functioning human being literally to travel in the inner cosmos. This is revolutionary. The sufi paradigm goes beyond consensus reality, while including it. Sufis are involved in everyday life, even though they are not *of* that everyday life. In other words, the process of becoming a sufi is the orienting of one's consciousness beyond ordinary space–time–ego reality, while still living in ordinary space-time.

This is not to say that contemplative practice is simply post-rational. Indeed, contemplatives start from a quite rational set of premises. First, any religious/spiritual truth must have evidence; second, that evidence is an outcome of a contemplative *practice*, a methodology; third, truth is tested in the laboratory of personal *experience*; and fourth, any transrational claims that come out of this laboratory of experience must be in accordance with the community consensus (over the centuries) by qualified sufis.

Transrational experience is inherently subjective, as is all experience in life. The difference between the shared empirical experience 'out there' and inward, non-sensory empirical experience is training. Most humans share an outer sensory world. Other worlds are not shared so commonly – like the discipline of mathematics, which is an inward, mental experience only shared with those who have studied mathematics for many years. Take for example, π (pi) or $\sqrt{-1}$ (the square root of minus one). These concepts can only be seen with the 'eye of the mind' and can never be seen with the sensory eye. Yet a community of trained mathematicians understands these symbols and can decide whether they are being used correctly. The same holds true for contemplative experiences, which are understood by a community of qualified contemplatives who can evaluate such experiences with authority. This does not mean contemplatives agree with each other – just as various types of mathematics are derived from different assumptions, sufis have different 'schools of interpretation'. To the untrained, neither the mathematical symbols nor the contemplative experience make any sense at all, because there is no shared background, either in mathematical training or in consciousness development. The untrained literally cannot perceive these (and other) unknown universes of human experience. In their worldview, these universes do not exist.

Sufis who have reached advanced stations on the sufi path – in transpersonal psychology, this is called reaching higher stages of transpersonal development – demonstrate a set of characteristics in their words and behaviour that is representative of that development. Even though the stations and the path can be rationally described, they cannot be rationally experienced, precisely because they are *trans*-rational. To have extended transrational or transpersonal awareness, more than as a fleeting experience, one has to develop beyond the rational stage of human development, just as one had to develop beyond the pre-rational stage of development after the age of seven to develop one's reasoning abilities. As adult rational beings, we move between the pre-rational and rational seamlessly. Contemplatives expand these options of experience to include the transpersonal as life situations unfold. It is easy to see how this post-rational/transpersonal realm could deeply trouble those who value linearity, predictability and rational order. In addition, there are too many who conflate the non-observed with the non-existent.

Muslim religious scholars, using their rational academic methods had, and continue to have, difficulties with sufis over differences of practice and language. Because sufis tend not to talk in a language that non-contemplatives can understand, contemplative knowledge is dismissed, or not even recognized as possible. We now come back to the same situation of the rational versus the post-rational spheres of knowledge and consciousness discussed above, but from a linguistic angle. It is not easy to explain what a fish is to a person from the middle of a huge desert, who has never heard of or seen a real fish or a picture of a fish. Normally this would not be a problem, because of shared language and cultural backgrounds. But language in and of itself is insufficient to communicate what a fish is without a certain amount of shared lived experience. This is true with just about all direct experience – the taste of a strawberry, the sound of rain on a roof, lightning, or driving a car. It is not surprising that most people ignore contemplatives and their transrational experiences, because they have no way to connect to extraordinary contemplative experiences. I can go and get a fish or buy one from the market and show it to someone, because we share a common sensory world, but when it comes to God (a placeholder term for the infinite context), no one can show God to anyone else in the sensory world. That requires, in the sufi context, to have travelled a certain way down the sufi path with a developed eye of the heart. Without this awareness of an awakened heart, God is merely a word, a concept. There is no common experience, only incommensurability.

Sufis over time created transformative practices to bring forth specific world spaces, which in turn are disclosed by transpersonal transformations. According to Thomas Kuhn,[16] this is how scientists proceed to create a paradigm, namely they follow an agreed methodology that will further a specific discipline. Successive paradigms are refined by a consensus of scientists in any given field, resulting in later paradigms progressively solving problems more effectively as time goes on. The same process has occurred with sufism. As we will see in Chapter 6, over time, a paradigm developed as a result of the development of more and more refined contemplative practices. In fact, as we will discover, more than one paradigm has emerged. These sufi practices require many years to master. As a frame of reference, Tibetan Buddhists estimate that 30,000 to 40,000 hours of supervised meditation are needed in their tradition to become qualified teachers. Contemplatives have their experiences verified over their training period, until they are able to discern good from bad data on their own.

Even though experience is mediated by concepts, language and religio-cultural background, just about all contemporary armchair philosophers have not realized that each experience is a context unto itself (e.g. taste a mango, parachute jump, have sex). Every experience is already contextual; the mind further contextualizes the experience on the basis of a particular religio-cultural-linguistic background. In a transrational context of contemplative experience, it is obvious that many of these experiences are influenced by religio-cultural factors, apart from pure consciousness events. However, the transrational context of the experience is also moulded by realities that are beyond these religio-cultural factors. Again, using science as an example, different socio-cultural and linguistic contexts do not prevent scientists from making apparently valid universal claims. In the same way, valid contemplative claims can, and do, go beyond any specific religio-cultural context. This is to be expected, because transrational experiences go beyond the sensory-rational world of the everyday consensus reality in any given society. The key point here is that contemplatives cannot help but be anchored in a specific religio-cultural context. This is a common human situation. However, their contemplative experience includes and goes beyond this cultural context. There is a transcendental aspect to the experience, which differentiates it from being a hallucination or a projection of religious dogma.

Quality control: Which sufi teachers are authentic?

Academics and Muslim religious scholars, the vast majority of whom are not experientially qualified in any kind of contemplative discipline, are not in a position to demarcate 'authentic sufis' from 'pseudo-sufis', because they have only been trained to look at texts and/or to observe the outward aspects of sufi activity. Therefore, if persons call themselves sufis, academics have no other choice but to take their word for it and seek to understand what is meant by that statement. From the preceding discussion we have seen how 'sufi' has a variety of connotations in a spectrum of contrasting activities, depending on the context and time period. When I was doing research in Pakistan, many people who had no idea that I was studying sufism would call me 'Sufi Sahib'. It was not clairvoyance on their part, but rather that, in the Panjab, any person with a longish beard was called a sufi.

'Sufi' is not a trademark, so anyone can call himself a sufi. In Indonesia there is a rapidly growing group called Majlis Dhikr, where they do a version of a recycled Islamic recollection exercise in a large group with no personal supervision or commitment.[17] As Muslims, they identify with being sufis. Bapak Rachmat in Jakarta has been initiated in a lineage going back to the legendary Sunan Kudus, one of the nine founder-figures of Indonesian Islam, the Wali Songa, and from there to the Prophet's cousin and son-in-law, 'Ali. Yet what Rachmat teaches is from the Ibn al-'Arabi school – which is not a sufi lineage, much less a sufi practice, because the massive visionary contribution of Ibn al-'Arabi (d. 1240, Damascus) to the discipline of sufism did not include a set of contemplative practices to be passed on from him to others. Rachmat formally initiates seekers, an initiation into a universal Islam that means 'universal truth.'[18] This notion of Islam contrasts sharply with the literal meaning of the Arabic word *islam*, submission to God, recognizable by the vast majority of Muslims worldwide. Another modern Indonesian organization, Intensive Course and Networking for Islamic Sciences (ICNIS), has a programme of instruction of contemplative practices developed by Nasruddin Umar. These exercises are not linked to any sufi lineage and do not require initiation. In 2002, Nasruddin Umar became a celebrity preacher on television.[19]

All of these activities, along with numerous others like them around the world, blur and recast the boundaries of sufism and the people who call themselves sufis. So, 'yes', from a postmodern academic point of view, people calling themselves sufis are sufis. From a sufi standpoint – and this has been an ongoing situation from the beginning of sufism – charlatans and imposters in sufi garb abound. It is a general principle that a person cannot evaluate something that is literally *beyond* his understanding and awareness, making the evaluation of sufis extremely difficult. Sufi post-rational experience goes beyond the intellectual worlds of academics and Muslim religious scholars, although one can be a scholar and a sufi.

Within the *institutional sufi* context worldwide, only some sufi teachers are designated legitimate, for a variety of conflicting reasons. Nahdatul Ulama (NU), one of the largest Islamic organizations in the world, based in Indonesia, has defined criteria for proper Islamic sufi activity. In 1957 they set up the Federation of Recognized Sufi Paths, defining a legitimate sufi path as one in which the sufi shaykh and his practices can be traced in an unbroken lineage back to the Prophet. The major difficulty with this criterion is that there is no textual documentation of a sufi lineage before the ninth or tenth century. In addition, all sufi teachings and practice must conform to NU's Islamic guidelines. As of 2000, there were 46 recognized sufi groups in Indonesia. This determination is not legally binding, but only applies to NU members, who are not supposed to follow unauthorized sufis.[20]

This NU determination of legitimate sufi activity considerably simplifies the diversity of sufi practice and ways of constituting legitimate lineages. On the other hand, they are attempting to exercise some quality-control mechanisms in an area where literally 'anything goes'. One of the most vexing issues for anyone determining the authenticity of an individual sufi is to first ask about the evaluator's qualifications. External criteria based on supposed lineage or lack thereof, and/or dogmatic considerations, cannot determine whether aspirants are in the process of transforming themselves and becoming closer to God. It is just not that simple.

The perspective shared in this book is that the litmus test for *the process of becoming a sufi* is the existence of a transformative practice that facilitates ethical development and/or furthers taming of the ego. The intentional process of 'becoming a complete human' constitutes one of the ways that sufis have expressed the goal of sufi practice. To be whole or complete means to realize the fullness of one's own nature, physically, emotionally, mentally and spiritually. The process of becoming a sufi is about cultivating unconditional love and becoming truly human. Sufis state that this wholeness is a human being's natural state and that the predominance of the ego-self is an indication of separateness from God. In short, no ego transformation or ethical development, no sufism. Everything else is appearance – including lineages and teaching certificates, distinctive hats, beards and sufi robes.

'Ali b. Ahmad al-Bushanji (d. 959), from a town in eastern Iran, said, '*Tasawwuf* is a name without a reality, but it used to be a reality without a name.'[21] One interpretation of this statement is that he saw many people called or calling themselves sufis, but much of their practice did not involve a process of transformation (the 'reality'). Another equally plausible interpretation is that what he saw as sufi practice in his environment did not correspond to what he thought sufi practice should be and he *assumed* that the reality of transformation was absent. Though we probably will never know what he meant, this is a reminder of the difficulty in assessing the transformational validity of an individual sufi and any given practice.

This also illustrates a common human proclivity to glorify the past. I am reminded of the well-known conversation of someone coming to Shaykh Hasan Muhammad Chishti (d. 1575) saying, 'In times past, there were men like Shaykh Nasir ad-Din [Chiragh-i Dihli], the Emperor of the shaykhs [Nizam ad-Din Awliya'], and the revered [Farid ad-Din] Ganj-Shakar. Now there is no one like them.' The Shaykh answered, 'In their time, men said the very same thing.'[22] Sufi treatises throughout their thousand years of history have continually bemoaned the absence of real sufi practice. Even if these statements were accurate locally, the transformative practice of becoming a sufi has continued throughout the world. In some places it dies out, but in others it gloriously appears, as if out of nowhere.

To embark upon the path of becoming a sufi, one usually finds a teacher or *shaykh*, formally makes a commitment through an initiation ritual and then proceeds to incorporate a transformative discipline into one's life (discussed later, in Chapters 5 and 6). An experiential transformational process is the root of the tree of sufism. Many, if not most, other activities associated with sufism take place in the branches and under the shade of this tree. It is important to keep in mind that these deep transformations do not necessarily take place for every person diligently practising sufism. At the same time, incredible transformations can occur to people who have never even heard of sufism and who have never learned any kind of transformative practice. For the majority of people, including transpersonal psychologists and academics, the process of human realization appears to be accidental at this stage of our very limited knowledge. Transformational practice only makes one more accident-prone.[23] From a sufi perspective, the transformational process involves God's grace, which is not accidental if one has the capacity to see the larger context of human action in the universe.

Who is qualified to discuss sufism?

Just about everyone has a partial perspective to share, but not all partial perspectives are equal. Scholars of aspects of sufism – historians, anthropologists, sociologists and psychologists – have their partial perspectives to share. Sufi aspirants have their personal experiences to discuss. Accomplished sufis are qualified to communicate their unitary experiences and the methods they used to get there – an expansively qualitative difference from anything in the scholarly realm. All of these categories of individuals – except probably the accomplished sufis – share a common principle, what I call the 'well principle'.

Once upon a time there was an ocean frog that visited a frog in a well. The well frog asked the ocean frog what the ocean was. The ocean frog noted first that the well was very small and it would be hard to describe the ocean. The well frog responded immediately that he had never heard of anything larger than his well, so what was this ocean? This question put the ocean frog in a difficult position, because it was so hard to describe something so qualitatively different from a well. All he said was, 'It is vast without any boundaries.' The well frog felt insulted and demanded that he leave because the ocean frog was obviously crazy and talking nonsense.

The vast majority of people who discuss and/or practice sufism are like the well frog – they only know their own tiny disciplinary or experiential world. Academics have their disciplinary silos and sufi aspirants have their limited local group and personal notions of what sufi practice is. They may nod towards the *idea* of radical ego transformation or unitary knowledge, but only the realized sufi has any lasting experience of the ocean. Ironically, these small wells eventually lead to the ocean one way or another. Yet there are very few 'ocean frogs'. Who *really* wants to look in his house for the key? Ocean frogs know that it is a waste of time trying to explain the ocean to a well frog. The only effective way is to teach the well frog how to navigate to the ocean one way or another. It is not about believing. The rational mind cannot *fruitfully* conceive of something so absolutely beyond, until the consciousness is deepened to the level of the ocean (as a start, there is no *thing-ness* to conceive of). The process of becoming a sufi is increasing awareness as a result of one's own confirmatory experience(s). Theologians spend their lives talking about God and trying to dumb down God to concepts understood at a rational level. Sufi masters do their best to bring aspirants to the actual experience.

This can be summarized by the old Buddhist story of the blind philosophers trying to work out what an elephant was by touching various parts of the elephant. One touched the elephant's tail, the other the skin along its side and the third, the elephant's trunk. Their differing reports had them bickering for a long time, as philosophers are wont to do. Collectively they had no idea of what an elephant was. But this enterprise of *really* knowing is not as straightforward as I am making it out to be. Not all well frogs are the same. Some have explored the depth of their wells more than others; some have tasted ocean water.

Transformative practice necessarily is a very narrow and constricting path – until one experiences a consciousness expansion to infinity. The scholarly enterprise, not bound by any religious dogma or contemplative practice, appears expansive like a broad flat plain. This perspective continues until one takes into account the consciousness contraction of cognocentrism – being locked into the extremely narrow band of rational thought. Then one realizes how two-dimensional and limiting it is. Nor are all philosophers equally blind. Plato, along with Mulla Sadra from Shiraz, Iran, and many other philosophers, do appear to have stepped out of the cave of duality into the sunlight of greater post-rational awareness.

Life is ever full of surprises. We can learn from the most unlikely people. I first heard about sufism from the books of the late Idries Shah (d. 1996), a prolific writer who wrote and sold many books on sufism. His books were full of entertaining stories, because Shah was an extremely good storyteller. After reading Shah's second book, I realized (as I had realized previously with Carlos Castaneda's second book) that Shah was writing a fictional version of sufism but passing it off as 'non-fiction'. I felt that I had been conned again. So I decided to travel to places where sufis were supposed to be and find out about sufism for myself. Fifteen years later, the degree to which I had been conned had become clear. Both Shah and Castaneda have been repeatedly exposed since the 1970s.[24] Not everyone realizes that they were both tricksters – they had a skilful knack to mix truth and fiction to create a story that most people believed was real. All kinds of things happen around tricksters and the activities they generate – and not all of the outcomes turn out as fortunate as mine. If my life depended on knowing which way to turn at a fork in the road and the only person I could ask were Idries Shah, I would stake my life on going in the opposite direction to the one he indicated. But not until I thanked him for lying to me.

This question of qualifications is not one that fits a set of outer pre-determined categories. This applies equally to sufi shaykhs and those writing about sufis. Consider how many more modern books on sufism are written by scholars of sufism rather than by sufis. There is a major imbalance – it is not easy to find a book written on scholars of sufism written by a sufi. Books are books. Meanwhile, most people know that human experience is not a straightforward, linear, discrete realm – and contradictory surprises abound.

Does one have to be a practising Muslim to be a sufi?

The answer to this question is both 'yes' and 'no'. Let's start by unpacking *islam* and *muslim*. In Arabic, the word *islam* means the submission to God and a person who submits to God is called a *muslim*. These are purposely italicized to indicate the Arabic and are written in lower case letters to indicate a difference from 'Islam', the established religion of over 1.7 billion Muslims, who define themselves as Muslims by birth or by conversion. According to a well-known saying of the Prophet, everyone is born in harmony with one's innate human nature and it is one's parents who determine what kind of religious path the child will follow. The Islamic consensus is that all of creation, as God's creation, is by definition innately submitting to God. All humans are born as *muslims*, but because they have free will, most of them, like their parents, end up submitting to their egoic nature rather than to their innate nature.

This turns things around a bit from the conventional boxes that people like to make. It means that any human being can be a *muslim*. Thus, a person who does not believe that Muhammad is God's messenger can be a *muslim*. It also means that a devout practising Muslim may not in reality be a *muslim*, an overall quality of the heart that (apparently) only God is able to discern. In the Islamic Shafi'i legal school, if someone asks another if he is a Muslim (the conventional meaning of the word), one is supposed to say, 'If God wills'. This indicates the provisional and unknown quality of one being a *muslim*. In the Islamic Hanafi legal school, the same question is supposed to be answered by: 'Thanks be to God.' This answer indicates membership in the larger Muslim community, not the inner quality of being a *muslim*.

Historically, sufism has been practised almost exclusively by Muslims. It has also gone beyond the human-created boundaries of the religion of Islam – or any specific religious form – to include anyone who seeks to submit to God and respond to God's call. Sufism is simply the Islamic expression of this urge to respond to God's call. Submission to God is not a monopoly of any human group. Indeed, in Islamic terms, no one has a monopoly on God or on the Prophet Muhammad, commonly known as 'the mercy to the worlds'. Sufis, as heirs to the Prophet, have followed the Prophetic example of inviting people to God. Sufis residing in largely un-Islamicized areas had many non-Muslims in their circles. Over time, people willingly converted to Islam or were required to convert at a certain point to continue more advanced sufi practices. Here, I am thinking of the non-Muslim sufi aspirants of both historical and present-day Turkey, Indonesia and India. Likewise, many sufi groups in the West do not expect their members to convert to Islam. Mirza Jan-i Janan (martyred 1781) taught Naqshbandi practices to Hindus, who have had an ongoing Hindu Naqshbandi sufi lineage for around 250 years. The late Irina Tweedie (d. 1999) kept a diary of her experiences in learning from a Hindu sufi of this lineage, which was later published as *Daughter of Fire*.[25] It is not until near the end of her 822-page diary that she realizes that she is being taught Naqshbandi sufi practices. This is yet another reminder that sufi practice often does not happen under the banner of sufism.

That being said, at least 95 per cent of historical sufi activity – if not more – has been enacted under the auspices of the religion of Islam. Sufis in many parts of the world probably never asked for a person's religious credentials to transmit sufi contemplative practices. Some sufi groups freely communicate the elementary practices to those who are sincere and ready to benefit from them, with the proviso that after tasting *islam*, at a certain point, they will need to convert to Islam formally to proceed further. Other sufi shaykhs, both in the West and throughout the majority Islamic world, require initial formal conversion to Islam. Contemporary teachers of contemplative practices in the Jewish, Christian and Buddhist traditions also differ in their requirements for religious affiliation.

From one perspective, attachment to a religion, in this case Islam, and developing a sense of superiority involving 'us versus them', could be considered to reinforce egoic behaviour. Attachment to religion is like being attached to nationality or ethnicity and can engender friction and disharmony between people. From another perspective, daily Islamic prayer and fasting during the month of Ramadan are custom-designed to fit in with contemplative practice. Such practices, performed sincerely, combat egoic behaviour and help one remember God. To resist becoming a practising Muslim can be as egoic as pride in being a practising Muslim. In a very really real sense, the transformation inherent in the process of becoming a sufi is the process of becoming a *muslim*. According to a saying of Muhammad, 'God does not consider your outer aspects or wealth, but rather God considers your hearts', as Muhammad pointed to his heart.[26] This hadith places sufi transformative practice and ethical behaviour at the centre of submission to God.

How is sufism central to the practice of Islam?

The easiest way to answer this question is to quote the famous hadith of the Prophet known as Gabriel's Hadith. It is so famous that it is the first hadith in some hadith collections. In shortened form it tells about a man with very white clothing and very black hair coming up to the Prophet and his companions. No mark of travel was visible on him, and no one recognized him. Sitting down before the Prophet he said, 'Tell me, Muhammad, about submission to God [*islam*]'. He replied, 'Submission means that you should bear witness that there is no god but God and that Muhammad is God's messenger, that you should perform the ritual prayer, pay alms, fast during

Ramadan, and make the pilgrimage to the House [the Ka'ba in Mecca] if you are able to go there.' The man said, 'You have spoken the truth.' Then he said, 'Now tell me about faith [*iman*].' Muhammad replied, 'Faith means that you have faith in God, his angels, his books, his messengers, and the last day and that you have faith in the measuring out, both its good and its evil.' Remarking that the Prophet had spoken the truth, the man then said, 'Now tell me about doing what is beautiful [*ihsan*].' Muhammad replied, 'Doing what is beautiful means that you should worship God as if you see him, for even if you do not see him, he sees you.' When the man left, Muhammad informed his astonished companions that the angel Gabriel had come to teach them about their religion.

Here is upright living in a nutshell, based on what one does (*islam*), what one has faith in (*iman*), and what one intends in one's heart that is exhibited in beautiful behaviour (*ihsan*). The point here is that each of these three religious dimensions is interconnected like a tree's roots, branches and fruit. Being a complete human being involves an integration of these three dimensions. The process of becoming a sufi is the third dimension, the root of action and faith, as the order of the three dimensions goes from outer (*islam*) to inner (*ihsan*). Muslims who deny sufi contemplative practice (sufi practice is not universally accepted by all Muslims) do not recognize this integral 'heart dimension' in Islam. The word *ihsan* can also be translated as 'virtue' or 'God consciousness' (though many usages of *taqwa* may be better translated in that way). One manifestation of *ihsan* is having a life focused around what pleases God, not what pleases the ego. It is the deepest way of submitting to God. Being a *muslim* and being a completed person, a sufi, are one and the same.

The vast majority of Muslims seek salvation through their daily practices, informed by a faith commitment. Becoming a sufi, on the other hand, encompasses the matrix of activities aimed towards the field of consciousness and experience, represented by acting in a beautiful manner. Such an enterprise assumes a firm foundation in faith and in the practice of submitting to God before achieving an extraordinary degree of proximity to God. Surely not all who call themselves sufis have achieved this advanced goal and not all of the apparently few who reach this stage are necessarily sufis.

In short, the vast majority of sufi practitioners have been practising Muslims. Their contemplative exercises (*dhikr*) are above and beyond the five daily ritual prayers, the month of fasting during Ramadan and other required Islamic practices. Sufi activity is not a substitute for standard Islamic practice. It is not a *sect* in Islam. Sufi practice is found in the two largest sects in Islam, both among the Sunnis (85 per cent) and Shi'is (13 per cent). In most parts of the Islamic world (Bosnia to Bengal to Indonesia) a sufi ethos of poetry and music is still deeply embedded in the culture. Until a hundred years ago sufism was normative in Muslim societies and the authority of Islamic law (which now occupies the headlines) was relatively marginal to people's lives.

Summary

This introduction, among other things, has demonstrated the incredible diversity of sufism and the limitations of making generalizations. I have endeavoured to elucidate principles outlining how inner transformation is not about the outward appearance of waving the banner of sufism or wearing a sufi costume. Just as the Muslim community does not have a monopoly on God or *islam*, sufis with lineage certificates or with fathers who declared them to be sufis do not have a monopoly on sufi practice. There is the reality of sufi practice without the name, as there is also the name of sufism without the reality of transformation. Only by tasting the fruits of companionship with a shaykh can we know, through our own direct experience, who deserves to be called a sufi. Everyone needs to have his or her own experience. Everything else is conjecture.

Look at this book as a kind of sufi tree. The roots of this tree involve an inner human transformation, an ethical and ego-shattering unitary experience nourished in the crucible of a daily practice and the shaykh–seeker relationship. The trunk of this tree is the history of sufi practice, beginning in Chapter 1, where it is demonstrated how sufis evolved from renunciation to doing formal practices. This is the formative period when a technical vocabulary developed from Qur'anic and non-Qur'anic Arabic, so that sufis could articulate their experience. Continuing up the trunk of the tree, Chapter 2 outlines how the techniques of contemplative practice developed, along with an institutionalization of sufism in recognized lineages. Part of this development resulted in sufis becoming involved politically. Chapter 3 explores some aspects of the most popular manifestation of sufis: visiting the shrines of deceased sufis. Because of its popularity we can say that this aspect of sufism is the foliage of the tree. These shrines dot the Islamic world like leaves on a tree. Unlike similarly coloured leaves on a tree, however, each shrine uniquely reflects the local environment in which it is situated, marvellously demonstrating the diversity of one of the great world religions.

Chapter 4 demonstrates how some sufi leaders ended up engaging in politics or how politics came knocking on their door uninvited. Chapter 5 returns to actual sufi practice, by exploring the dynamics between the shaykh and the student. Chapter 6 explicates some examples of sufi contemplative practices, focusing on the Naqshbandis and the Mevlevis. These practices, built upon a millennium of contemplative experience, came to the fore in the seventeenth to twentieth centuries and indicate how contemplative practice continues to evolve over time.

Chapter 7 introduces two women sufi shaykhas through interviews. Here the reader is reminded that there probably were extremely few, if any, sufi *brotherhoods*. Such a term is a holdover from male-oriented Orientalist scholarship, where sufi lodges were compared with Christian monasteries – ignoring the parallel convents of nuns. Women have in fact been active participants in sufi transformation from the beginning. In addition, the reader is reminded that sufi practice is not a doctrine or philosophy (these are dead branches on the tree), but a vibrantly alive *human* endeavour that bears fruit as the transformed human heart comes alive in all its glorious infinity.

1

QUR'AN, TRANSFORMATIVE PRACTICES AND THE DISCIPLINE OF SUFISM: 700–1000

Introduction

IN 610 A NEW RELIGIOUS PRACTICE – Islam – and afterwards, an ethico-renunciate practice within that new religion, later called sufism, burst on the historical scene. It is not clear what happened during the first three centuries, since we only have scattered historical potsherds in the form of written sources that provide brief glimpses of the early stages of sufism. There are accounts of altered states of consciousness, which eventually contributed to a shared sufi vocabulary. Another set of sources established sufism as one of the recognized Islamic religious sciences. Stemming from the Qur'an, itself a source of facilitating altered states of consciousness, commentaries on the Qur'an and theological treatises blossomed. Muslim

30

contemplatives used these Islamically recognized disciplinary formats and vocabulary to legitimize sufism, communicating their experiences to future generations.

Retrospective historical accounts of sufism's early centuries typically portrayed an orderly development of sufism, smoothing over messy and awkward episodes to demonstrate the compatibility of sufism with what had become the Sunni Islamic mainstream and a 12-er Shi'i orthodoxy. Legendary accounts, a common aspect of historical narratives, created a coherent picture of sufism. Early sufis became effectively connected to what in later centuries was considered proper sufi practice and behaviour. It made for a step-by-step and orderly story. Let's not forget, however, that what we think we know about early sufi history is exponentially less than what we do not know.

In this chapter I will outline a history of sufi practice and how a specialized, technical sufi vocabulary came into being. To some extent such a narrative details how personal subjective *experience* was shared collectively over time and how sufis discovered principles of transpersonal human development on the basis of these shared experiences. Sufis, like contemplatives in other religions, observed a sequence of developmental stages, preliminary to advanced, and the dynamics associated with each of these stages. This enabled conscious cultivation of experience that, in turn, was repeatedly verified over centuries and became a set of parallel guidelines, the process of becoming a sufi.

But this *inner* subjective evolution of sufism did not happen in a vacuum. There was an *outer* socio-religious history in which sufi contemplative practice developed alongside the developing *Islamic* context of Muslim contemplatives. The Islamic context impacted directly on the interpretation, if not the content, of contemplative experiences. In particular it determined, on the linguistic and conceptual level, the vocabulary that sufis used to report their experiences, which was in part derived from the Qur'an. Islamic contemplative currents, jostling with jurist and theological understandings of religious possibilities in increasingly Islamic societies, took a few centuries to become labelled as 'sufism'. The resultant practice and discipline of sufism necessarily developed harmoniously in parallel with what was to become mainstream Sunni Islam.

The religious strand of early sufism was, therefore, intimately intertwined with the story of Islam and an understanding of Islamic history will help to illuminate the development of the knowledge strand also. It was in 610 that Muhammad received his first revelation, in a cave outside Mecca, and he continued to receive revelations until his death in 632. For the first 12 years, Muhammad's small Muslim community was persecuted in Mecca until they migrated to nearby Yathrib (later named Medina, 'the city of the Prophet') in 622. By the time Muhammad died, ten years later, the disadvantaged Muslim minority had become triumphantly successful – having converted, at least nominally, the majority of the population of the Arabian Peninsula. A vast expenditure of intellectual and spiritual energy by billions of people has been channelled in the direction of Islam since Muhammad's *experience* that night in a cave, when a voice called out repeatedly, 'Recite!' In 656 the compilation of what Muslims have considered the verbatim word of God, known as 'the recitation' (the Qur'an), became standardized in its consonantal form by the third caliph after Muhammad, 'Uthman. Recorded memories of the Prophet's sayings and behaviour, the hadith, were compiled and edited for accuracy of transmission two centuries later. Using these foundational sources, Muslim jurists developed a set of laws and ethical guidelines (the sharia) to order the ritual and social life of the Muslim community. Over the first few centuries, more specialized religious sciences developed, including Arabic grammar (to interpret the Qur'an), theology and jurisprudence. Sufism as a religious science, with a specialized vocabulary and literature, also developed alongside these other religious sciences, forming the knowledge strand of early sufism.

The formation of the Umayyad dynasty, centred in Damascus, began in 661, with regular armed conflicts over political and religious leadership continuing beyond 680, when the Prophet's grandson Husayn and other family members and followers were massacred at Karbala, in Iraq. Pious Muslims, proto-sufis if you will, surfaced historically in Basra. The legendary Hasan al-Basri (d. 728) is the best known of these early renunciate contemplatives. After a major civil war, lost by the Umayyads, the new Abbasid dynasty began in 749–50 and the capital was moved to Baghdad in 762. During the next 100 years or so Baghdad, the capital of a huge empire, became a major centre of sufism.

The practices of sufism were not restricted to Iraq, since the Islamic Empire stretched 6,000 kilometres as the crow flies, from Spain in the west to the Talas River in present-day Kazakhstan in the east. In the middle of this expanse we find two centres of Islamic contemplative activity in Iran's eastern province of Khurasan, situated between present-day eastern Iran in the west and Tajikistan in the east, which is why Afghanistan and Tajikistan are Persian-speaking countries today. One group of pious contemplatives, known as 'the Blameworthy', lived in the city of Nishapur, in northeast Iran. Further east in present-day Tirmidh (Tirmiz), in Uzbekistan, the Hakimiyya focused on the teachings of Hakim Tirmidhi (d. 912). There were other sages (*hakim*s) in the region, but they were known as scholars or theologians. By the end of the tenth century, the vast majority of these pious contemplatives, from Iraq to Central Asia, had become known as sufis. This is the geographical strand of early sufism.

Islam, as a religious tradition, followed the trajectory of other world religions with founder-figures (for example, Buddhism and Christianity). Each founder-figure had a set of extraordinary experiences of non-ordinary consciousness and shared these insights with those around him. When he died there was an institutionalization, a crystallization, of these experiential insights. Max Weber called it the 'routinization of charisma', charisma being as vague a concept as mystic/ism. Thus a *religion* came into being that was suitable for the default consciousness level of the masses, manifesting in doctrines, rituals and ethical principles.

In the Islamic case, there were a few centuries of intense endeavour and conflict after Muhammad had his revelations, resulting in the demarcation of two major orthodoxies – the Sunni majority and the Shi'i minority – in addition to some other minor orthodoxies. If one's beliefs and religious praxis fitted into these boundaries, then one was recognized as a Muslim; otherwise one was outside the community. The primary boundary marker stemmed from the Islamic attestation of faith declaring there to be one God, with Muhammad being the last prophet. These are non-negotiables in an Islamic worldview. Such doctrinal boundaries usually go hand-in-hand with political power, so Muhammad's extraordinary experiences eventually became institutionalized in politics of one kind or another – minus most, if not all, of the inner experience.

Counterbalancing these doctrinal–political imperatives, sufis, like their contemplative counterparts in other religions, formulated a methodology to emulate the founder-figure's extraordinary experiences. They developed a set of practices above and beyond the ritual practices incumbent upon Muslims. Over time, sufi groups also became institutionalized, consolidating into lineages and funded sufi lodges. In some cases, major sufis became political leaders or advisors to influential political leaders. This is the path of an institutionalization of a contemplative practice. In the shuffle from extraordinary experience to institutionalization, *experience* usually is the first to go. On the other hand, one can argue that this institutionalization preserved the practices of sufism, isolating sufis to some extent from the outside world and thus allowing them to further develop transformative disciplines. Century after century, sufi contemplatives have been able to preserve their practices, while modifying them for local conditions, enabling these practices not only to survive, but arguably to become more sophisticated over time.

Early in the history of sufism we find opposition between jurists and sufis, where jurists often have the clout of the rulers to enforce their version of Islamic practice. Jurists, trained to interpret the Qur'an and the hadith, have tended to focus on the outer ritual dimensions of worship (the *islam* dimension of Gabriel's Hadith) to an utterly transcendent God. On the other hand, sufis' non-ordinary experience of God and God's attributes verify God's utter immanence. Both groups, as well as those sufis who are also religious scholars/jurists, appeal to the Qur'an. The sufis cite the Qur'an (50:16 and 55:26) stating, 'God is closer to you than your jugular vein' or that 'wherever you look you see the face of God'. Jurists cite more numerous verses demonstrating God's transcendent aspect. This creates a standoff, since a great variety of conflicting perspectives can be justified through recourse to scripture. I have chosen this example because understanding sufism is greatly enhanced if one takes a 'both ... and ...' approach. Is God immanent or transcendent? Both. God is beyond the beyond the beyond, which includes both the immanent and transcendent.

The issue between jurists and sufis goes deeper and is intimately connected with different levels of knowing. Think of the gap between hearing about strawberries and tasting a strawberry. There is a major difference between knowing something intellectually and knowing it experientially. Then consider the gap between reading about love and experiencing love. This is the difference between rational understanding and post-rational/transrational experience. Although sufis understand the everyday rational jurists' understanding of Islam, jurists who do not have any experiences beyond their book learning have no idea about sufis' experiences and ways of knowing. As Abu'l-Qasim Qushayri (d. 1072) says:

> Whoever has a difficulty concerning the legal rulings for the enjoined and the forbidden refers to the jurists for the rulings of God. Whoever has doubts about a matter concerning the knowledge of spiritual wayfaring on the path of God refers to the experiential knowers of God. The jurist abjudicates about God; the knower of God speaks about God.[1]

Abu Yazid Bistami (also known as Bayazid) chastises jurists' book learning, saying, 'You have had your knowledge from a dead man who had it from a dead man while we had our knowledge from the living one who never dies.'[2]

An aware jurist who knows that he does not understand sufi experience, simply does not comment on something he cannot grasp. But a narrow-minded and less aware colleague might, and many did, vehemently oppose sufis. An uneducated sufi would defer to jurists in their nuanced knowledge of Islamic practice. The burden was placed upon the sufis to practice and publically declare their experiences in a socio-culturally acceptable manner, because the vast majority in society had no clue of what the sufis were about. Harmonizing sufi activities with the developing set of Islamic societal norms took centuries.

Sufis started attracting attention by communicating divine inspirations and being associated with the unusual events that happened around them (miracles). Some religious scholars found this kind of sufi activity contrary to one of the dogmatic corollaries of Muhammad's being the last prophet, namely that prophets are *in essence* different from all other non-prophet humans. Muslims were to follow the example of the Prophet – his sunna – but when sufis started having inspirations from God, these inspirations (*ilham*) needed to be of a lower, non-prophetic order than prophetic revelation (*wahy*), otherwise the finality of the Qur'an would have been called into question. If events in Muhammad's presence appeared to bend the normal laws of nature (*mu'jizat*, miracles), then if similar phenomena happened around sufis, they must have a non-prophetic quality and were called *karamat*. Otherwise it could imply the status of prophethood to someone after Muhammad, who is considered the last prophet according to Islamic dogma. These are some examples of how sufis ironed out discrepancies between their religious experiences and religious dogma. It is ironic that religious experience, originally a revolutionary event, not only becomes institutionalized with standard rituals and dogma, but the new institutions curb further religious experience which may upset the new status quo. Sari Saqati (d. *c*.867, Baghdad) declares:

> Sufism (*tasawwuf*) is a name for three things: he [the Sufi] is the one in whom the light of knowledge does not extinguish the light of scrupulosity. In his inner self he does not speak of any knowledge contradicting the external meaning of the Book or the Prophet's custom (sunna). [His] miracles (*karamat*) do not cause him to violate the sacredness of the divine prohibitions.[3]

This enforcement of dogma also happened with Muhammad's ascent through the seven heavens. The Qur'an (17:1) briefly alludes to this journey. 'Glory to the one who took his servant on a night journey from the place of prayer in Mecca to the furthest place of prayer, which we have blessed so that we could show him some of our signs. He is the all-hearing, the all-seeing.' Qur'an commentaries and hadith elaborated this Qur'anic account of Muhammad's ascent. In one hadith, Muhammad mounted a white beast that took him to Jerusalem (interpreting the 'furthest place of prayer' to be Jerusalem), where he met the angel Gabriel. He visited the prophets Adam, Jesus, Joseph, Enoch, Aaron, Moses and Abraham in their respective heavens. One could say that Muhammad received their 'stamp of approval' in this process.

About 260 years later, Abu Yazid Bistami (d. 874) reported a heavenly ascent through the seven heavens to God's Throne, whereupon the spirit of each prophet, including Muhammad, greeted him. It appears that Bayazid was banished more than once from his hometown for reporting such experiences, since the authorities thought that only Muhammad could embark on such heavenly journeys. Most sufis, by that time, described their experiences in terms of stations or stopping-points on a path towards God and thus avoided controversy. If they happened to visit previous prophets – which many did in their contemplative journeys – the experience was not couched in terms of a 'heavenly ascent'. Note that Muhammad b. 'Abduljabbar Niffari (d. after 977 in Iraq), perhaps deliberately, wrote enigmatically about his experiences journeying through the seven heavens as a confidant of God.[4] Most sufis learned to use technical language that did not overlap with Muhammad's prophetic experience and did not get mis-interpreted by non-sufis.

As with the formation of institutional Islam in the same period, sufism had its own internal growing pains. Some other contested issues included: whether living a life of poverty was better than a life with wealth, whether one could ignore performing ritual prayer and other Islamically mandated actions after arriving at a certain place on the sufi path, and whether it was possible to see God in this world. It was a tumultuous beginning. Some contemplative experiments succeeded and became part of the later sufi repertoire, while the practices that were abandoned either disappeared or became markers of fringe activity denounced by most Muslims, whether sufis or non-sufis. Through a three-century organic process of subjective inquiry channelled by Islamic societal constraints, a new paradigm of human spiritual development came into being. By the end of the tenth century this new science of introspective practices, principles, concepts and rudimentary spiritual maps was called 'Sufism'. The initial capital letter in 'Sufism' indicates the name of an Islamic religious science, not the experiential, transformative process of becoming a sufi.

On renunciants and sufis: The evolution of piety and formal sufi practice

Before ninth-century Baghdad and in tenth-century Khurasan, 'sufi' was not the common term for those who frequently experienced altered states and who endeavoured to tame their egos. They were known in the biographical compendia by many names *other* than sufis, e.g. ascetic/renunciant (*nasik*, *zahid*), spiritually poor person (*faqir*), worshipper ('*abid*) or an upright person (*salih*). These descriptions in the biographical compendia emphasized various forms of outward piety valued and respected at the time. Early pious Muslims emulated the piety and sincerity of Muhammad and the early community of Muslims. Their renunciant piety was glorified when brought into high relief by the extravagance of wealth and power in the Umayyad and Abbasid dynasties. Renunciation is a general orienting principle from which the science of introspection and ethical/moral development evolved. In its most rudimentary form ascetic/renunciant practice included physical austerities, such as fasting and little sleep, and other driving mechanisms (see below) that induced altered states of consciousness. Over time renunciation became less focused on the physical body and became a set of more internalized, if not contemplative, practices. Further shared experiments facilitated a rudimentary paradigm of introspection, ethical/moral development and transformative processes with shared concepts and vocabulary.

An 'inner' renunciation is the process of rejecting a world-centred life and cultivating a God-centred life. It is a way of living piously in everyday society. Think of the Nasrudddin story, mentioned in the introduction, which encourages one to consider going inside one's house (to become intimate with God) instead of focusing on the world, symbolized by looking in vain for the key under the street light outside. This ascetic tendency was found among some companions of the Prophet. Abu'l-Darda said, 'God despises the world [because] only in the world do we offend him, and without renouncing the world we obtain nothing from Him.'[5] Abu Dharr Ghifari (d. 652, Medina) said, 'It is through asceticism that God makes wisdom and goodness enter men's hearts.' Note that Muhammad criticized Abu Dharr for his desire to be celibate.[6] There are legends of the 'people of the veranda', who chose to remain poor and who used to live under the overhang along the wall of the mosque adjacent to the Prophet's house, devoting themselves to God. Among the generation of those following the companions, other expressions of piety emerged that were to foreshadow the sufi emphasis on the heart. Mujahid (d. 722), who edited the first Qur'an exegesis of his teacher Ibn 'Abbas, said:

> The heart is in this form [showing an open hand]. If a man commits
> a sin, it becomes like this', and he curled up one finger; 'then another
> sin, like this', and he curled up one finger; then three, then four. Finally
> at the fifth sin, he closed the fist with the thumb and said, 'Then God
> seals the heart.'[7]

Here is a clear example of a practice emphasizing ethical behaviour and connecting this behaviour with the locus of inner transformation, the heart. For sufis the primary subtle centre is the heart and it is located overlapping the location of the physical heart. It is a major centre of consciousness in Tibetan Buddhist and Taoist practice also (see Chapter 6).[8]

Al-Zuhri (d. 741), when asked about asceticism in the world, said, 'It is denying your ego-self all forms of desires.'[9] The move from the outer trappings of renunciation to an inner transformation is revealed in the saying of Sufyan al-Thawri (d. 777), 'asceticism is putting little hope in things of the world rather than wearing a tough woollen robe'.[10] Fudayl ibn 'Iyad (d. 803) juxtaposed contentment with renunciation by saying that '[t]he origin for renouncing this world is contentment with God'.[11] Asceticism is also based on trust in God according to Shaqiq al-Balkhi (d. 809 in Afghanistan). Ascetics and sufis disagreed with one another – and still do – over the extent to which renunciation should include material poverty. Abu Talib al-Makki (d. 996), the sufi and hadith scholar mentioned above, said that asceticism is choosing poverty. Ahmad ibn Hanbal (d. 855, founder of the Hanbali legal school), speaking from the viewpoint of a religious scholar, said that it is fine to have money as long as one is not happy if it increases or unhappy if it decreases.[12] The principle here is non-attachment. One necessarily needs to be in the world, but does not have to be *of* the world. He goes on to say that renunciation for the common people is to avoid the forbidden; for the religious elite, it is abandoning the surplus of what is permitted; and for those who know God, it is abandoning whatever keeps one from God.[13] According to this formulation, every observant Muslim is an ascetic to some degree.

Another characteristic of renunciation and other forms of introspection – but not restricted only to introspective activity – is having a sudden, but fleeting, experience in a state of consciousness other than our waking consciousness. In sufism this is called a state. Shaqiq al-Balkhi and Sari as-Saqati discussed these states in early sufism.[14] Modern scholars of consciousness call these states 'altered states of consciousness'. Some examples of these altered states are dreams, states caused by the injestion of mind-altering substances and meditative states. Altered states can be also produced through driving mechanisms, such as repetitive drum beats, sensory deprivation and fasting, and communal rituals. Precisely because altered states are so qualitatively different from normal waking consciousness, altered states facilitate new symbols, concepts and vocabulary. So powerful are many of these experiences that some are convinced that they have experienced God because of the clarity and suddenness of the experience. This does not mean that a person actually has had an experience of God. Accumulated subjective experience, mediated by inter-subjective verification, resulted in sufi practices and methodologies to promote and evaluate altered states in the context of transformation. This experimental process went hand in hand with symbols and concepts becoming formalized in the first few centuries of sufi activity.

Dramatic as they may be, altered states are closely examined by experienced sufis because often the visions or experiences are only valid in the altered state, but not in ordinary consensus reality. In other words, what occurred in an altered state of consciousness cannot necessarily be applied or extrapolated to everyday consensus reality. Many times, experiences in altered states are delusions in both non-ordinary and ordinary reality, even though they seem as real as a mirage. Altered states were not considered by the majority of sufis to be valid on their own if they contradicted the Qur'an or hadith, and, later, the creedal tenets developed by Muslim jurists. At the same time, most sufis recognized that the textual authority of scripture was best understood and applied in daily life with direct transformative experience to bring it deep into a heart realization. The development of the sufi process of transformation was based on a mutual interaction between personal, subjective experience and the evolving Islamic socio-religious tenets. Later, both Abu Sa'id al-Kharraz ('the cobbler', d. 899, Baghdad) and Qushayri emphasized the necessary harmony between the outer and inner, saying, 'Every law (shari'a) not supported by reality is unacceptable. Every reality not bound by law is unacceptable.'[15] In this fashion, the science of sufism, based upon the accumulated experience of subjective 'laboratory data', became compatible with Islamic jurisprudence. Sufis managed to integrate two levels of existence, the everyday tangible, linear, rational world of sharia and the intangible, nonlinear, transpersonal world of sufism, forming a synthesis – one that implicitly included the dimension of faith.

Early pious Muslims evolved so that they had one foot in ordinary reality and the other foot in non-ordinary reality. It was a move from an outer, isolated physical asceticism to an inner-directed renunciate lifestyle in the world. What good is an altered state, regardless of whether it is achieved through asceticism or another driving mechanism, if one is still ruled by the ego-self? Muhammad, his pious companions and successors, and the proto-sufis and sufis following them, all share a common process of becoming more God-centred persons. In the beginning, these pious Muslims were described by a handful of terms, which over the centuries coalesced into a common descriptor, 'sufi', by the end of the tenth century. The goal to get closer to God, described differently with multiple method-ologies of introspection, shows a progressive development of technical sufi vocabulary and sophisticated concepts. This came as a result of a collective exploration of inner lives, altered states and visions.

Some noteworthy contemplatives in the sufi tradition

A set of practices and perspectives called 'sufism' apparently originated in Iraq. There was another contemplative path: that of the Blameworthy, centred in Nishapur, in present-day Iran. The Blameworthy reacted to the relatively widespread renunciant Karramis, a group named after Ibn Karram (d. 869), who put on public displays of piety and asceticism. According to their opponents, Karrami activities were more exhibitionist than Islamically pious. We do not know what the Karramis did because we only have their opponents' accounts. With that in mind, one observer of the Karramis notes, '[T]hey do a lot of praying, fasting, and are humble but I do not see the light of Islam in these actions.'[16] Note the criterion of mainstream Islamic praxis as the litmus test of appropriate practice. The Blameworthy were prominently bazaar craftsmen and tradesmen, who kept a low profile and blended in with the urban society around them. Blame was to be focused on one's ego-self.

Abu Sa'd Khargushi (d. 1016), in an attempt to show the superiority of the Blameworthy, characterized them as everyday working people of confirmed experiential knowledge. The sufis, on the other hand, were portrayed as unemployed, wearing patched clothing, artificially cultivating spiritual states through ecstatic dance and listening to music and poetry.[17] 'Abdurrahman Sulami (d. 1021, Nishapur, Iran) outlined four levels of people: two associated with transmitted book knowledge and a third, which he called sufis, who lived in everyday society and focused on altered states. The fourth (probably the Blameworthy) 'are the chiefs of the community. It is difficult for others to know their states just as their reports about themselves are not free of ambiguity. Their station has been fortified through authentication of their affinity to the Real'.[18] By the end of the tenth century, there are very few pious individuals still described as Blameworthy – they had taken on an ultra-low profile. Sufi had become synonymous with pious Muslim contemplatives. Textual evidence in one compendium of sufi biographies lists only five Khurasani sufis at the beginning of the tenth century and 46 a hundred years later.[19]

It is now time to put some human faces on the development of sufism. The following six individuals should give you a flavour of the glorious geographic and experiential diversity of the early centuries of proto-sufi and sufi practice.

Hasan al-Basri

Hasan al-Basri (d. 728, Basra, Iraq) began his young adult life participating in the Arab conquests in Sistan, a region that today saddles southeastern Iran and Afghanistan. At some point, he settled in Basra to spend the rest of his life there. In the early sources it appears that he was concerned with developing God consciousness and defining corresponding behavioural ideals. Listening to the Qur'an with the heart was the best means to develop God consciousness for Hasan. 'Faith is attained neither by hopes nor by good appearances. It is rather attained by what is revered in the heart and confirmed by deeds.'[20] One of his guidelines for daily living was to scrupulously abstain from any thing or any action that was not ethically beyond reproach. Those who knew him noted his morose moods, reflected in his saying, 'Continuous sorrow in this world is what makes a pious act fertile.'[21] Others have noted, 'You seldom see al-Hasan but (grieved), as if just struck by a disaster.'[22] On the other hand, it appears that this sorrow was tempered by a genuine sincerity: 'Ah! If only I could find life in your hearts! Men have become like specters; I perceive a murmur, but I see nothing that loves. Tongues are brought to me in abundance, but I am looking for hearts.'[23]

It seems that Hasan's austere piety was shared by many of his contemporaries. Later in the tenth century, Basran sufis were keen to promote Basra and their group as the founders of sufism and Hasan was the perfect choice as a founder-figure.[24] So tenth-century Basrans acclaimed Hasan as the founder-figure of sufism, even though this genealogy was not generally acknowledged beyond Basra. As later biographical compendia reconstructed a smoothed-over version of early sufism, Hasan became one of the key founder-figures of sufism over the centuries. This retrospective on Hasan has him proposing a framework for heart knowledge and talking about altered states. Whether it was Hasan's framework or not – for there is no way of knowing – it had become included in the science of sufism by the tenth century.

Ibrahim ibn Adham

Ibrahim ibn Adham (d. c.777) came from Balkh, in present-day Afghanistan. The legends say that he abandoned his father's kingdom for a life of poverty, in much the same way that the Buddha-to-be had renounced worldly kingship. His sufi orientation follows that of Hasan al-Basri and others from Basra, Iraq. He practised contemplation, a more profound mode of introspection than reflection, in addition to being one of the first to mention a deeper way of unitary knowing through experience (*ma'rifa*). He defined three levels of asceticism. The first was renouncing the world and then renouncing the satisfaction of having renounced the world. The final stage was to not even notice the world.[25] Ibrahim says:

> If you wish that God should love you and that you should be the friend of God, then renounce this world and the next; do not desire them, empty yourself of the two worlds, and turn your face to God; then God will turn His face to you and fill you with God's grace.[26]

It appears that he lived outwardly as a renunciant, who often fasted for long periods and went out in the winter wearing only a fur covering without shoes or hat. Ibrahim was a frontier soldier who died fighting the Byzantines on the Syrian coast.

Dhu'l-Nun Misri

Dhu'l-Nun ('the one with the fish') Misri (the Egyptian, d. 859) is known to us through fragments of his sayings and anecdotes cited by later sufis. On one hand he writes, '(Drink) the wine of God's love for you, as long as God is making you drunk on your love for God.'[27] This is easily the type of verse that could lead to ecstatic states. Indeed, Dhu'l-Nun was said to be one of the first advocates of poetry/musical sessions where such altered states were facilitated for specially trained individuals. With this experiential background, Dhu'l-Nun categorized different levels of altered states, as well as the stations of increasing intimacy with God (from responding to God's call to total reliance on God). The sufis of the next few centuries, Sahl al-Tustari (d. 896), Qushayri (d. 1072), and Ghazali (d. 1111) built upon his 'spiritual travel maps'. Dhu'l-Nun precisely specified the meaning of direct knowledge of God (*ma'rifa*) as the attributes of oneness. He also specified three ranks based on knowledge: that of common Muslims, that of scholars and sages, and that of the friends of God, 'who see God with their hearts'.[28] Dhu'l-Nun contributed significantly to the growing lexicon of technical vocabulary in sufi practice. This is not to be mistaken for 'doctrine', which results from rational thought instead of disciplined introspective experience. These distinctions in kinds of knowledge and altered states over the centuries were to result in a particular type of knowledge associated with the process of becoming a sufi.

Pithy dialogues are characteristic of narratives transmitted about Dhu'l-Nun and other early sufis. One has Dhu'l-Nun wandering along the seashore when he meets a woman. He asks her: 'What is the end of love?' She answers, 'O simpleton, love has no end.' Then he asks why and she answers tersely, 'Because the Beloved has no end.'[29] This love is deeply rooted in the Prophet Muhammad. Dhu'l-Nun says, 'I knew God by God, and I knew what is besides God by the Messenger of God.' ... 'The sign of the lover of God is to follow the Friend of God, i.e. the Prophet, in his morals, and his deeds and his orders, and his customs.'[30]

Muhasibi

Muhasibi ('a person who diligently introspects', d. 857, Baghdad) considerably expanded the sufi technical lexicon. Like other sufis, he scrupulously observed the canonical duties outlined in the Qur'an and the example of the Prophet. Following renunciants before him, he felt sadness towards things of the world and was not distracted by the apparent joys of the world. As we have seen, this is a common theme in sufi practice, for one cannot have a God-centred life while being attached to worldly concerns. He emphasized inner actions of correct intention and sincerity, which he called 'actions of the heart'. For Muhasibi inner actions form the basis of correct outer action. Thus, by examining one's actual intentions through diligent introspection, one could avoid hypocrisy. With this as a basis, Muhasibi formulated a discipline that constantly subordinated one's thinking and behaviour to one singular goal: heart-felt service to God. Obedience to God went far beyond simply performing the ritual duties of prayer and fasting. Muhasibi's practice fostered altered states of consciousness that in turn engendered a direct unitary knowledge of God (*ma'rifa*). He isolated contemplation of God as the best means of purifying the ego-self, which in turn purified the actions of the heart (sincerity, certitude, gratitude and humility). This is a practice that 'is harsher on the body than enduring the night prayer (*qiyām al-layl*), fasting during the day and spending one's wealth in the path of God [that is, actions pertaining to all Muslims]'.[31]

Junayd

Junayd (d. 910, Baghdad) is a pivotal figure in sufism, representing an approach to sufism that integrated well with mainstream Sunni Islam. Early in life he migrated from Iran to Baghdad and became a grandmaster of sufism. He did not give much importance to altered states of consciousness, much less outward expressions of ecstasy. Once, as people were being moved to ecstasy by music, someone asked Junayd if he was moved. Junayd replied, 'You see the mountains and think they are fixed: but they pass like the clouds.'[32] (Q. 27:88). Junayd's apparently sober behaviour simply concealed his inner ecstasy. The goal of sufi practice, according to Junayd, was to annihilate the ego in God (a preliminary step), and then come back to one's daily life transformed in order to experience an innate profound love permeated by the attributes of God (the mark of realization). He outlined three levels of annihilation in God, the final stage being:

> [P]assing away from your ecstasies as the sign of the real overpowers you. At that moment you both pass away and abide, and are found truly existent in your passing away; through the found existence of your other; upon the abiding of your trace in the disappearance of your name.[33]

Not only did his outward sobriety protect him from harassment, but he was particularly well placed as a jurist to reconcile his practice with the norms of Islamic law and jurist understandings (and misunderstandings) of proper ways of living life as a Muslim. It was this jurist background that enabled him to avoid the persecution of Ghulam Khalil in 877 (explained below). As a jurist, he declared scriptural knowledge to be more reliable than the limitations of subjective experience that some sufis claimed to be the direct experience of God (*ma'rifa*). Subsisting in God non-ecstatically, like the Prophet, was to set the example for future mainstream sufism. Junayd rejected Hallaj's (martyred 922) open expressions of 'being one' with God, because he was well aware that religious scholars and common people were not in a position to understand. Their misunderstandings – and Hallaj's execution is the best example – could have dire consequences. Sufis after Junayd tended to follow his example through silence or by expressing their experiences and ideas in a way that only fellow sufis could understand.

Bayazid Bistami

Bayazid Bistami (d. 874), from northwestern Iran, is often used to represent the ecstatic mode of sufi expression, because of his many ecstatic utterances. It appears that Bayazid brought about these altered states by a severe solitary ascetic lifestyle. He relates:

> For twelve years I was the smith forging my self, for five years I was the mirror of my heart; for one year I observed both my self and my heart; I discovered a belt of infidelity (*zunnār*) around me, and I took twelve years to cut it; then I discovered an inner belt, which took me five years to cut; finally I had an illumination; I considered the creation; I saw it had become a corpse to me, and I [...] buried it and it did not exist for me any more.[34]

Bayazid used to focus on the Prophet's ascension as he meditated on the Qur'an. He was trying to duplicate the Prophetic journey through the seven heavens. There are many different accounts of Muhammad's night journey to Jerusalem and his ascension through the heavens, many including him riding on a white horse-like animal called Buraq. One outcome of this process had Bayazid asking God in one of his ecstatic utterances to 'seize me in Your oneness so that when Your creatures see me they will say, "We have seen You."' Junayd noted that Bayazid was very close but not at the goal yet.[35] The other outcome of this introspection was getting banished from his home town of Bistam various times for claiming to have experienced the Prophetic ascension. One of his best known ecstatic sayings is, 'Praise be to me!' (instead of 'Praise be to God'), which has been frequently discussed over the centuries. Hallaj commented, 'Poor Abu Yazid! He was at the threshold of divine speech (*nutq*) and it was from God that the words came (to his lips). But he did not know it, blinded as he (still) was by his (persistent) preoccupation with the one named "Abu Yazid."'[36] Over the centuries, many other renowned sufis in addition to Junayd and Hallaj have considered altered states and ecstasy to be markers of the beginning of the path.

The Qur'anic role in the development of sufism

The Qur'an is for Muslims as Jesus is for Christians. For Muslims the Qur'an is the word of God manifesting in a text; Jesus for Christians is the word of God manifesting in a human being. When people asked Muhammad to perform miracles, he only acknowledged one miracle: the Qur'an. When challenged by his opponents of composing poetry, Muhammad in turn challenged them to compose anything in Arabic as sublime as the Qur'an, which they apparently were unable to do. The Qur'an was the starting point for all Islamic religious sciences, including sufism.

The Qur'an is an embodied scripture; literally Muslims embody the Qur'an. In a pre-modern environment, the first step for young boys in their educational endeavours was to memorize the Qur'an. Still today a significant proportion of the Muslim community learns many suras (the Qur'anic equivalent of chapters) of the Qur'an. They learn it *by heart* and strive to recite it with an open heart. The Qur'an, meaning recitation, is not a book but is the human recitation of God's words – which practising Muslims enact five times a day in ritual prayer. The Qur'an often embellishes the façades of mosques and calligraphic representations of the Qur'an decorate the interiors of many buildings, including people's houses. Islamic culture is where the Qur'an, radiating from hearts, permeates everyday life via prayer, recitation, architecture and the visual arts.

It is natural that much of the evolving technical vocabulary of sufism came from the Qur'an, especially since many pious Muslims memorized it and used it as a basis for their meditations and introspection (see fig. 1.1). In addition, the Islamic monotheistic universe communicated via

FIGURE 1.1 Qur'an (2:4–20) written in Naskhi script by Hasan ibn Ahmad al-Qarahisari (d. 1556, Turkey) for the Ottoman Sultan Salim II. Most of the inscriptions in the Süleymaniye Mosque are the work of this calligrapher.

the Qur'an must have framed much of sufi experience. Muslims learned that by reciting and listening to the Qur'an in a synoptic, non-linear way, beyond literal and discursive meanings of the Qur'an, they could shift their awareness and consciousness. Another way of eliciting inner Qur'anic meanings was through the process of *istinbat* (from the root meaning of extraction of water from a well), which in a Qur'anic context was to extract meaning from the source of the Qur'an. As a ninth-century commentator, Muslim Khawwas noted, 'At first, since my reading of the Qur'an lacked sweetness, I began to read it as if Muhammad were dictating it to me; then, as if I could hear Gabriel announcing it to Muhammad; finally, as if I could hear God Himself; and all the sweetness was given to me.'[37] Another method of reading the Qur'an was to recite it in its entirety (at that time people read with their lips moving). After a vocalized reading of about 40 hours, over and over, seekers of God would find inspiration and multiple levels of meaning spontaneously evoked in the experience. Compare this method of relating to scripture with the rational, linear, piecemeal textual dissection employed by most of the later Qur'an exegetes and religious scholars ('*ulama*). This 'inspired reading of the Qur'an' could easily have been a stimulus for altered states and a direct experience of God's attributes.

So when we consider early sufi contemplatives after they emerged from their altered states, it was natural to use the vocabulary gushing from the Qur'anic source of God's words to communicate their experiences. Louis Massignon lists about 50 words used in sufism that are derived from Qur'anic vocabulary.[39] As other religious disciplines of specialized religious knowledge developed over the first 300 years, religious scholars also created technical vocabulary for their disciplines derived from Qur'anic vocabulary. Technical vocabulary of Arabic grammar and theology cross-fertilized sufi terminology. The key difference was that this process of developing a contemplative vocabulary (versus a theological, juristic vocabulary) came about through experience instead of through discursive reasoning. It is

INTERLUDE

The late Islamic studies scholar Nasr Abu Zayd (d. 2010) memorized the Qur'an by the time he was eight years old and forgot it quickly after going to a secular school. He notes, however, that:

> [F]orgetting did not affect the intimate personal connection with the Qur'ān which became an essential component of my identity; my memory could easily recall a passage of the Qur'ān when evoked by a single word. Later on, as a scholar, this intimacy became problematic to the extent I had to consult an English translation of the Qur'ān in order to establish a space of 'otherness'.[38]

easy to see how religious scholars – or common Muslims for that matter – who did not have this experiential knowledge, would look askance at sufi discourse. Some of this vocabulary, like the path to God along with states and stations on the path, included 'road maps' and descriptions of the stations one could encounter. These signposts made it easier for other seekers to follow, but made little sense to those without an inclination to go beyond the mainstream version of Islam.

One of the controversial outcomes of Qur'anic recitation was intentionally using particularly melodious recitation to induce ecstatic altered states. Poetry also served the same function. Dhu'l-Nun Misri, Junayd and Hallaj considered this practice legitimate only on the condition that one had control over the ego-self. The Khurasani Blameworthy, honing their low profiles in practice and in society, saw these ecstatic gatherings in Baghdad as a front for sensuous expression and dubious behaviour – like gazing at beardless boys or tearing one's clothes off. In the beginning, such ecstatic states were the spontaneous outcome of listening to the Qur'an. Altered states were not the goal, because they were an ephemeral 'high'. Later other sufi groups made ecstasy an end in itself and many sufis and non-sufis were, and continue to be, scandalized. Abu'l-Husayn al-Nuri (d. 907, Baghdad), a contemporary of Hallaj, died in ecstasy as he walked barefoot into a patch of freshly cut reeds.

Sufi interpretations of the Qur'an: Ja'far al-Sadiq and Sahl al-Tustari

Qur'an interpretation (exegesis) encompassed another expression of experiencing the Qur'an. One of the early Qur'an commentaries by Ja'far al-Sadiq (d. 765), a pivotal individual in many sufi lineages and also the sixth Shi'i Imam (after whom the Ja'fari school of jurisprudence is named), is known through a compilation by Sulami written around 980. Ja'far's commentary has a clear ethical perspective, while utilizing a vocabulary derived from experience, e.g. the ego and the heart, proximity to God, subtleties and realities. Ja'far was probably the first to use *al-haqq* (the Real, the Truth) as the principal synonym for God that later became common usage in sufi writing (note Hallaj's ecstatic utterance, 'I am *al-haqq*!'). Ja'far delineated four levels of Qur'an commentary: 1. literal interpretation for the common people; 2. an extended interpretation based on allusions for religious scholars; 3. a subtle mode of interpretation for those in close proximity to God; and 4. an interpretation of realities for the prophets. This hierarchical principle would later be reflected in degrees of human awareness (commoners, elite and the elite of the elite) and the various stations (levels of consciousness) to locate a person on the path to God.

The human heart is the focal point for God consciousness. Ja'far, commenting on 'God has made ships to travel on the ocean by command' (Q. 14:32), says, 'God has made the heart of the believer of service to God's love and God's knowledge. God's share of the slaves is their hearts and nothing else, because the heart is the receptacle of God's gaze and the repository of God's trust.'[40] In short, the heart is the ship upon which we navigate God's ocean. His comment on 'God bought from the believers their lives and wealth' (Q. 9:111) is that this purchase serves as a means for love to come through their hearts, allowing them to be connected to God.[41]

Ja'far integrated spiritual rank (the friends of God), direct experiential knowledge (*ma'rifa*), and stations along the path to God (trust, faithfulness, certainty and love). His was one of the first commentaries to make what was later to become a sufi quest, explicitly grounded in Qur'anic verses. Unfortunately we do not have any personal diaries to understand the correlations of this introspective commentary and Ja'far's own personal introspection. If it is authentically Ja'far's commentary, however, it is very likely a result of his own experience, because in this early period Muslim contemplatives did not have to justify their experience by linking it with scripture. It was later in sufi history that manuals on sufism continually used Qur'anic passages to justify some sufi concept or teaching in order to legitimize sufism as an Islamic religious science.

Sahl al-Tustari (d. 896, Basra), a native of Tustar in southwest Iran, stands out as an early sufi commentator. From his youth he went on a quest to realize closeness with God, travelling to Iraq and the holy cities of Mecca and Medina. He visited the frontier retreat fortress at 'Abbadan, located on an island near the present-day Iran–Iraq border, where other contemplatives and renunciants lived. A transformative experience occurred while he was there, which Sahl included in his commentary on 'God, there is no god but God, the living, the everlasting' (Q. 2:255):

> This is the greatest verse in the Book of God. It includes the supreme
> name of God which is written in the sky with green light in a single line
> from east to west. I used to see it written like that in the Night of Might
> when I was at 'Abbadān.[42]

After returning to Tustar, Sahl lived a secluded, ascetic life contemplating
the Qur'an for two decades before becoming a public figure, teaching a
circle of seekers. He declared himself as the proof of God and the proof
for the friends of God of his era. Other non-sufi religious authorities with
political connections disagreed with this assessment, so he was forced to
flee to Basra. His commentary on the Qur'an, recorded by his students and
often quoted by Hujwiri (d. *c.*1075) in his sufi treatise, *Revealing the Veiled*,
is his most prominent legacy.

Sahl apparently did not meditate on the Qur'an per se, but instead
allowed a word or phrase from the Qur'an to trigger associations in a larger
context – and to facilitate a field of associations for other people who had
immersed themselves in the Qur'an. Gerhard Böwering, whose pioneering
work on Sahl's Qur'an commentary informs this discussion, says, 'The
actual shape of Tustarī's *Tafsir*, with its layers of contents, its clusters of
aphorisms, and its samples of illustrations, represents a direct reflection
of this open-ended and in-gathering way of Qur'an interpretation by
association.'[43] It is impossible to separate Sahl's Qur'an commentary from
his inner world because this visionary, transpersonal realm is a unitary field
and experienced as such. Literally, there is a quranization of consciousness
– a process that is not a monopoly of sufis (as Nasr Abu Zayd reminds us
above).

Like Ja'far al-Sadiq, Sahl begins his commentary by contextualizing
it within four meanings inherent in every Qur'anic verse: 1. a literal
meaning which is beautiful recitation; 2. a hidden meaning of understanding the verse; 3. a meaning limiting what is lawful and unlawful;
and 4. a transcendent meaning revealed through the heart as understood
by God.

Sahl gives an example of inner and outer levels of meaning in his interpretation of 'That you may warn [people of] the mother of cities [Mecca],
and those around it' (Q. 42:7):

> In its outward meaning, it (the mother of cities) refers to Mecca. In its
> inner meaning it refers to the heart, while those around it refer to the
> bodily members. Therefore warn them, that they might safeguard their
> hearts and bodily members from delighting in acts of disobedience and
> following (their) lusts.[44]

Some of Sahl's technical vocabulary utilized in Qur'an interpretation
expresses a subtle psychological structure of the human being. In
this enterprise of mapping out a subtle psychology, he was joined
by his contemporaries, Muhasibi (purifying the ego), Nuri (levels
of the heart) and Tirmidhi (the ego-self versus the heart). Like
other sufis before him, Sahl located the locus of God consciousness
in the heart (*qalb*) and the innermost heart (*sirr*). This innermost
heart, literally 'the *secret*', is already alluded to in a hadith attributed
to Muhammad, 'Truly within hearts there is a *concealed secret*
pertaining to knowledge, which belongs to God, Exalted is God;
the Aware – God informs you of what is [hidden for] you in the
unseen.'[45] Commenting on 'O humans! It is you who need God'
(Q. 35:15), Sahl says, 'The servant should feel the need for God in
his innermost secret, cutting himself off from all other than God,
so that his servanthood becomes pure; for pure servanthood is self-
abasement and humble submission.'[46]

In his commentary on 'Those who were given knowledge before
it (the Qur'an), when it (the Qur'an) is recited to them, fall down
prostrate on their faces' (Q. 17:107), Sahl notes that: 'there is nothing
which affects a person's innermost secret like listening to the Qur'an.'[47]
The innermost heart is the seat of experiencing and inclining towards
God – that which connects God's word to each person. It is the heart
and innermost secret where God consciousness is cultivated and from
which authentic sincerity radiates. Indeed, the heart and innermost
heart reflect the subtle physiology of contemplative practice that other
sufis (and non-sufi contemplatives) have discovered through centuries of
collective experience. Early sufi Qur'an commentary was consistent with
what became the discipline of sufism and a paradigm of contemplative
practice.

The paradigm and science of sufism c.1000

Over a period of 300 years, sufis created their own sets of practices and developed a generally common paradigm of contemplative practice compatible with what became the Sunni and Shi'i orthodoxies. We have seen how early sufis had difficulties with the religious authorities, who often had political clout. Jurists, as religious scholars, were trained to memorize texts, the Qur'an and hadith, and to produce other texts (usually legal texts and rulings) using these scriptural sources as their basis. Some Muslim religious scholars had a tolerant, inclusive stance towards something they realized that they knew little about. Others, seeing themselves as 'defenders of the faith', took it upon themselves to have an antagonistic stance towards sufis and sufism. This is quite understandable. Sufism, like any contemplative practice, is beyond the intellectual, rational realm of jurists and scholars. No wonder they rejected it – it made no sense to them. For example, Sahl asserted (probably from his own experience) that one can contemplatively witness God. He was accused of sacrilege, because the doctrine of the jurists declared that God could not be perceived visually until the Day of Resurrection. The jurists had no idea that Sahl was talking about the eyes of the heart, not physical eyes. What Jalaluddin Rumi (d. 1273) said 300 years later applies to Sahl's time also:

> In the same way the great scholars of the age split hairs on all manner of sciences. They knew perfectly and have a complete comprehension of those other matters which do not concern them. But as for what is truly of moment and touches a man more closely than all else, namely his own self, this your great scholar does not know. He pronounces on the legality or otherwise of every thing, saying, 'This is permitted and that is not permitted, this is lawful and that is unlawful.' Yet he knows not his own self, whether it is lawful or unlawful, permissible or not permissible, pure or impure.[48]

The burden continues to be on the sufis, operating out of a larger context, to accommodate juristic understandings. The typical Muslim jurist never went through a contemplative process of discovering himself (though many sufis were also jurists). Sufis claim that there are higher domains of awareness, experience, love and truth. These claims are not the result of armchair speculation, Islamic dogma, or even Qur'anic assertions. Instead, they are the result of what became centuries of cumulative inter-subjective experience, the result of intentional experimental transformative practices that in turn were tested and verified in the crucibles of experienced contemplative communities, who often disagreed with each other. In parallel with the insights of sufi Qur'an interpretation, a science of Sufism developed that set the foundation for future contemplative practice. Some of the domains of this science are explained below.

Subtle physiology

The heart is already mentioned in the Qur'an as a critical part of human subtle physiology, the locus of one's conscience and sincerity, where humans are connected to God (note where God intervenes between a person and the heart in Q. 8:24). The expansion of the chest, metaphorically a heart transformation, is mentioned three times in the Qur'an.[49] Qur'an commentaries elucidate the crucial significance of the heart and the innermost heart, while various sufi masters contrasted the heart with the ego-self and/or the spirit. Through actualizing the heart, sufis discovered a common subtle physiological phenomenon (relating to the corresponding human subtle body) that is shared in other contemplative traditions.

Other early sufis further developed the subtle physiological system they discovered. Hasan al-Basri conceived of the material body (lit. 'mould'), in which there were various interpenetrating subtle bodies. His students named these subtle bodies, from coarse to more subtle: ego-self, heart, spirit and mystery, conceiving each of these subtle bodies as veils separating one from the divine essence.[50] Abu'l-Husayn al-Nuri identified the knowledge of God in one of four levels of the heart: the chest (*sadr*) associated with submission to God, the heart (*qalb*), the inner heart (*fu'ad*) and the innermost heart (*lubb*), where one experiences God's unity.[51]

Love

Rabi'a (d. 801, Basra) is usually the only woman most people can think of when the discussion turns to early women sufis, though we know from Sulami's works that there were dozens of prominent early sufi women.[52] Like other early sufis, we only know of Rabi'a through pithy phrases, anecdotes and stories written after his death. There are even stories of her rejecting the marital proposals of Hasan al-Basri, another legendary figure who had already died when she was a child. One of these stories has Rabi'a saying to Hasan that if he wanted to marry her, he would have to ask God because she was under his command. He asks:

> O Rabi'a, by what means did you attain this degree?
> By losing in God everything I'd attained.
> How did you know God?
> You know the how [answered Rab'ia]. We know the no-how [lit. without how, *bila kayf*].[53]

So-called history and fact are one thing, and teaching sufi ideals is yet another. Rabi'a modelled a very austere life, based on extreme reliance on God, to meet her needs. Her contribution, or the contribution to sufism in her name, is a love of God simply for the sake of God. In a more explicitly sufi version of what could have started out as a Nasruddin story six centuries later, Rabi'a was asked why she was carrying a candle in one hand and a water pitcher in the other. She replied, 'I want to throw fire into Paradise and pour water into Hell so that these two veils disappear, and it becomes clear who worships God out of love, not out of fear of Hell or hope for Paradise.'[54] Love of children, a husband or even the Prophet only distracted her from loving God. In this focus on the love of God, Rabi'a's emphasis on divine love contrasted with that of many of her contemporaries, who focused on being scrupulous, fearing God and putting the emphasis on Islamic ritual practice.

The emphasis on love continued after Rabi'a and still continues today. Yahya Razi, from Rayy near present-day Tehran (d. 871, Nishapur) declared, 'one mustard seed of love is better than seventy years of worship

INTERLUDE

Here is a humorous contemporary example. Around 1987, when Tibetan monks first saw neuroscientists putting electrodes all over a monk's head to measure EEG activity, they burst out laughing. The neuroscientists thought that they were laughing because 20 electrodes on a human head looked strange. They were surprised to find out later that the Tibetans were laughing at the placement of the electrodes on the head, when all the actual contemplative activity, as far as the monks were concerned, was related to the heart region. Think of putting a stethoscope on a person's big toe to measure the heartbeat. Twenty-five years later the neuroscientists still apparently have not heard what the Tibetan contemplatives have been trying to communicate to them.

without music'.[55] Sari Saqati (d. 867, Baghdad) declared that love is the primary motivation and experience to get closer to God. This love is a burning love that has to be experienced to be understood. Sari refrained from elaborating more on his experience since love is beyond linguistic understanding. Nuri, a student of Sari Saqati, is an example of a sufi's manifesting unconditional love of God, like Rabi'a. His definition of love was to prefer others to himself, even to the point of putting his own life in jeopardy. In 877, Ghulam Khalil, a zealous jurist, rounded up sufis who professed 'desire or love for God', because in his mind God was to be feared, not loved. They were to be charged with heresy and then probably executed. Nuri volunteered to be the first one to be killed. This moved the Caliph so much that he dropped the charges and let them go free. At the same time, Nuri took it upon himself to reprimand people if they did not follow Islamic law in their lives. For him, sufism 'consists not of (outward) appearances and sciences but of high moral qualities.'[56]

Developmental stations on the path and corresponding ranks of aspirants

Shaqiq al-Balkhi focused on an extreme version of relying on God (like Rab'ia) by advocating a life without working at any kind of paying job. This probably was considered more extreme for a man, who was expected to be gainfully employed, than for a woman. Shaqiq mapped out a sufi path to God, with a graded set of way stations. This path was developmental in that the characteristics at the early stages of the path – fear of God and ascetic practices – were contrasted to a fervent love at the advanced levels of the path. Shaqiq outlines four levels of sincerity:

1 Renunciants
2 Those who fear God
3 Those who have a strong desire for paradise
4 Those who focus on love of God, whose hearts bask in the light of God.

Abu Sa'id al-Kharraz discussed the path towards God and its many stations in his *Book of Truthfulness*. As the sufi wayfarer progressed, he became more truthful. Like schema of other paths toward God, Kharraz's started with repentance and trust in God and, many stages later, ended in intimacy with God. Shaqiq identified various altered states of consciousness, along with more permanent developmental stations, leading closer and closer to God. Junayd denied any reality to altered states, while Hallaj saw them useful for the beginner, though he cautioned against seekers becoming attached to altered states.[57]

Annihilation and abiding in God

Like Junayd, Kharraz commented on the annihilation of the ego in God (*fana'*) and abiding in God (*baqa'*). He outlined ranks of sufi aspirants, like Shaqiq. For Kharraz, there were various ranks of people:

1 Religious scholars who have intermittent glimpses using allusions in their search for God,

2 Those who have varying experiences of altered states and various levels of those privileged by God,
3 Those who are immersed in an ocean of sincerity and who experience pure love,
4 Those who have stabilized their altered states and have control over them,
5 Those who see reality unveiled and are conducted to God from a place beyond space-time.

According to Kharraz, only the last group fully abides in God.[58] Each of these ranks has its own transformative practice, which in turn determines a specific set of experiences and the language to describe those experiences.

The textual synthesis of the sufi tradition

Most of the previous discussion has been derived from primary sufi experiential sources and sufi Qur'an commentary, a subset of the experiential sources. However, there were also sources seeking to establish sufism as one of the recognized religious sciences, that is, writing *about* sufism. These sources include retrospective historical accounts of sufism's early centuries and explained sufism in a plausible manner to largely non-sufi audiences. Rather than stemming from transpersonal experience, these texts seek to establish a discipline of Sufism on a par with the other Islamic religious sciences, legitimizing sufism for the non-sufi Muslim majority. They also gave sufism a scholarly, respectable lineage for future generations.

Abu Nasr al-Sarraj ('the saddler', d. 988, Tus, Khurasan) wrote one of the earliest surviving books that surveyed the topic of sufism, *Flashes of Light in Sufism*. Travelling from Tus in northeast Iran to the Middle East, Sarraj talked personally with 39 sufis to write about 200 in all.[59] When Sarraj did express his own perspectives, they were in accordance with Junayd's path of sufi practice and mainstream Sunni practice and belief. Much of *Flashes* discusses a range of controversies – from ecstatic utterances ('I am God!'), listening to music and extreme ascetic behaviour, to more Islamically controversial beliefs, such as dispensing with ritual practices, being able to see God in the physical world, and incarnation of God in human form.

It appears that he did a very credible job of communicating mostly Iraqi sufism to his Khurasani audience. He was very specific and inclusive about who the *real* heirs of Muhammad were, namely jurists, hadith scholars and sufis. In the last case, authentic sufis were those who lived according to Qur'anic dictates and the Prophetic sunna.

Further east, in present-day Uzbekistan, Abu Bakr al-Gulabadi (d. *c*.992, Gulabad, Uzbekistan) wrote his *Introducing the Way of the Sufis*,[60] which expressed the variety of sufi perspectives through the lens of their respective theological orientations. In many ways, this was a translational project seeking to explain sufism in a context that educated readers already knew. Gulabadi made sufism accessible to jurists, theologians and those already acquainted with Tirmidhi's wisdom legacy by fitting sufism into the existing framework of Islamic religious sciences. Both of these authors effectively explained a predominantly Iraqi sufism to a Khurasani and Central Asian audience.

Most of the sufi literature in the early centuries contributed to the formal development of a discipline called Sufism, namely a paradigm of knowledge acquisition, interpretation and verification. In the eleventh century sufi pedagogy was emphasized – perhaps because of greater numbers of people participating in sufi practices. From the titles of these treatises, there was an emphasis on correct conduct and behaviour for sufi aspirants and methods of recollecting God (*dhikr*). For the ethical/moral dimension of sufi practice, a relatively large number of sacred sufi biographies (hagiographies) were written. These texts detailed a continuity of exemplary behaviour, from the Prophet through the generations of sufis, all of whom were to be emulated. Treatises on listening to music also started to appear in the eleventh century, probably to provide guidelines to practitioners in response to controversies.

In *The Nourishment of Hearts*, Abu Talib al-Makki (d. 996, Baghdad) combined guidelines for living a pious life – both inwardly and outwardly – with the dictates of the Qur'an and sunna. He emphasized the unambiguous superiority of heart knowledge, the result of a devotional life, over the book knowledge of scholars. Makki makes it very clear that those with heart knowledge are the sincere heirs of the Prophet, not the government-employed jurists and religious scholars, who were preoccupied with their lucrative salaries and social prestige. Because of the ethical principles transmitted from Sahl al-Tustari's students and frequent quotes from Sahl, some modern scholars situate *The Nourishment* as a continuation of Sahl's teaching.[61]

'Abdullah Ansari (d. 1089, Herat, Afghanistan), in sharp contrast to Makki, outlines a more formal sufi pedagogy, particularly focused on stages along the sufi path. His treatises, *A Hundred Stations* and *Travelers' Way Stations*, are classics in sufi literature of 'contemplative maps' that describe the developmental path sufis take. Lest one 'mistake the map for the territory', Ansari counsels, 'Know that the wayfarers through these stages are very different from each other, not agreeing on a specific order, and not standing on a common goal.'[62] This is a good reminder that the sufi path – often called the pathless path – is subjective and open-ended. One is reminded of a saying attributed to many sufis, and to Muhammad, 'There are as many paths to God as there are human breaths.'[63]

Abu'l-Qasim Qushayri (d. 1072, Nishapur, Iran) was a master of various Islamic religious sciences: Qur'an exegesis (note his sufi commentary, *Subtleties of Allusions*), jurisprudence (the Shafi'i school), and theology (the Ash'ari perspective). He wrote the *Treatise* (on sufism) from this impressive background. Beginning with the common refrain about the decline of sufis of his generation, he then started outlining a jurist-friendly version of sufism, highlighting the pivotal importance of Junayd. Qushayri details 83 sufi biographies before his relatively extensive coverage of sufi technical vocabulary, stations and states, and correct sufi behaviour. For its time this was a masterpiece of sufi learning, incorporating various Islamic religious disciplines.[64]

Revealing the Veiled was the first Persian compendium of sufism. The patron saint of Lahore, 'Ali b. 'Uthman al-Hujwiri (d. *c*.1075, Lahore, Pakistan), nicknamed 'the one who bestows treasure', wrote this book towards the end of his life. As with most of the writers mentioned in this chapter and qualified sufi teachers since then, there is a concern about increasing numbers of people setting themselves up as sufis. The quote by 'Ali b. Ahmad al-Bushanji (d. 959), '*Tasawwuf* is a name without a reality, but it used to be a reality without a name' is from Hujwiri's book. In *Revealing the Veiled*, there are discussions concerning sufi robes, clothing and paraphernalia, because for common people these outer markers were equated with authenticity. Earlier sufi authors, including those mentioned above, focused on a few normative versions of sufism while Hujwiri 'was the first to tackle the issue of diversity head on'.[65] *Revealing the Veiled* was a useful indication for his readers and for us today that the practice of sufism is a quite diverse rainbow of phenomena.

Across an area between Iraq and present-day Uzbekistan, extending 2,500 km east–west, one necessarily finds diversity in sufi practices and written interpretations of these practices. This literature overview has briefly summarized some of the diverse facets of sufism overlapping with the 'process of becoming a sufi', whether ethically or contemplatively. Sarraj and Gulabadi, in particular, promoted sufism under the rubric of inner ethical and contemplative practice across the eastern Islamic world. Their writing about the foreign, and perhaps even the exotic, subject of Iraqi sufism for a Khurasani and Central Asian elite audience helped to put sufism in the foreground, subordinating the Blameworthy and Hakimiyya contemplative currents. By 1100, most sufis conceived of their practice as the quintessence of *islam*, with sufis as the true heirs of the prophets (instead of jurists and scholars). The compilation of sufi biographies (hagiographies) between the time of the Prophet and contemporary times set the stage for sufi lineages, as we will see in the next chapter. Thanks to Gulabadi, Qushayri and Hujwiri, who incorporated more theological and juridical perspectives in their expositions, sufism became all the more attractive to religious scholars and jurists, some of whom began on the sufi path themselves. Sufism ended up being quite compatible with mainstream Sunni practice and belief.

The polymath Abu Hamid al-Ghazali (d. 1111, Tus, Khurasan), one of the scholarly giants in the Sunni tradition, is generally accredited with the grand synthesis of sufism with the other Islamic religious sciences.[66] Ghazali represented the mainstream sufi emphasis on moderation and low-profile conformity within society, which set the stage for sufi activity to include many who were eager to benefit from the blessings of those who were close to God, without embarking on a rigorous path of contemplative practice themselves. His seminal work, *Enlivening the Religious Sciences*, rests on the shoulders of the pioneering work of the relatively unknown sufis mentioned in this chapter.

As a concluding remark, the early sufis, like those who followed them, have continued to be masters in harmonizing Islamic practice and local cultures – spearheading the indigenization and vernacularization of Islam globally. Although the discussion in this chapter has highlighted the role of the Qur'an and other dynamics internal to the religion of Islam, it should be obvious that *any* set of religious practices is coloured by the local language, history and culture. The success of any religious practice to successfully move from one culture to another is directly a function of its practitioners' ability to adapt to local cultures – otherwise no religion could ever spread beyond its original geo-cultural sphere. I wish I could list the common qualities of the people who have facilitated the flourishing of sufism in so many places and in so many ways. Perhaps then I could figure out the corresponding set of characteristics of people whose families originated in the Arabian Peninsula and who have not contributed anything connected to sufi practice or lineage in the past 1,000 years (with the exception of Yemen and very sporadic activity in Oman and up the coast).

2

INSTITUTIONALIZATION OF SUFI PRACTICE

Sufism through verbal instruction [only] *is like building* [a house] *on dung.*

ABU SA'ID ABU 'L-KHAYR[1]

BY THE ELEVENTH CENTURY, sufi practice shifted from informal groups of sufi practitioners to more institutionalized forms of sufi activity that included lineages, founder-figures of these lineages and sufi lodges. Historians have yet to piece together how this momentous transformation came about. Looking at how institutions develop in contemporary sufi practice, we see that when the number of people in a contemplative group gets too large to meet in a home, they require a larger space. Mosques then and now (especially now) are not usually available for such activities. The new venue requires additional resources. Institutionalization often begins here, fuelled by increased demand for sufi expertise. At a certain point the shaykh, who might have had another occupation, becomes a full-time teacher, which in turn requires additional finances, often provided by affluent members of the group.

That increasing numbers of people are visiting sufis does not necessarily imply that there is a proportional increase of seekers engaged in transformative sufi practice. As today, most of those going to sufis were not aspiring to engage in a rigorous discipline, but looked for assistance in worldly affairs, healing, amulets and blessings. In the contemporary world, middle-class seekers tend not to use amulets or opt for spiritual healing. Most are not all that keen to abandon their existing lifestyle habits and replace them with a practice that takes hours a day. This should not be surprising. The demands of transformative practice, like the human egos they seek to tame, have not changed that much over time.

Institutionalization often moves to another level when the shaykh's eldest son inherits the large majority of his father's students, becoming the custodian of the sufi lodge and a new tomb. Hereditary succession with a tomb attracting regional visitors was well underway by the eleventh century. Sometimes the spiritually most qualified student set up a new sufi lodge away from the shaykh's family after the shaykh had given him his prayer rug, cane and rosary as tangible and blessed signs of authority. Practices varied. The Khalwatis, whose founder-figure was 'Umar al-Khalwati (d. 1397), were also known as the Halveti lineage in Turkey. They often had hereditary succession and others, like the Naqshbandis, whose founder-figure was Baha'uddin Naqshband (d. 1389) in Bukhara, Uzbekistan, tended to choose the spiritually most qualified student. In either case, sufis were in demand as they adeptly adapted to local customs, replicating the community of Muhammad and his companions. In the thirteenth century, when the Mongol hordes devastated Iraq and Khurasan, the new Mongol dynasties patronized sufi lodges. When the Mongols converted to Islam over the next century, it was likely at the hands of the sufis. We know about some of the major sufi players of the time from texts. The vast majority of sufis, as now, however, lived and worked in textual, and therefore historical, obscurity.

The role of holy men was a commonly shared feature in both Christendom and the Islamic world, as friends of God (alive and dead) became intermediaries between people and God. Sufi shaykhs often became enmeshed in the local socio-political fabric in their role as intermediaries across economic and social classes. In an urban setting, the rulers patronized influential sufis, who in turn legitimized and often worked in harmony with them. Typically there were close ties between the ruling elite, the learned elite and the sufi elite.

My educated hunch is that, at some point, the supply of qualified shaykhs, always low, could not keep up with the demand of the masses and opportunists rushed in to fill the demand. This prompted sufis to respond with the same mode of quality control that hadith scholars had developed centuries before to verify the accuracy of what the Prophet Muhammad had allegedly said or done (the hadith). After people started fabricating hadith, scholars made their countermoves and determined reliable transmitters in each generation after Muhammad to verify that each reliable hadith had a bona fide chain of transmission. Likewise, a probable first response to the burgeoning demand for sufi shaykhs in the tenth century was to document sufi lineages. These lineages came into being as each sufi documented his teacher, his teacher's teacher, and so on until the initiatory 'chain' connected to the Prophet. It did not take much to falsify these hadith and sufi chains, but *something* had to be done.

Along with lineages, sufi lodges soon became a common feature throughout the Islamic world, alongside mosques (the government) and madrasas. Sufis attracted resources that were accumulated through decentralized pious endowments catering to local needs. Sufi affiliations also extended to men's clubs and guilds, thereby extending sufi connections to organizations that had a stake in a stable social order. When one had an entire guild associated with a sufi lineage, donations were continuous and compounded over time. Sufi lodges promoted a potent mode of conviviality, in that they brought people together across socio-economic classes in a way that the former centralized caliphal bureaucracy in Baghdad, which had ended by the middle of the tenth century, could never have accomplished. Sufi ways of bringing people together, as we will see, were very personalized. They created a transformative liminal space in sufi lodges that replicated the community of Muhammad and his companions. The extensive institutionalization starting in the eleventh century, therefore, is likely to have been a direct function of sufism's relatively sudden popularity.

Why did sufi shaykhs become mainstream?

If we start with what is easily observed, we notice that people in many contemporary majority Islamic countries consult with sufi shaykhs and sufi shrine custodians. Sufis provide a unique and varied set of services.

Unlike the modern West, most of the Islamic world has very few profes-
sional psychologists and counsellors, though this is changing fast in
countries where the middle class is growing. Instead sufis often perform
these functions. Western biomedical medicine is often too expensive. There
are many alternative forms of effective and affordable medical treatments
with fewer side-effects, such as Greek medicine, homeopathy and herbal
remedies. Sufi healing is another medical modality – free with no side-
effects and available without prescription. Since physical disease has been
thought to result from spiritual disease, efficacious cures have depended on
unquestioning faith in the sufi master, who is perceived to be close to God.
Although sufi medical anthropology has hardly been studied, I can attest
that in each culture where I have lived, people usually know where best to
go for a given ailment. Here is a modern example from Morocco.

> In the morning, I decided to go to the *fqih* [functionally equivalent
> to a sufi in this case]. My husband said, 'No it is necessary to go to the
> hospital.' I answered, 'No, it is not an illness for the hospital, it is an
> illness for the *fqih* and the saint. When an infant falls sick and has fever
> and breathes with difficulty, it is an illness which is for the *fqih*. But
> when a child eats and vomits, when he is sick in the intestines, then it
> is an illness for the hospital. Also, if he chokes when he vomits, it is an
> illness for the hospital. I learned to tell them apart from the neighbours.'[2]

My sense is that, at some point in history, sufis replaced the former
specialists who performed these kinds of services. Sufi lodges began in
northeast Iran – Nishapur to be exact – and spread throughout much of the
Islamic world. Perhaps sufis filled in a vacuum of wandering Manichaen and
Zoroastrian holy men. To the west of Iran there were pre-Islamic shrines,
e.g. the tombs of ancient prophets, but these and other holy places remained
non-Muslim domains until most of the population were Muslims. If the
extrapolated data of Richard Bulliet are correct, then Iran and much of the
Middle East did not become a 90 per cent majority Muslim area until the
eleventh century.[3] It could have been this critical mass of urban and rural
Muslims and their healing and spiritual needs that propelled the populari-
zation of sufism. The average person would probably go to a sufi shaykh,

who was trained to deal with these everyday practical needs, rather than a religious scholar, whose main qualification was the number of the books he had memorized (at least in most of the eastern Islamic world). The former non-Muslim specialists lived in a bygone world, or had converted to Islam. Perhaps in a newly Islamicized Middle East, sufis were the human face of Islam, mediating between the pre-Islamic past and the post-conversion future. If there were a 'find wali' game, the *wali* (the sufi) would usually be in the mediating middle.

It would not take much for a sufi to become popular. Consider how fast entertaining stories about miracle working, telepathy and flying to Mecca in the evening for a pilgrimage could spread. I have heard about miracles of sufi shaykhs living in the United States from Euro-American students – almost always about someone else's experience. After hearing so many stories, I too started to think at least *some* may be true, particularly when credible people are so convinced. It is hard for us in the modern world to understand how fast the reporting of events, including miracles, could be in a society without the internet or mobile phones. Living in Cairo in the late 1970s, when only select people had landlines, we used to call this phenomenon of apparently instant communication the 'Arabic telephone'. I can imagine how sufis became inundated with people suddenly requesting assistance, as stories of their feats became more and more embellished.

The process of 'status inflation' increases in the environs of the sufi lodge. A first-time visitor immediately encounters the group dynamics created by the shaykh's students. Often there is considerable awe and hyper-respectful behaviour toward the shaykh, which also influences the newcomer, who picks up the cues to the new environment. Other sufi shaykhs have attracted people because their practices facilitated altered ecstatic states, e.g. listening to music (*sama'*) and recitation of poetry. This became synonymous with sufi practice in many quarters. With no corresponding ethical or behavioural discipline, some might say that this was no more than a legal 'high'. But for many these experiences were – erroneously according to some sufis – equated with becoming closer to God. Again, the vast majority in the outer circles of sufi activity did not go to sufi shaykhs for rigorous ego-disciplining, but to receive God's blessing to ease their daily lives. Over time, people in each locale came to know when it was appropriate to go to a sufi for healing or other assistance.

If we look at this rise in popularity from a socio-political perspective, then from 945 the Abbasid Empire, centred in Baghdad, started breaking up into a dynamic and expanding network of successor states governed by independent rulers. For the next six centuries, much of the Islamic world was decentralized in various communities where the local elite legitimized and mediated the power of regional military commanders. In a social system where patronage and loyalty determined political power, the mediatory expertise of sufis was in demand. The inward 'anti-structure' of sufi lodges (as will be detailed below) transformed individuals, while legitimizing Islamic institutions maintained by large landholders and other outer politico-economic structures of society. Sufis' integrating, mediating role was critical in an agrarian system with weak central government, as they successfully embodied the central symbol of authority, Muhammad.

Sufi shaykhs also became popular, and thereby powerful, because they were perceived to have direct connections with God. When some travellers asked Abu'l-Hasan al-Kharaqani (d. 1033) to pray for their safety, he advised them to set out on their journey in the name of God and call out his (Abu'l-Hasan's) name if they ran into trouble. Then highway robbers attacked the caravan. Those who called on the shaykh were saved and those who called on God were robbed and killed. Abu'l-Hasan explained later that those who called on God directly petitioned a reality they did not know and so received no aid. Those appealing to Abu'l-Hasan used the name of a person who knew God and who could intercede and assist them.[4] This mediating authority ultimately connected to the Prophet Muhammad via the definitive chain of holy men connecting the sufi to Muhammad.

Genealogy as a source of sufi legitimization and authority

> Baha'uddin Naqshband, when asked about sufi lineages, replied,
> 'No one gets anywhere [solely] through a *silsila* [sufi chain].'[5]

There was probably more going on than word-of-mouth popularity and politico-economic convenience to legitimize sufi authority. Undoubtedly the sufi connection to the compelling pan-Islamic reverence for the Prophet authenticated the figure of the sufi shaykh. This was accomplished in many ways. The most formal and recognizable way of connecting to the Prophet was through a spiritual genealogy. When a seeker becomes initiated to do the practices of a given sufi lineage, he clasps the right hand of the shaykh. This is a symbolic, if not literal, shaking of the Prophet's hand, since this handclasp was said to have been passed down from the Prophet to his companion and so forth from shaykh to shaykh to the seeker. This series of physical handshakes form a chain that connects the seeker directly to the Prophet. Simultaneously these are the spiritual links that transmit divine grace and auspiciousness (*baraka*) from God. As mentioned before, the chain of sufi transmitters parallels the same kind of chain used to authenticate a hadith report from the Prophet. In a traditional Islamic learning environment, *all* religious knowledge has to be transmitted from recognized teachers, going back to the founders of those disciplines (and implicitly back to the Prophet and his companions). This is the paramount Islamic knowledge validation principle – until recently when 'internet shaykhs' can write whatever they please.

But this is simply the cover story. There is a more encompassing principle: the personal encounter between two reliable transmitters. Religious knowledge in Islam is much more than just factual information that can be written in a book or flashed on a PowerPoint presentation. Instead it has two modes: oral knowledge and knowledge of the heart. This principle begins with the 'first pillar of Islam', the profession of faith, saying, 'There is no god but God and Muhammad is God's messenger.' Although this is spoken, it has no *real* validity unless it is affirmed in the heart. Especially in sufi practice, but also in the other religious sciences, there is emphasis on the heart being actively engaged in the learning process. Most of the time this manifests in memorizing the text at hand (learning by heart). The key pedagogical factor is an intimate spiritual communication between human hearts that transforms ordinary intellectual knowledge into religious wisdom inherited from the prophets. We have sufi reports of being in the presence of the Prophet himself after a hadith session with a religious scholar.[6] It may be difficult to relate to terms like 'heart knowledge' and communications with 'potency of the heart'. These have not been a part of modern public or private education, much less a part of the digital revolution.

But there is more going on. Hadith scholars back in the day also had major problems with the way sufis validated their initiatory chains, even though both groups used the same principles of transmission to verify authenticity. In a linear, rational world one assumes that the people in any given transmission – whether hadith or sufi – both lived at the same time and were old enough to have been learning with each other. This assumption works for hadith scholars but not for sufis. In sufi lineages there are transmitters whose death dates are separated by more than 100 years. How could Abu Yazid Bistami (d. 875) have met Ja'far al-Sadiq (d. 765), or even more outrageous, how could Abu Yazid Bistami have met Abu'l-Hasan Kharaqani (d. 1033)? The response of scholars has been to dismiss these sufi genealogies as 'fabricated'. If this were the case, then one would not expect their arithmetical skills to be so deficient. An eight-year-old could have done a better job.

For sufis, who live in a context that includes transrational experience and the unseen worlds, these historical inconsistencies do not exist. They cite the precedent of Uways al-Qarani, who is said to have met the Prophet in a visionary experience without ever having seen him in the physical world. Thus there is an 'Uwaysi connection' that is the model for initiation, by the imaginal form of a deceased shaykh appearing in a visionary experience. Those acquainted with the New Testament can think of St Paul having his visionary experience and deriving his authority from that. Shaykhs in established lineages very often are suspicious of those claiming Uwaysi authority because there is no standardized way of validating the authenticity of the experience. Being certified to teach in a dream means that there are markers in the dream to validate the experience. Validation is by experts only and they may not agree among themselves. Dreams are at least as deceptive as waking life. If you remember the Indonesian organization of Nahdatul Ulama, mentioned in the first chapter, you can now smile at their well-meaning efforts. They do not recognize recent Uwaysi initiations in their efforts to determine who is a valid sufi, yet they consider 'established lineages' to be legitimate. Evidently no one has informed them that these established lineages have Uwaysi links in them.

Outside of sufi specialists themselves, there is currently no way of validating the qualifications of someone who has received permission to teach from a living teacher either. In a fascinating study of living sufi practitioners in Egypt, Valerie Hoffman discovered that, as I found in the Panjab and Kyber Pakhtunkhwa areas of Pakistan, there was very little transformational practice with the hereditary shaykhs of established lineages. In contrast, she found that groups with Uwaysi shaykhs were much more likely to be dynamically teaching transformational exercises.[7]

A word on hereditary lineage is in order. Very often when a shaykh dies without designating a successor, there is disagreement over who should be the principal successor and inheritor of the sufi lodge and buildings. Custody of the grave is also a big issue. At least as early as Abu Sa'id Abu'l-Khayr (d. 1049), there was hereditary succession to members of the family. Depending on the circumstances, such a process has continued until the present day. In an ideal world, perhaps, only the spiritual qualifications would determine the main successor. But what if that person were unqualified to manage a 'small village' of buildings and the sufi lodge? The late Shaykh Ma'sum used to ask those who had hereditary shaykhs whether they would have surgery performed on them by someone whose only qualification was being the son of a surgeon. This is a convincing point. Yet, in some cases there is more going on and the issue of hereditary succession and the existence of transformative practice need to be pursued on a case-by-case basis.

In the next chapter we will see that shrines are almost always administered by descendants of the deceased shaykh and there is no pretence of transformative sufi practice. These shrine custodians have many other activities to perform in the community.

Recognized sufi lineages

From the eleventh century, pan-Islamic sufi lineages were named after their founder-figures (see fig. 2.1). One of the earliest was the Kazaruniyya (or Ishaqiyya), named after the patron of traders and seafarers, Abu Ishaq al-Kazaruni (d. 1035 in southern Iran). During his lifetime this lineage had a network of 65 sufi lodges on trading and pilgrimage (*hajj*) routes, which extended from Edirne in Turkey to the port city of Quangzhou

FIGURE 2.1 A tree of sufi lineages, beginning at the bottom with Allah, the angel Gabriel, Muhammad and the first four caliphs, and culminating at the top with the Sanusiyya lineage.

in eastern China. The Qadiriyya lineage began with 'Abdulqadir al-Jilani (d. 1166, Baghdad) and soon became the most widespread lineage in the Islamic world. Other major lineages (in chronological order) include the Suhrawardi lineage from Abu Hafs al-Suhrawardi (d. 1234, Baghdad), the Chishti lineage in India from Mu'inuddin Chishti (d. 1236, Ajmer, Rajasthan, India) famous for its *qawwali* singing (if you do not know what *qawwali* music is, check out Nusrat Fateh 'Ali Khan on YouTube), the Mevlevi lineage from Jalaluddin Rumi (d. 1273, Konya, Turkey), so named because Mevlana is the honorific given to Rumi in Turkish and famous for its popularly named 'whirling dervish' ritual, better described as coming face to face with God' (see fig. 2.2), and the Naqshbandi lineage from Baha'uddin Naqshband (d. 1389, Bukhara, Uzbekistan).

Naming a lineage after a well-known sufi was a new phenomenon. Of all the sufis in the lineage, why did one person stand out to become the founder-figure? My sense is that the principal transformative practices were pioneered, or were seen to have been pioneered, by founder-figures. We will see below how the Naqshbandi lineage itself became renamed, through a series of major revisions in contemplative practice.

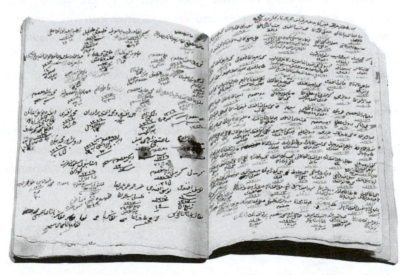

FIGURE 2.2 Mevlevi lineage records of dervishes in the Yenikapı sufi lodge associated with Ali Nutki Dede (d. 1804), with the dates of their 1001-day retreat.

As a lexical note, what I am calling a lineage is known in the original languages as a method or path (*tariqa*), again emphasizing the importance of the contemplative practice of each group. Readers who have read other books on sufism may have noticed authors talking about sufi 'orders'. There are orders of monks and nuns in Christianity and Buddhism, with very clear and often common rules and contemplative practices. In sufi practice, celibacy is rare and there is very little 'order' in sufi practices. Multiple sufi groups stemming from the same sub-lineages exist in one city, such as Istanbul or Delhi, with minimal overlap in contemplative practices. Sufi lineages at any given time are not interconnecting networks, since the shaykhs in each individual branch – even in the same city – hardly ever communicate with each other. It is a tree-like network that allows considerable independence. Each sub-sub-branch centres around the shaykh as its pivotal point.[8]

A second indicator that the naming of sufi lineages is related to contemplative practice is that many *were* named in reference to actual practices. Devin DeWeese, who has painstakingly investigated and tried to figure out the most complex sufi lineages in Central Asia, notes how some names of sufi lineages are attributed to contemplative practices and principles. Khalwatis and Helvetis (both come from the Arabic word for retreat, *khalwa*) used retreats as part of their practice and are associated with vocal remembrance of God and hereditary succession; Shattaris (technical translation of *shattar*: flying with daring intensity) saw their techniques as fast; and 'Ishqis (*'ishq* is Arabic for ardent love) emphasized love. DeWeese reminds us that what a sufi lineage meant historically is not necessarily what it means now – an unbroken chain of transmitters going back to Muhammad. He wonders why certain people ended up being founder-figures, even though after the person's death the group did not change its name to reflect the founder-figure until many generations later.[9] It is apparent that sufi lineages are much more complex than this introductory discussion indicates.

Examples of actual sufi lineages

Here we will explore some of the many ambiguities of early sufi-lineage history. Scholars have still not figured out a plausible account of how

'Abdulqadir al-Jilani became one of the paramount sufi shaykhs of all time (note his dictum: 'My foot is on the necks of all friends of God.'), when apparently, from textual descriptions, he was primarily a charismatic preacher when alive.[10] From the sources, which can easily exaggerate, it seems that he must have been an extraordinary personage – no building in Baghdad, the capital of the Abbasid Empire, was large enough for the number of people who wanted to listen to him talk. It is said that entire non-Muslim communities in Baghdad converted to Islam by his efforts – a common comment when glorifying someone in an Islamic context, but not usually verifiable. In addition, he was a sufi shaykh who initiated students by giving them a robe and expected them to abide by a set of rules in his sufi lodge. Not only is there little information about 'Abdulqadir outside of his writings, it is still anyone's guess why the Qadiriyya is the most widespread sufi lineage today.

Erik Ohlander has intricately researched the early institutionalization of the Suhrawardi lineage by focusing on the life of its founder, Abu Hafs al-Suhrawardi. One of his opening remarks is noting the 'disciplinary practices' (which presumably are not contemplative practices) of Suhrawardi's sufi lodge:

> Suhrawardi clearly delineates a number of core characteristics which mark them out from others, the most visible being comprised of a shared body of disciplinary practices which, in the urban milieu of late 12th–early 13th-century Baghdad, were often constructed institutionally.[11]

Suhrawardi pioneered a system of organization in his sufi lodge, together with a specific contemplative practice. His mission, centred in Baghdad, was bolstered by a very close relationship with the Caliph al-Nasir. Suhrawardi declared sufi knowers of God to be the only true heirs of the Prophet. He recognized the necessity of religious scholars, but their knowledge was generally inferior to that of their sufi counterparts, because only sufis imparted the kind of experiential knowledge that the Prophet communicated to his companions. For Suhrawardi, sufis have achieved the highest rank of following the Prophetic exemplar, making them the best qualified to keep the Prophetic example alive in each generation – which again bolsters the claim of being the true heirs of the Prophet.[12] It was the sufis who:

> in particular distinguished themselves through their pious actions, illuminated spiritual states, and renunciation of the world and its vanities, gathering together in the corners of mosques in the manner of the 'Folk of the Veranda', [the pious who lived under the overhang along the wall of the mosque adjacent to the Prophet's house] developing a specific science and technical language to delineate and describe that which had been passed down to them.[13]

In this way Suhrawardi legitimized sufi practice, both behavioural and contemplative, as a branch of the religious sciences. This included awareness of the ego-self, together with a methodology to eventually subdue the commanding nature of the ego. Suhrawardi also included a set of procedures to observe one's thoughts through a process of disciplined and exacting introspection. Another dimension of practice included the experiencing of various stations of contentment, renunciation, renunciation of renunciation and divine love. The student was also taught how to accomplish contemplative witnessing to experience the really real. We find specific mention of the subtle centres of the heart, spirit and ego that became elaborated over the next four centuries. As much as Suhrawardi created his own institutionalized path, with its praxis and conduct to be communicated to his students and then to their students, he reminds us not to get hung up in 'order'. 'Every station is a path in and of itself, and the respective paths of the Sufi masters differ because their station and states differ. Every master devises a path which accords with his state and station.'[14] The paths or methods do not necessarily imply organized sufism or even organized transformative practice. The quote continues,:

> Some of them follow the path of assembling with people and training them while others select only a selected group or individual [to train]. Still others follow a path consisting of the recitation of many litanies, extensive fasting, prayer, and the like. Others pursue a path of serving people by carrying firewood and hemp on their backs and selling it in the market, being honest in its price.[15]

Another component of sufi institutionalization included pivotal texts associated with what became the Suhrawardi lineage – in this case Suhrawardi's *Knowers of Inner Knowledge*. It became 'an instrument of affiliation, identity, and authority'.[16] This probably assisted in creating a Suhrawardi identity, which over time replicated forms of Suhrawardi organization and praxis that eventually became a tradition established over generations. From the available sources, it is not clear when aspirants identified themselves as 'Suhrawardis'. And when they did, what did that mean?

Why did Suhrawardi's path thrive and survive and not al-Qushayri's? We know that Qushayri's sufi robe was passed among his successors at least until the fourteenth century and the Qushayri sufi lodge, led by his family line, existed at least until the middle of the thirteenth century.[17] Yet no sufi lineage called the Qushayriyya resulted. Although Qushayri wrote many books, no further books glorifying him or his family appeared. We do not know about any contemplative practices associated with the Qushayri sufis.

Probably dozens of sufi lineages have become defunct for every one that has survived until today. My theory about the 'right stuff' for thriving sufi lineages is that they splendidly adapt to the needs of local seekers, and at least in the early generations, they are successful to some degree in transforming human egos. That every master creates a path harmonious with his own states and stations also implies that he attracts students who will be in harmony with his methodology and path. It is an inter-subjective undertaking. No students, no shaykh. No shaykh, no sufi practice.

We have more documentation for the Naqshbandis. Originally a Central Asian sufi lineage, the Naqshbandi lineage was named after its founder-figure, Baha'uddin Naqshband, continuing 'the way of the Masters' that had begun with 'Abdulkhaliq Ghujduwani (d. 1179). In Central Asia, the Naqshbandis were closely allied with the sedentary middle and lower classes and linked many different groups, for example artisan guilds in towns and village peasants. Naqshbandi shaykhs were to be respected and their assistance (and wrath) was perceived to have implications for one's life after death. Timur (Tamerlane, d. 1405), the founding member of the Timurids, chose to be buried next to Baha'uddin's sufi guide, Amir Kulal (d. 1370).

In the following century, 'Ubaydullah Ahrar (d. 1490) became the most significant Naqshbandi in Central Asia, as he was one of the largest landowners and de facto ruler of most of the eastern Timurid kingdom. His lineal and spiritual descendants dominated the Indian Naqshbandiyya, as they became allied with the first Indian Mughal ruler, Babur (d. 1530). By the time of Akbar's rule (r. 1556–1605) in India, Naqshbandis had intermarried with many of the leading Mughal families. The first Naqshbandi to arrive and teach in Istanbul, 'Abdullah Ilahi (d. 1490), went from Anatolia to learn from Ahrar and then returned to Istanbul to teach. Isma'il Shirvani came from the Caucasus, was trained by Ahrar, and then went to teach Naqshbandi practices in Mecca. Ahrar continued to send his students throughout the eastern Islamic world and they in turn sent out their students.

Ahmad Sirhindi (d. 1624, Sirhind, India), the founder-figure of the Naqshbandi-Mujaddidi (henceforth Mujaddidi) lineage, was the next founder-figure after Baha'uddin Naqshband. Sirhindi, initiated into the Qadiri lineage by his father Abdulahad, met his paramount Naqshbandi shaykh Baqibillah (d. 1603) in Delhi. After a short period of three months, Baqibillah gave him permission to teach. His followers proclaimed him the 'Renewer of the second Islamic millennium' (*mujaddid-i alf-i thani*, hence Mujaddidi). The reigning Mughal emperor Akbar ignored Sirhindi's attempts to reform government practices, but many members of Akbar's court were Sirhindi's students. Akbar's successor, Jahangir (r. 1605–27), imprisoned Sirhindi for a year, apparently because of Sirhindi's claim to have reached a station higher than the first caliph, Abu Bakr. In the context of contemplative practice, Sirhindi vastly expanded the contemplative repertoire of the Naqshbandiyya, so much so that apparently it became the top sufi contemplative technology of the day. Kalimullah Jahanabadi (d. 1729), a prominent Chishti shaykh of Delhi, says, '[T]he Naqshbandi path is very widespread. Since all paths are found in you, why should you remain a stranger to the way of meditation? Train people in this way also, for by God! It is the shortest of paths. There is no doubt concerning the greatness of this order.'[18]

The next major development of the Naqshbandiyya occurred when a Kurdish disciple of Ghulam 'Ali Shah (d. 1824, Delhi), Mawlana Khalid (d. 1827, Damascus), became the founder-figure of the

Naqshbandiyya–Khalidiyya lineage. He further tweaked Mujaddidi contemplative practices, which then spread throughout the Ottoman lands (more on this below). The Mujaddidi lineage is still active in the eastern Islamic world and is now found in most parts of the world, having globalized like other sufi lineages. Naqshbandi contemplative practices are remarkably diverse, even in Naqshbandi lineages of the same city. Istanbul, for example, has the Iskenderpaşas, the followers of Süleyman Hilmi Tunahan, and separate practices led by Shaykh Mahmut Ustaosmanoğlu, Osman Nuri Topbaş and many others.

Mawlana Khalid initiated the third phase of the Naqshbandiyya. In around 1810, Mawlana Khalid met a disciple of Ghulam 'Ali and started travelling to India. After arriving in Delhi, Mawlana Khalid first denied the ideas of Ahmad Sirhindi, but after receiving divine grace from the Mujaddidi lineage, Mawlana Khalid eagerly acquired a copy of Sirhindi's *Collected Letters*, translated into Arabic. In his nine or ten months of discipleship in Delhi with Shah Ghulam 'Ali, he completed the contemplative exercises and received unconditional permission to teach. Mawlana Khalid consciously expanded the lineage by pioneering 40-day retreats and enforcing a concentration on his image, even by students of his authorized students. These were both effective, intensive training measures, because he could not count on keeping aspirants for a long time in any one place, given the political and economic uncertainties at the time.[19] When Mawlana Khalid died in 1827, five years after immigrating to Damascus and 16 years after returning from India, the Khalidiyya had become a thriving lineage, quite different in many respects from its Mujaddidi counterpart in Ghulam 'Ali's sufi lodge in Delhi.

It is very telling how the three Naqshbandi founder-figures (Baha'uddin, Sirhindi and Khalid) become prominent because each was a pioneer in contemplative practice. According to Naqshbandi tradition, Baha'uddin was taught silent remembrance of God (*dhikr*) via an Uwaysi initiation from 'Abdulkhaliq Ghujduwani, in spite of his physically present shaykh Amir Kulal, who practised vocal *dhikr*. Baha'uddin's Uwaysi experience justified his break with Amir Kulal, which probably caused a bit of a stir at the time. Baha'uddin was a reformer of sufi practice like Sirhindi and Khalid.

The following account gives us a window on disagreements over the proper way to do transformative practices and shows how sufi transmissions of knowledge had conflicting interpretations. It has an air of truth, simply because I have been in situations with sufis where similar kinds of disagreements have happened. They turned out exactly as this account did. This Central Asian account concerns succession and the differences in interpretation concerning silent versus vocal *dhikr* in the lineage of 'The Masters', which later became the Naqshbandiyya.

> Master 'Arif Riwgari (d. 1219) departed the world, leaving Master Mahmud Anjir Faghnawani (d. 1317) as his successor to summon people to God. After Master 'Arif, they began the vocal dhikr, which prior to him had not existed in their path. Neither Master 'Arif, who was the shaykh of Master Mahmud, recited vocal dhikr, nor did 'Abdulkhaliq Ghujduvani (d. 1179). Mahmud introduced vocal dhikr of the tongue. When Master Awliya' (a successor to 'Abdulkhaliq), in Bukhara, heard that Mahmud was doing vocal dhikr, he went with his companions to Mahmud, saying, 'This is not the practice of the great master 'Abdulkhaliq and vocal dhikr did not exist prior to him so why are you doing this?' Mahmud said, "Arif licensed me to do so in his last breath,' saying, 'I have licensed you in summoning people to God and to perform dhikr of the tongue.' Then Master Awliya' said, 'My brother, 'Arif was a man who discerned the true nature of things and was among the men of discernment of this age. Your shaykh referred to the tongue of the heart and opposed this method you have taken up.' Master Mahmud ignored him and traveled the path doing vocal dhikr; and Master Awliya' went away continuing to travel the sufi path doing silent dhikr, the method of 'Abdulkhaliq.[20]

If you read the literature, you may find that scholars identify Naqshbandis with silent or heart remembrance of God (*dhikr*). In actual practice, *dhikr* depends entirely on the individual shaykh and his group. Many Naqshbandis practised and still practice vocal *dhikr*. Once, in the Pushtun-speaking part of Pakistan, I asked a prominent Naqshbandi shaykh why his students practised a *very* loud *dhikr*, and he replied, 'The modern world is very noisy and our *dhikr* needs to be heard above the noise.' In Damascus, the Naqshbandi 'Abdulghani Nabulusi (d. 1731, Damascus) argued that singing and music were permitted in certain circumstances as long as it did not keep one from recollection of God – a viewpoint that was shared by the Kurdish Ibrahim al-Kurani (d. 1690), who lived in Medina. Transformative practices vary considerably and morph when needed to suit the local circumstances. This process has often happened in sufi lodges ever since the twelfth century.

Sufi lodges

As previously discussed, most of the aspirants who came to sufi lodges never progressed beyond the most elementary stages of sufi practice. At a minimum, they behaved respectfully while conforming to the rules of the sufi lodge. Because of what they had heard before coming to the sufi lodge, the vast majority of people honoured the shaykh's exalted status and assumed that it resulted from his access to God's grace. The sufi shaykh was a mediator between the divine and human worlds who could poten- tially assist them with their worldly difficulties. For the small initiated minority, being in the company of the sufi shaykh was a qualitatively more intense experience than they had experienced in previous learning environ- ments. Few who entered this intimate relationship considered doubting the shaykh's authority any more than the average person would question a surgeon's choice of scalpel or a commercial jet pilot's navigational skills. Sufis skilfully re-created the dynamics of the original community of the Prophet and his companions – and did so while also responding to local needs. Sufi lodges were the institutional brick-and-mortar evidence of the increasing popularity of sufism.

Although the institutionalization of sufism may have been associated with 'sudden' popularity, one cannot explain the development of the sufi lodge solely on surging numbers. When Ibn al-Faraji (d. after 903) went with 120 sufis to visit Abu Turab an-Nakhshabi (d. 859), the group stayed in mosques during the entire trip. Abu Yazid al-Bistami supposedly had a visit from Ahmad b. Khidrawayh with 1,000 students. Abu Yazid did not have a sufi lodge, but he did have a room large enough to store all their walking sticks. When sufis came to Herat to visit the famous 'Abdullah Ansari (d. 1034), they lived as guests of a different person each day.[21] Generally if a house was insufficiently large, they moved to a nearby mosque. Sometime in the tenth century, learning activities slowly moved from a mosque to an Islamic school or a sufi lodge, depending on the type of learning. Some buildings were both madrasas and sufi lodges.

Locating a sufi lodge outside the main population centres was often intentional, so that the sufi shaykh could appear to be aloof from any specific worldly faction and function effectively as a mediator. While the sufi shaykh embodied the paradigmatic figure of the Prophet, commanding obedience and psychological compliance, his authority was sometimes tested and contested by outsiders. Rulers were known to verify the spiritual qualifications of shaykhs in a variety of ways, including the administering of poison. Most sufi shaykhs survived these tests, to receive funding for the establishment and running of sufi lodges. The elite established pious endowments for sufi lodges throughout the Islamic world, often stipulating the daily offering of prayers and blessings on the benefactors' behalf.

Sufi lodges, and therefore institutional sufism in one form or another, flourished because sufis were able to replicate an anti-structure or what Victor Turner calls *communitas*.[22] The sufi shaykh in the lodge attempted to recreate the *ideal* community of the Prophet with his exemplary companions – which by definition diverged from *everyday* social reality. Any given society has *structure* that justifies economic, hierarchical, age and sex differences. *Communitas* is created in an intentional temporary micro-community, designed for transformation, that stresses the equality of individuals. This is not something peculiar to a sufi lodge. Anyone who has ever gone on a worthwhile retreat may find initial re-entry into the everyday world to be disorienting.

By the time sufi lodges had become popular, the political counterparts to the Prophet had often surrounded themselves with ostentatious wealth and strong-armed others with military force in order to maintain themselves in luxury. The environment of a sufi lodge was an attempt to temporarily implement Islamic ideals among a small group of people; it was an attempt to bridge ideals and actual practice. From the visitors' perspective any donations going to the shaykh went to the community kitchen to feed the poor and travellers. The shaykh did not publically accept honours and gifts, but channelled these resources into pious endowments. Anyone could come and publicly request assistance from the shaykh. The sufi lodge also functioned as a refuge and asylum, and those who had received help from his divine intervention often returned with gifts to thank him. This was all done in public. Word spread quickly as people recounted the 'miracles' happening around the shaykh. Later these were embellished with legends and stories that were recorded in pious hagiographies.

Since the *communitas* of the sufi lodge reversed the normal day-to-day order, the weak and inferior were given power and the strong and powerful were humiliated. In the anti-structure of the sufi lodge, weakness is associated with a minimal ego, while strength is the ego unleashed upon the world. Thus, the sufi lodge gave great symbolic value to poverty. In hagiographical accounts, we read how sufi shaykhs were just as oblivious to abject poverty before becoming a shaykh, as they were to the abundant resources that surrounded them in the sufi lodge. The sufi shaykh lived in an in-between state – a liminal state of poverty – not the literal poverty experienced in everyday society.

Abu Saʿid Abuʾl-Khayr wrote one of the first manuals outlining appropriate behaviour in a sufi lodge. Lest anyone denounce sufi lodges as an innovation, the institution of the sufi lodge was declared to be based on the practices of the Qurʾan and the sunna of the Prophet. The sufi lodge was to be a contemporary shelter for the poor and ascetics, much like the 'companions of the veranda', who apparently slept under the overhang along the wall of the mosque adjacent to the Prophet's house. The first group of injunctions enjoined constant recollection of God – *dhikr*. Everyone must maintain ritual purity and have clean clothing, so that they can pray or recite the Qurʾan at any time. Residents had detailed directions for what to do before the dawn prayer and after the prayer until sunrise. Everyone was always expected to eat in the company of others and not leave each other without mutual consent. Free time was for religious study, earning a livelihood or comforting another person. Of the 120 residents noted at Abu Saʿid's lodge in the eleventh century, 80 were temporary residents and half of the remaining 40 would remain less than three years. Presumably only the most advanced seekers remained there for long periods. Over-exposure could cause the lodge *communitas* to lose its extraordinary quality and just become one more tedious ego-clashing experience in group living.[23]

There were many levels of ritual in the sufi lodge. The first was the set of rituals shared by pious Muslims, including performance of the five ritual prayers, the sunna prayers before and after each of these, night prayers (*tahajjud*), and the regular recitation of litanies. One did not need to come to a sufi lodge for this level of ritual. The next level of ritual was designed specifically for a sufi environment: initiation to a sufi lineage, inculcating and performing group *dhikr* and bestowal of sufi robes. The patched sufi robe had the Prophetic precedent of his giving a robe to Ka'b b. Zubayr. Not all visitors participated in these rituals, but all observed them. A third level of ritual was the set of rules governing behaviour in the lodge itself. Abu Sa'id describes the cumulative effect of these overlapping sets of rituals and rules. 'At first a rule is something people adopt with difficulty, but then it becomes a habit. Then that habit becomes second nature and finally, what is second nature becomes reality.'[24]

The creation of *communitas* around the sufi shaykh enabled sufis to be the prime agents for the Islamization of society. The sufi lodge became a vehicle for incorporating local culture into Islamic society, while the veneration of Muhammad and his central place in the hearts of Muslims influenced the sufi community. To the extent that sufi shaykhs were able to renew the kind of transformative community experienced by Muhammad's companions, sufi practice would remain a reality. A sufi master in his local community was akin to the Prophet in his universal community. This process is still operating as the following contemporary account reveals:

> A third-generation Khalwati sufi shaykh from a village near Luxor in Upper Egypt, Shaykh Muhammad Ahmad al-Tayyib, does more than just act as a sufi shaykh. He is an arbitrator and acts as an intermediary with government officials. Like his father and grandfather before him, he is perceived to be someone who is close to God – his very worldly authority is seen as a result of God's favor, which in turn is derived from his closeness to God. There are weekly distributions of food after *dhikr* rituals and considerable expenditures for celebrations in Cairo,

all of which require substantial funds. His lodge is open to all and is a center for social services. A man of God, like the Prophet, is generous to all and is very powerful. His real power is invisible and any apparent worldly power is only a small trifling to what is not seen.[25]

In this incredible expansion of institutional sufism there were, as now, ties to people with power and money, along with sufi-lodge activity that did not come close to measuring up to the Prophetic precedent. Just as many early sufis mentioned above reacted to the pomp and ease at the centres of the Umayyad and Abbasid dynasties, four centuries later there were groups of sufis who distanced themselves from what they considered dubious behaviour in the name of institutional sufism.

The founder of what became the 'counter-cultural' Qalandariyya sufi lineage, Jamaluddin Savi (d. 1233), broke away from his conventional sufi master 'Uthman Rumi. He rejected not only his sufi training, but also a career as a sufi master. Soon the term 'qalandar' became a word, like 'dervish', that people used to describe a wandering beggar who flagrantly flaunted societal norms. Sometimes these dervishes shaved all their facial hair, while others openly drank wine and smoked hashish. We do not have much detailed information on qalandars, except from their detractors, so these stereotypes might not represent qalandars in reality. Sometimes the outward guise of a qalandar was merely a cover for sociopaths and criminals. There are records of qalandars' unprovoked aggressive behaviour towards established sufis, such as Baha'uddin Zakariyya Suhrawardi in Multan, Pakistan, and Fariduddin Ganj-i Shakar Chishti in what is now Pakpattan, Pakistan. People looking like qalandars attempted to assassinate Nasiruddin Chiragh-i Dihli and Ibrahim Gilani (prominent sufi masters), for no apparent reason.

Yet qalandars and other anti-establishment sufis had their own lineages, founder-figures, distinctive clothing and practices. The shaykh–seeker relationship was as central to them as it was in the established sufi lodges. Many of these dervishes and qalandars came from the cultural elite and one would have expected them to enter a recognized sufi lineage.[26] Whether discussing a prestigious sufi or a dervish beggar, back then or now, I am reminded of Abu Sa'id al-Ziyadi, who, '[w]henever he looked at those

[s]ufis who dressed in patched clothes and worn wraps, would say: O my friends! You have hoisted your flags and played your drums. I wish I knew what kind of men you really are in the engagement.'[27] I wish I knew also.

From sufi lineages to sufi lodges to shrines

As we have seen, sufi lineages were probably a way to verify authentic sufi practice – a logic that followed the same logic as the chains of transmitters that had been used for centuries in attempts to verify authentic sayings of the Prophet. Though there is no specific point in the historical record to declare a sudden increase in numbers of sufi shaykhs, it seems to me that sufism had started to become much more popular by the eleventh century. With such a great demand for sufis and a short supply, people began wearing patched robes and touting sufi paraphernalia, setting themselves up as sufi shaykhs in the same way as non-authentic hadiths multiplied over the centuries. Thus, a complete sufi lineage connecting with Muhammad potentially acted as a quality control mechanism. Within a few generations, lineages were named after founder-figures with transmitted ritual practices, clothing and contemplative exercises. It appears that a set of practices became identified with lineages and sub-lineages – though these practices varied considerably. At the same time, sufi-lodge environments replicated the dynamics of the Prophet and companions. The following chapter discusses the new tomb complexes built adjacent to some sufi lodges. When the sufi master died, sometimes his tomb became a place of auspicious blessing, where visitors could come and request his intercession. In some cases the activities around the tomb became more popular than the former sufi lodge had ever been.

3

SUFI SHRINES: DOWN-TO-EARTH, DAY-TO-DAY, DEVOTIONAL SUFISM FOR THE MASSES

Muslim [sic] *shrines and tombs of Sufi Saints represent Muslim* [sic] *culture, traditions and its benevolence in totality. These Sufi Saints still rule over the hearts of Pakistanis and Muslims of other countries. With the passage of time the number of devotees has increased. The visit to shrines by millions of people every year is an abiding testimony of their absolute and undisputed sway over their followers and of their divine blessings emanating from their hallowed graves.*

FROM A PAKISTANI TOURISM BROCHURE,
JOURNEY INTO LIGHT

VISITING SUFI SHRINES is probably 90 per cent of the world-wide activity associated with sufism. If transformative practice is the inner circle of sufism, then visiting sufi shrines is one of the outermost circles. It appears that, as in the case of going to sufi lodges, alleviating worldly difficulties, healing and attaining contentment are primary reasons people visit these shrines, an activity that has been going on for at least a millennium. My suspicion is that people's healing experiences in the vicinity of deceased sufis' tombs consist of a combination of self-healing effects, which activate a person's self-repair mechanisms, and conditions that would have changed anyway without intervention, much like the results of modern psychiatry. However, visitors to shrines report a wide range of phenomena that modern science cannot explain, perceiving their experiences as manifestations of spiritual power or *baraka*. In this sense, visiting sufi shrines can be included as one of the 'paranormal' experiential dimensions associated with sufism.

It is divine grace or *baraka* that often motivates people to travel some distance to a tomb-shrine. *Baraka* is a beneficial flow of healing and auspicious energy that can positively affect people and objects, imbuing them with this energy. In Arabic, *baraka* originally meant plentiful rain or a camel chewing its food, and then feeding young camels with it. *Baraka* was the term associated with a father putting his saliva into the mouth of the newborn child and thereby transferring blessings and protecting the child.[1] It was a common practice of the Prophet to heal people using his saliva. *Baraka* is a counter-force to unintentional malevolent forces associated with jealous or envious glances, commonly called the 'evil eye', or actual intentional harm through the employment of black magic and curses. The function of amulets, easily attainable at many tomb-shrines, is to keep these kinds of forces at bay.[2] Objects can be imbued with this blessedness and are called '*tabarruk*', meaning literally 'objects concentrated with *baraka*'. Possession of the deceased sufi's *baraka*-impregnated relics legitimize the head custodian at his shrine in the same way that the Abbasid rulers of eighth-century Baghdad used the Prophet's mantle to indicate that they were his rightful successors.

In Senegal, the disciples of Amadu Bamba, founder-figure of the Muridiyya lineage (d. 1927), consider him and his family as sources of *baraka*, offering protection, healing and prosperity (see figs 3.1, 3.2, 3.3 and 3.4). Very often Murids, students in Bamba's lineage, touch his photos to their foreheads or kiss wall murals to receive blessings. *Baraka* is like

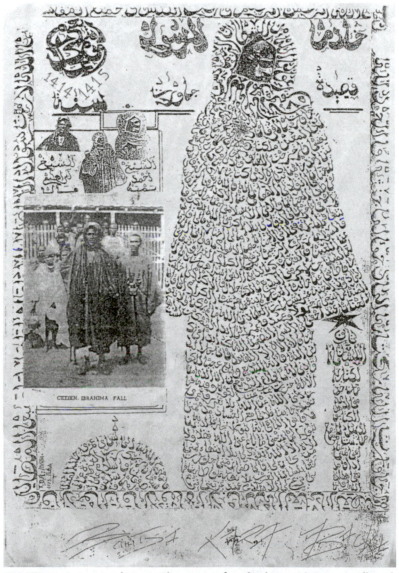

FIGURE 3.1 Artist unknown. Photocopy of a calendar, 1994. Paper, cardboard, and tape: 42.1 x 29 cm. FMCH TR99.37.83. This calendar shows Bamba's turban and robe, composed entirely of calligraphy. The writing consists of Qur'anic verses. (Reproduced with permission of the UCLA Fowler Museum of Cultural History, Los Angeles from Roberts and Roberts, *A Saint in the City*, 57).

FIGURE 3.2 Artist unknown. Calligram. Glass-covered découpage: 48 x 32.5 cm.
FMCH TR2002.5.7. The calligram of a person in a prayer position is popular in
North Africa and the Middle East and has been recreated as a découpage in Senegal.
It can be found in the homes of pious Muslims and *marabout* holy men. Calligrams
of Amadu Bamba were undoubtedly inspired by these works of art. (Reproduced
with permission of the UCLA Fowler Museum of Cultural History, Los Angeles
from Roberts and Roberts, 57).

FIGURE 3.3 Elimane Fall. Amadu Bamba and *khassaid* (a litany to remember God), *c.*2000. Paint on paper: 161.5 x 205 cm. FMCH TR2002.1.2. Mr Fall states that this work 'is a khassaid to protect the world. It incorporates mystical calculations. I have put the [Qur'anic] verses in this painting, but I also work with numbers, and there is numerology embedded within the text. If one wants to be protected from the evil eye and the evil tongue that spits venom, then one must read this. And if you want to avoid the evil that comes from the hand of man, then you must absolutely read this. Therefore I have put many hands, hands of men, women and children, and in all different colors. That stands for humanity.' (Reproduced with permission of the UCLA Fowler Museum of Cultural History, Los Angeles from Roberts and Roberts, *A Saint in the City*, 171.)

an energy field surrounding a sufi, his relics and his tomb. As is the case in many African and other societies around the world, this *baraka* is also perceived to be inherited by immediate descendants.

Visiting shrine-tombs is significantly different from travel associated with tourism and holidays. It may seem that these two modalities of travel have a lot in common, since both types of travellers arrange for transportation, take time off from their everyday lives and buy souvenirs. One could even consider the 'pilgrimage trade' to be a precursor to the tourist industry.

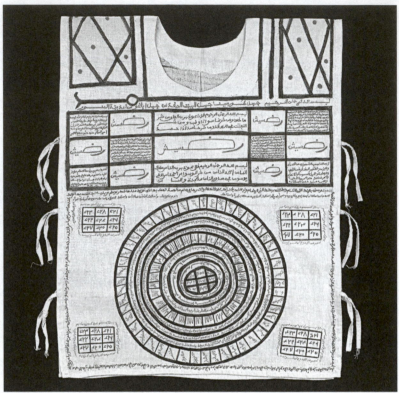

FIGURE 3.4 Serigne Batch. Shirt covered with calligraphy and *khatems* (devotional prayers), late twentieth century. Cotton cloth and ink: L:76.3 cm. FMCH X99.56.48. Among the most powerful of healing objects are shirts inscribed with verses that Serigne Batch prepares as he chants *zikrs* (remembrances of God), creating a mystical link between the image and sound. The circle at the centre of the front of this shirt is a metaphor for the *dahiras*, or worship groups that tie Mourides together in blessed solidarity. (Reproduced with permission of the UCLA Fowler Museum of Cultural History, Los Angeles from Roberts and Roberts, *A Saint in the City*, 182).

Think of the huge bazaars in Mecca or Mashhad, Iran. But these economic enterprises around pilgrimage sites are small 'lemonade stands', compared to the principal draw of holy pilgrimage sites – *baraka*. Each potent pilgrimage site, metaphorically if not literally, exists as a nexus of 'heaven and earth', generating blessings or divine grace. Pilgrim-visitors usually come for *baraka* first and foremost, in spite of how many pictures they may take or souvenirs they may buy. The more blessings pilgrim-visitors receive, the more blessings that emanate from the potent shrine, because the popularity of a shrine is probably a function of its potency. More demand automatically brings more supply. There is always an abundance of *baraka* for those ready to receive it.

Compare this with the tourist. The tourist travels for the exotic. Tourism these days is often an imaginary escape from the monotony of info-industrial modern life. Observe groups of tourists moving from their buses to an interpretive tour, hundreds of camera and video clicks mediating and distancing them from their environment. Then they return in the buses to their sanitized hotels to eat familiar food. Tourism degrades the human and spiritual environment. Millions of people can visit a shrine over thousands of years with increasing *baraka* year after year. Yet a couple of decades, or less, of tourism can obliterate the spiritual contours of a sacred site and adversely affect the experience of those working there. Tourism is the process of treating place and people as objects to be photographed or purchased in some form.

Pilgrimage is human-to-human sharing. People bring their troubles and their devotion to the deceased holy person and/or his living representative, in the hope of receiving *baraka*. If the desired changes occur in their lives, they usually return to give something to the shrine and, in many cases, then visit on a regular basis. There is an ongoing relationship. The qualitative difference in these two kinds of travelling is clear. The intentions for travelling are radically different, as are the assumptions once one arrives at the destination. Both pilgrim-visitor and tourist may share pictures and videos after the trip, but some returning visitors to tomb-shrines report experiences that differentiate them from tourists, as we will see.

I have painted a black-and-white picture here to demonstrate that travel to sufi shrines can be qualitatively different from a stereotypical tourist trip. Having said this, 'devotional tours' are big.[3] These tours can happen under the rubric of tourist agencies, but are also sponsored by sufi groups. In 2006, I was invited to go on a tour to visit the nine 'super friends of God' (the Wali Songa) of Java, Indonesia, sponsored by the Tarekat Qadiriyah Naqsabandiyah sufi group based in Suralaya.[4] There were 15 full-length buses and a few cars totalling around 820 people. It was impeccably organized – name badges, charts on the bus door with each person's name, a 'visitor's guide' with a very detailed notebook of the itinerary and explanations – this was the seventeenth year they had organized this event. In our bus there was a person on a citizen's band radio talking to the lead car where my host, with flashing lights and siren, was clearing the way. He had contacted the police in each town before our arrival to stop the side traffic at major intersections, so our 15 buses could pass through without stopping. This caravan ended up in Tasikmalaya, where each person filed in to kiss the handkerchiefed hand of the grandshaykh.

Boundaries are very blurry between a busload of sincere pilgrims getting off at a shrine clicking cameras and the next busload of tourists who descend upon the same shrine, both buses coming from the same hotel. Who is the pilgrim and who is the tourist? Anyone can happen to wander into a shrine and have an unexpected life-changing experience. Weird unexpected things happen in life. I suspect that these kinds of non-linear events probably happen more frequently around shrines, though my experience is very limited.

The shrine experience that sticks most firmly in my mind was simultaneously the worst experience and the most amazing experience I have ever had at a sufi shrine. It all happened in less than the space of an hour. The occasion on the first day was to witness one ageing sufi ritually designating his successor at a relatively recently constructed sufi tomb-shrine. The second day inaugurated the shrine's most special ritual day of the year, the anniversary of that sufi's death. These events took place adjacent to a much more established and popular sufi shrine in one of the poorest neighbourhoods of a very poor country. The outward signs of tourism were the five modern buses from five-star hotels parked outside the sufi shrine, which brought wealthy devotees from around the world to witness this event. I am purposely vague because this is not an exposé of the leaders of this sufi group, but a report of an experience shared with a good friend (D. A. Sonneborn who has read this over, and has confirmed what I am relating).

Some background information is in order. First, I have never seen or heard about a sufi shrine in this country that closes its doors during usual opening hours (roughly sunrise to 10 pm or a couple hours after sunset) to *anyone*, other than to keep women from entering the inner precincts of male sufi shrines or to keep men from entering the corresponding areas of female sufi shrines. Second, on the death anniversary of the person buried in the shrine, not only are the doors open, but everyone, near and far, is invited to partake in sharing food. So when they announced an open invitation for the anniversary festivities, everyone was welcome. But that is not how it turned out.

In the early evening of the death anniversary day we had to leave the gathering in the more recent sufi shrine before the festivities had ended. Walking toward the exit, the first thing we noticed was loud shouting. We could see from a distance that there was no way to exit the way we had entered, because the eight-metre-high, heavy wooden doors were bending inwards from a crowd of shouting people on the other side. My friend, who emailed the leaders soon after this event said:

> At the front doors the scene was pandemonium. It bordered on violence, people fighting and clamoring to get in, two or three men at the door hammering at hands reaching inward, pushing and straining to close the doorway. I watched two women struggle through the mass and enter, visibly shaken, clothes and hair askew. It was clear that there was no way to leave.

There was another exit and we went to the shrine office to find the way. When we explained what was going on, the person there said, 'It's not my job', even though we emphasized that the situation bordered on violence. We left. Since we had some time before our next engagement, we decided to visit the tomb of the well-known sufi nearby, expecting the usual crowds. As we walked through a hallway towards the entrance to the courtyard of the tomb, we encountered about ten men along the way, some in twos and threes, walking towards us. Each of them stopped, gazed into our eyes, and shook our hands. This was an unusual experience for both of us. Then the biggest surprise of all – the tomb was entirely deserted. As my friend, who had been at the shrine many times before, said, 'Unlike any other time I've been there, there was no one present within the courtyard except one man seated outside the entrance to the tomb.' We went into the tomb and I immediately went into a meditative state. Some time later, I opened my eyes and saw people walking towards the tomb. The following day my valiant friend went to discover what had happened with the 'door episode'. The loud shouting we had heard came from angry neighbourhood people who had been excluded from participating in the anniversary activities. He says:

> I was disturbed that such an event, advertised as open to the public, one to which I had been told that all were welcome, could have men stationed at the public entrance to the shrine beating away people trying to enter with fists, slamming the door shut upon them.

The worst was yet to come. I wrote about what had happened to the new sufi leader, whom I knew personally. No answer whatsoever. My friend wrote very compassionate emails to three other leaders. No answer. About five years later, yet another high-ranking sufi leader in the same group came to visit me at home. I told him what I have just shared with you. It was as if I had been casually discussing the weather. His answer was, 'Hmmm, that is interesting.' I am understating the utter dreadfulness and appalling nature of this experience and its follow-up, because in life I put these kinds of things out of my mind.

The most wonderful part, which like a fragrant rose is hard to put into words, is much easier to access. It was clearly an altered state that I experienced going towards the other shrine and this was followed by incredible peacefulness after spending that time alongside the tomb. It lingered the following day – I did not feel like going anywhere. In turn, the experience next to the tomb directly connected to my being able to get married near that same tomb where I had meditated. A prominent sufi in Delhi 'saw' my connection to the deceased sufi buried in the tomb and arranged for my marriage there. Although this may seem very straightforward, as I try to communicate it to you, it ranks up there among the many inexplicable events in my life.

I wonder as I write whether I should thank those sufi leaders for their lapses in responsible behaviour – because otherwise I might never have had that set of incredible experiences.

Sufi tomb-shrines: An overview

One underlying principle of Muslims visiting tomb-shrines is the presupposition, shared as an operating principle by almost all sufis, that the Prophet is still alive. It follows that deceased sufi *heirs* of the Prophet are also alive. A minority opinion, particularly among contemporary modernist/ Wahhabi Muslims, asserts that the Prophet is dead and buried.[5] Thus, if he can no longer intercede for humans, until the Day of Judgement, then neither can anyone else, such as sufis. For these Wahhabis, the Prophet's legacy is the Qur'an and his sayings, the hadith. End of story. This bookish interpretation of the Prophet is not convincing for those who have experienced Muhammad and/or his sufi heirs in dreams, some even in waking consciousness. Nor is it convincing to the millions who continue to visit deceased sufis every year, including numerous non-Muslims. Regardless of theological perspectives, the reality on the ground is that tombs of sufis are visible signs of *baraka* to those who visit. Once buried, the deceased is automatically considered to have been 'a friend of God', especially if healing or other life-changing events occur after petitioning there. Sometimes there is not even anyone buried there and it does not make any difference (more on that later).

If a living sufi was considered to be a friend of God who could have powers of intercession, it follows that one should not only come to ask for his advice and blessings while alive, but also after he has passed away. The Qur'an says, 'Do not think that those who were slain in God's way are dead. They are living with their Lord and sustained by him' (Q. 3:169) and 'Do not say that those slain in God's way are dead; they are living, but you are unaware' (2:154). There are numerous hadith with the same message, e.g. 'The prophets are alive in their graves praying' and 'No one sends greetings to me without Allah returning my spirit to me so that I return his greeting'.[6] Naturally, those opposing intercession by live or dead friends of God can also find Qur'anic passages and hadith to support their views.

It is unlikely that visitors to sufi tomb-shrines consulted the Qur'an or hadith for references before leaving home. There are very long-standing cultural patterns at work. At least half the planet's population acknowledges the permeability between the world of the living and the world of the dead.

Consider ancestor veneration in East/Southeast Asia and Africa and then add three-quarters of the Islamic world. That we live in a multi-dimensional universe, populated by beings and life-forms that are less densely embodied than we are is the common assumption – and in some cases, experience – for the vast majority of people historically and people living in most world cultures today. This contrasts sharply with the monolithic physical cosmos of scientific materialism – if it is not visible, then it does not exist. Those who exclusively focus on the material world are prone to ignore, much less appreciate, other dimensions of reality. They find themselves in what Max Weber calls the 'iron cage of modernity' (or its graphene post-modern simulacrum). Reality is far more than we can perceive with our physical senses. Just think of your mind and keep on going.

At the same time, a lot of what happens around shrines is a function of local cultural patterns (though I prefer not to reduce everything to this), regardless of whether there is intercession or not. In that light, we have comments about visitors to Helveti shaykh Sha'ban Veli (d. 1569) in the Kastamonu province of Turkey:

> Non-Muslims from the protected religions other than Islam come with candles and sacrifices, and they bring the sick and other people struck by calamity, and they visit and request things. Even this poor one [Fu'ādī] was himself aware [of this ...] When they prayed, I prayed for their faith and their submission [to Islam]. At present, they still have not stopped coming and going, and when the poor one asks them about their coming with candle and sacrifices to visit, they reply, 'we request favor and help in our important affairs and in our times of confusion with pain and suffering, and we vow candles and sacrifices. We are satisfied through his sacredness, and our pain and suffering are taken away.'[7]

The famous Ottoman scholar Katip Çalabi (d. 1657) noted how an entire industry had developed to supply shrine visitors with lights and other paraphernalia. 'Thus it was hopeless to try and stop the foolishness.'[8] This reinforces that throughout Islamic history there have been those who were not pleased by the rituals that they observed at shrines.

A contemporary example (without any overt value judgement) is the shrine of La'l Shahbaz Qalandar (d. 1274), who is buried in the village of Sehwan, Sind, Pakistan (see fig. 3.5). Wasim Frembgen notes:

> Some toss their heads ecstatically and many rotate their heads to the beat of the *dhol* [a double-skinned barrel drum] [...] Some of the dancers become really wild, frenzied, and feverish, disrupting the order with their abrupt leaps into the air. In between there are dervishes dressed in black with shaven heads, who raise their horns or wooden clubs in supplication. These clubs are used to crush hemp in mortars to prepare intoxicants. Isn't the trance inducing *dhamaal* (which literally means noise) [but in this context is the name of ecstatic dance] an ecstatic dance par excellence? Is the trance-like frenzy mainly due to the effects of hashish and opium which are consumed on every street corner in Sehwan?[9]

Yet at the same time there is more going on than the transgressive outward show. The same author generously shares his own experiences there:

> I enjoy the togetherness, the harmony and feeling of security in the *dera* [a place where people gather in the village]. It is an island of leisureliness; [*sic*] inhabited by a community of pious pilgrims and seekers of a spiritual goal, intoxicated by Allah, the Qalandar [La'l Shahbaz Qalandar] and hemp – frugal, altruistic, without possessions, and sharing a fraternal spirit. Arif Sain [the author's friend] and his dervish companions are *ahl-e dil* (people of the heart), who by their example show me that other people are more important than oneself and one's ego. Here there are neither Islamists nor secular Muslims. Denominations are unimportant. No one asks whether someone is Sunni or Shia, Muslim, Christian, or Hindu. My companions in the tent are enraptured by the love of the Prophet, of Maula Ali, Lal Shahbaz Qalandar and Allah and wish to benefit from the power of the saint's blessing.[10]

Unless I lapse into historical data and talk conceptually about the topic of visiting deceased holy people, it is hard for me to make sense of what

FIGURE 3.5 A modern rendition of La'l Shahbaz Qalandar in ecstasy, depicted in a sufi poster available at the shrine.

is going on at *any* shrine. I have respectfully visited shrines around the Islamic world, as I would visit any cemetery, and each shrine is like a unique individual with its own dynamics – which vary hour-to-hour and day-to-day. The people going there with requests are not going to visit a shrine-tomb, but are going to visit the *person* buried there. A tourist or a casual visitor, on the other hand, is more likely to admire the architecture or watch the exotic 'spectacles'. There is the potential for two entirely different sets of experiences at the same place, depending on prior intentions.

Instead of texts – which hardly anyone reads – visitors to tombs access God through the intermediaries of local deceased holy people and their caretakers. It includes an immediate tactile experience, such as the *baraka*-laden strips of cloth, water, amulets, sweets and flowers. Think of it as an incredible local manifestation of blessings open to all, men and women, rich and poor, expressed eloquently in the vernacular local language of the shrine. All visitors can express their devotion to God and supplicate for their needs. Until you personally visit a sufi shrine and have your own experiences, you may not necessarily understand very much of the ritual vernacular language of the shrine. Learning a language, whether ritual, cultural or linguistic, takes many years.

Tombs of holy people also attract the dead. Millions of Muslims over the centuries have gone to great efforts to be buried near holy people, whether near Muhammad's tomb in Medina, 'Ali b. Abi Talib's tomb (Muhammad's son-in-law and cousin) in Najaf, Iraq, or Husayn's tomb (Muhammad's elder martyred grandson) in Kerbala, Iraq. Sufis' tombs have brought people to be buried in the Al-Qarafa cemetery in Cairo, the Shah-i Zinda cemetery in Samarqand, Uzbekistan, Touba in Senegal, and Khuldabad, Deccan, India. The logic of being buried near these friends of God is that, when they go to heaven, those near them will accompany them. These are some well-known examples. The majority of shrines in the Islamic world, however, are found in villages, where a tomb of one of the local pious holy ones has become the local centre of spiritual blessedness protecting the village.

Tomb visitation often includes the visitation of previous sultans, kings, and modern heads of state (Ataturk in Turkey, Jinnah in Pakistan, Sukarno in Indonesia, Khomeini in Iran). Snouck Hurgronje (d. 1936), advisor on native affairs to the colonial government of the Netherlands East Indies (now Indonesia), wrote in a report to the Governor-General, 'The Javanese still visit the graves of the most cruel tyrants, who resided in Mataram, as if they were the final resting-places of saints, and approach these creeping and stooping, full of fear and awe.'[11] Hurgronje should have known that in Indonesia, as in pre-Islamic Persia and many other places in the world, kings were perceived to 'have the mandate of Heaven', and, as such, were at the pinnacle of the hierarchy of sacred persons. In other contexts – like Mughal India – the emperor is pictured with the cup of Jamshid, a symbol associated with King Solomon (a prophet in Islam) and the lineage of ancient Sassanian Persian kings.

It is difficult to know historically how some shrines became more popular than others. As a general rule, older shrines have precedence over newer shrines. The nine super friends of God in Indonesia, the Wali Songa, are considered to be the ones who first propagated Islam, and their shrines are the most popular on the island of Java; 'Ali and his son Husayn, the first and third Shi'i Imams respectively, buried in Iraq, are probably the most visited tombs in Iraq (the tomb of the second Imam, Hasan, was desecrated by the Saudis); Data Ganj Bakhsh ('Ali b. 'Uthman Hujwiri, d. *c*.1075) is the earliest sufi buried in Lahore and also its patron saint (see fig. 3.6); Mu'inuddin Chishti (d. 1236, Ajmer, Rajasthan, India) is the founder-figure of the Indian Chishti lineage and his is probably the most popular sufi shrine in India. The tomb of Eyyüp Ansari, the buried companion of the Prophet, is the most popular shrine in Istanbul.

Rulers have often built or rebuilt stunning sufi shrines. The Mughal Emperor Akbar built a beautiful city, Fatehpur Sikri, around the humble residence of Salim Chishti (d. 1572) and later Mughal rulers built a lavish marble tomb for Salim. The Ottoman Sultan Selim I (r. 1512–20) rebuilt Ibn al-'Arabi's shrine in Damascus,[12] which has a steady flow of visitors. Since the fifteenth century, much vocabulary for sufis and associated architecture has been borrowed from their royal court analogues. For example, king (*shah*) is an honorific for sufis; a royal court (*dargah*) is the building built around the venerated sufi grave (*mazar*); and a sufi's turban is often called a royal crown (*taj*). Once the rulers began donating money and shrine caretakers became dependent upon these sources of income, the government's interests soon overlapped with the shrine's interests. Mughal and

British rulers in India used the custodians at shrines to collect taxes from the peasants, for example. This mutually beneficial system worked well in agricultural economies from Morocco to China.

Then there is the other side of government involvement. All sufi shrines were closed in Turkey from 1925 to 1950, except Rumi's, which was made into a museum in 1926. When the ban was lifted, visiting shrines commenced as usual, but often there were signs demarcating proper behaviour, e.g. reciting the Qur'an for the benefit of the sufi's soul was acceptable, but asking for intercession or any vows associated with these requests, including the tying of cloth on trees or railings was discouraged. In 1950 the Ministry of Culture allowed the opening of tombs of 'great and famous Turks' to the public, as architectural exhibits, though only civil servants could work there.

The Soviets began to 'close down' tomb-shrines in around 1927. Many times it was not possible to close down shrines, unless they bulldozed them away – which they did. Usually officials prevented people from visiting shrines by administrative means and through public pressure. Many shrine custodians were exiled and imprisoned. In Daghistan, the chief religious

FIGURE 3.6 The modern government-constructed shrine of Data Ganj Bakhsh ('Ali Hujwiri, d. c.1075) in Lahore, Pakistan.

scholars of the North Caucasus Muslim Spiritual Board, who were ordered by the KGB to write anti-shrine visitation tracts, benefited from shrine visitation, because the scholars received a cut of the donations. Some of the big sufi shrines in Central Asia became museums and visitors bought a ticket, while shrine custodians got jobs working in the 'museum' (e.g. the Yasawi shrine in the city of Turkestan). Here we have examples of attempts at state regulation of shrine protocol and a reminder that activities at shrines can change over time.[13]

Sufi shrines in the Indian subcontinent: Two brief case studies

Mihr 'Ali Shah

Mihr 'Ali Shah (d. 1937), a Chishti buried outside Islamabad, Pakistan, in Golra Sharif, was succeeded by his only son, Ghulam Muhyiuddin (d. 1974). When Ghulam Muhyiuddin died, his two sons took over the activities of the shrine; one presides over shrine rituals and the other administers the shrine. The shrine centres on the tombs of Mihr 'Ali Shah and his son – marble structures decorated by calligraphic verses from the Qur'an, surrounded by marble flooring outside. The tombs are draped with cloth covers and the scent of incense pervades the air. The doors close at 9 p.m. and women are not allowed inside the tomb itself. Nearby is Mihr 'Ali Shah's daughter's tomb, where only women can enter. In the compound is a tree with bits of cloth tied by women who have made vows to Mihr 'Ali Shah. When their wishes are fulfilled, they untie the piece of cloth and contribute what they have vowed to give to the shrine. Every day there is *qawwali* singing – one of the keynotes for the Chishti lineage – for an hour in the late morning. Any devotee is allowed to stay in one of the shrine's 70 guest-rooms for three days, after which permission is necessary. There is a public kitchen that makes food for 500–1,000 people a day. The shrine owns about 650 acres of village land, has a dairy farm and collects rent from about 50 shops around the shrine. Donations by devotees add to the shrine's income. There is a staff of about 160, run by retired administrative experts.

Specialists are in charge of the smooth organization of visitors and oversee amulet production, answering mail and teaching. Most of these employees are also devotees, so their salaries are minimal. There is a room with all the *baraka*-impregnated objects that belonged to Mihr 'Ali – his turban, rosary, prayer rug and spittoon. It is only opened twice a year – for Eid and for the annual death anniversary. At Mihr 'Ali's shrine, as with just about all other shrines, the most important day of the year is that celebrating his death, often called his 'marriage with God' (*'urs*).

To become a formal devotee, the person comes to the head custodian in a ritually pure state with the head covered. He takes the hand of the head custodian and repeats some Qur'anic verses and then prays in the congregational mosque. Then the head custodian supplicates to God and the person becomes a formal devotee. This initiation is supposed to set the formal devotee towards a pious life, protected by the head custodian from negative influences. In the case of female disciples, there is no handshake, but the shaykh and devotee hold the ends of a piece of cloth. There are group activities to remember God (*dhikr*) like reciting, 'There is no god but

FIGURE 3.7 Mihr 'Ali Shah and his tomb, as depicted in a poster available at the shrine.

God and Muhammad is God's messenger', and visualization of the shaykh, but research has not indicated whether this is a disciplined practice on the part of the formal devotees.[14]

Apparently the primary reason to come to the shrine is for economic security – this correlates with the reports of more experienced observers at other shrines in India. When a devotee gives crops for the public kitchen, he hopes that the rest of the crop will remain and be profitable.[15] Owners of buses and trucks come to Mihr 'Ali because they would not think of driving a new vehicle without a holy person blessing it, not only to prevent accidents, but for overall business success.

Managers of sufi shrines that cater to truckers (not Mihr 'Ali Shah's shrine) make it easy for drivers to donate to the *baraka*-exuding shrine by setting up kiosks with attendants along busy highways. The drivers slow down at these sufi kiosks and throw out bundles of paper money to be fetched by the attendants. If you happen to be on the Peshawar–Islamabad road, there is one near Taxila on one side and a second near Jhelum on the other side.[16]

The next most common reason for visiting Mihr 'Ali is for healing. Women typically come for blessings to have a male child or for the sufi to bless a child. Some come for other worldly difficulties or to have Mihr 'Ali or the head custodian forgive them for past actions they regret. One common way of administering remedies is for the head custodian to recite verses from the Qur'an and blow on a glass of water, which is then drunk by the petitioner (see fig. 3.8 for how this is done in Senegal). For those possessed by spirits (*jinn*), the head custodian often ties a thread around the person's neck. Often the next step is to pick up an amulet from a keeper of the shrine. Observers at Mihr 'Ali's shrine agree that approximately 95 per cent of the people requesting amulets are women.[17]

To temper my idealistic portrayal of visiting sufi shrines at the beginning of this chapter in comparison with tourism, we have an account from a 1949 Indian government committee inquiry about open corruption at Mu'inuddin Chishti's shrine in Ajmer:

> [A]s soon as a pilgrim gets down at the railroad station, Ajmer, he
> is met by a horde [of shrine custodians]. To avoid a conflict among

FIGURE 3.8 A Qur'anic board and the *qalam*, or sacred pen, 1990s. Wood and reed: height of board, 23.7 cm. FMCH TR99.37.55. These are the principal instruments of sufi calligraphers/healers in Senegal. Such boards are used to write prayers and mystical squares that are then washed off, and the resultant water and ink are consumed by patients in an act of devotional communion. It is said that the 'drinking of the Qur'an' is the highest form of prayer and memorization of the sacred verses that is possible. (Reproduced with permission of the UCLA Fowler Museum of Cultural History, Los Angeles from Roberts and Roberts, *A Saint in the City*, 177).

> (themselves) [...] the man is put to sale and whoever makes the highest bid becomes his guide. The sale proceeds are distributed [among the custodians]. The [custodian] who becomes the guide is anxious to make as much profit out of the transaction and tries to extort, by all means, fair or foul, the last [bit of money] out of his victim.[18]

In 1976–7 there were 1,400 people working at Mu'inuddin's shrine and people have reported that many of these people still wait at the railroad station, bus terminal and hotels to snag clients.[19] With the internet, it is no longer necessary for the shrine custodians to leave the comfort of home. Here is how it is digitally done these days:

> If you need protection from Black Magic or people are jealous of your prosperity or if you have any type of problems like work problems, engagement problems, marriage problems, family problems, Business problems, child problems, or you are already grabbed in fraud's hands then you can call me without any hesitation or tension [...] Here In Ajmer Shareef Please Call Me. Inform your near & dear ones, friends, relatives, anyone about this information & help them all. Immediate Result Is Just A Phone Call Away.[20]

The next Indian sufi is much lower profile, but we have more detailed information.

Abu Bakr Tusi Haydari-Qalandari (aka Matki 'claypot' pir, d. c.1235)

Philip Lewis, the author of *Pirs, Shrines and Pakistani Islam*, had the advantage of being able to visit Mihr 'Ali's shrine many times over the six years he worked at the Rawalpindi Christian Studies Centre. It appears, however, that he only talked with the English-speaking shrine staff, rather than the Urdu- or Panjabi-speaking devotees. Kumkum Srivastava, on the other hand, has presented us with a ten-year study of Abu Bakr, having spoken with a wide range of men and women devotees (an advantage of being a female researcher) in Hindi/Urdu.[21]

This shrine, unlike the other shrines discussed above, is small, like dozens of other sufi shrines in Delhi. It is the only Islamic shrine in Delhi on a mound, so one has to walk up 54 steps to reach it. There are no institutions, as at Baba Farid's or at Golra Sharif, or any other buildings like an office, hospital, library, mosque, kitchen or guesthouse. There are only two shops at the entrance to the shrine. Other than Abu Bakr and his successor, there are no other graves. Three brothers and their sons take care of the shrine part-time and they need other jobs to make ends meet. Now it is the only qalandar shrine in Delhi (Bibi Fatima's shrine near Nizamuddin's no longer has a sign indicating that she was a qalandar). Abu Bakr is called the 'claypot pir' because of thousands of people taking refuge at his shrine during the looting and pillaging in 1947–8 when the British partitioned India. The refugees used claypots for water and cooking. To protect the pots they often hung them from trees, which now has become a tradition, in addition to placing them in other locations (see fig. 3.9).[22]

The custodian's outer credentials are very similar to those of the head custodians in other shrines, large or small. Srivastava asks a mock (pun intended) set of questions to the current successor to Abu Bakr. 'How can you be the current successor without a certificate of succession or without being a descendant since Abu Bakr was celibate and there is no knowledge of any of his relatives?' He points to the certificate on the wall that came from his father. 'But that certificate is from your father, who like you was neither a successor or a recognized member of Abu Bakr's family.'[23] Herein is the situation with head shrine custodians. To the devotees, they are shaykhs and the custodians usually think of themselves as such, because people coming to the shrine reinforce this identity every day. The head custodian at Abu Bakr's shrine, Muhamamd Naseem, calls himself the principal successor (*sajjada nishin*) of Abu Bakr, and sees his prime duty as service, which includes preparing amulets and *baraka*-laden water to help clients with worldly problems.[24]

One servant of the shrine, Chand, specializes in spiritual cures. He has read a lot of books on how to make amulets and has prayed at various sufi shrines, while regularly visiting Abu Bakr. One night he fell asleep and stayed overnight at the shrine, which the head custodian interpreted as Chand being chosen to work at the shrine. He converted to Islam in 1994

FIGURE 3.9 Tomb of Abu Bakr Tusi Haydari-Qalandari in Delhi. Note the claypots on the roof of the enclosure.

and became an apprentice to Muhammad Naseem, the head custodian, to specialize in spiritual cures.[25]

All the donations to Abu Bakr's shrine go to meet the expenses, mostly electricity, and to support the extended family of the head custodian. Srivastava estimates a monthly income of the shrine to be around US $400 (£260), but she does not specify whether this is gross or net after meeting the expenses of the shrine. Roughly 8,000 to 10,000 devotees come to the shrine during the three-day death anniversary celebration. Hindu businessmen of old Delhi pay for the expenses (roughly US $2000 or £1,300). In the ten-year period Srivastava was researching the shrine, all kinds of improvements have occurred – roofing of courtyards, additions of new rooms and fitting of lamps and fans around the shrine. Almost all of this renovation was financed by Hindu devotees, who are about 75 per cent of the people coming to Abu Bakr. Since it is common for people to donate money to the shrine if their problems are solved, the expansion and refurbishment of the shrine is very likely concrete evidence that people associate Abu Bakr with improvement in their lives.[26]

The head custodian never asks for compensation for spiritual remedies or other consultations. Some people give him 100 rupee notes (US $2 or £1.30), and others just touch his feet. Bills are often folded into small squares and confidentially slipped under his cushion, in mutual recognition that these kinds of services are not performed for money. About 60 or 70 people come to Muhammad Naseem and Chand for spiritual remedies each Thursday and Sunday, mostly from lower socio-economic classes. Many more women come than men. Srivastava notes that women take more time, because they are keen to talk about their personal lives in a way, it seems, they cannot do with anyone else. They have no problem airing their difficulties in front of the other women. Men, on the other hand, tended to speak briefly and in lowered voices, sometimes even requesting privacy. Men always paid, while women paid much less, if at all. There is not more than around US $160 (£100) a month income from these consultations and the head custodian's brothers get a share of it.[27]

Srivastava frankly discussed others' generic criticisms of shrine activities with Muhammad Naseem, e.g. the commercialization of shrine activities and shrine caretakers receiving special political favours. He agreed with these criticisms in theory, but what was he to do? He did not want to turn people away. People keep coming to him insisting that he help with their difficulties and then they recommend others to come and do likewise. He affirmed that political involvement is not agreeable, but in Delhi one cannot get water or electrical connections, have sewer lines constructed or have any of this properly maintained without political connections.[28] It is easy to point fingers from armchairs afar.

Islamic shrines on the Indonesian island of Java: The Wali Songa

On the largest Indonesian island of Java, the friends of God with the highest rank are the nine Wali Songa (pronounced Songo). They are seen as the major Muslim pioneers, mostly from India and China, who first taught

Islamic practices to Javan Indonesians in the fifteenth and sixteenth centuries. It is likely that they came to Indonesia as traders or religious scholars. From the very scanty information available, nothing points to sufi connections. Legends of these Wali Songa were recorded centuries later and the contemporary understanding of the Wali Songa is based upon Solichtar Salam's *Regarding the Wali Songa*, published in 1960. Sunan Ampel Denta (Sunan is an honorific meaning 'The Venerable') is often accorded historical precedence, but others give spiritual precedence to Sunan Giri. Many regions put their regional *wali* in the most prominent position. Some high-ranking Wali Songa were associated with kings, e.g. Sunan Kudus in Demak and Sunin Kalijaga in Mataram.[29] Legends report their skilful means in communicating Islamic teachings in local cultural idioms. It is said that the Wali Songa used Indonesian shadow puppet theatre (*wayang*) as a means of teaching about Islam before becoming *wayang* figures themselves (see fig. 3.10). Holy men are buried all over Java and Indonesians of all religions piously visit them.

Thanks to Jamhari, we have insights into visitors' conceptions of *baraka* – an important consideration, since it is unlikely that *baraka* has a constant signification across cultures – or even within a culture. At Sunan Tembayat's tomb-shrine, some think that *baraka* is God's reward and others argue that it comes from the deceased friend of God because he/she is close to God. Others classify *baraka* into 'pure *baraka*', which benefits a person spiritually, and 'profane *baraka*', which can be used for worldly benefit. *Baraka* can include all kinds of worldly expressions, such as well-being, prosperity, good luck and success in studies. In any case, it is a reward from God. One shrine custodian at Sunan Tembayat functionally noted that the perception of receiving *baraka* 'provides motivation and courage to support people in achieving their goals'.[30] Another custodian explained:

> As Sunan Tembayat continues to receive *barakah* from God, his *barakah* overflows. Therefore visitors search for the *barakah* that overflows from Sunan Tembayat. In addition, Sunan Tembayat does not need *barakah* any more. The *barakah*, then, is given to visitors who need it.[31]

Signs in dreams indicate *baraka* and the head custodians of Javanese shrines (*juru kunci*) are expected to interpret dreams for pilgrims. Dream interpretation is one of the main modes of *baraka* transmission. In Bayat, the location of Sunan Tembayat (between Yogyakarta and Surakarta), the head custodian leads shrine rituals and unlocks the tomb. Because of constant contact with Sunan Tembayat, his *baraka* (and that of other shrine custodians) is acquired through a process called *kesawaban*, a word also used for the power that the wife of a president acquires because of her husband's position.[32] Sunan Tembayat is like a postman who delivers messages to God. Visitors who give their messages to Sunan Tembayat directly or through his head custodian believe that they have a greater chance of having God hear their plea.

Sunan Tembayat, converted to Islam by Sunan Kalijaga, is said to have been a major figure of those who communicated the practices of Islam

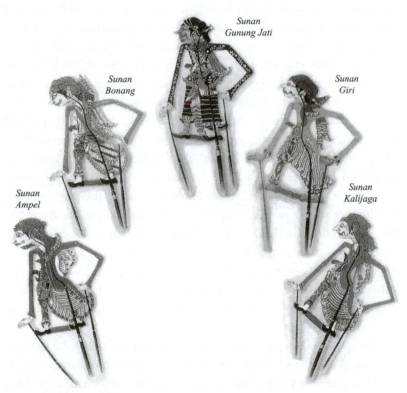

FIGURE 3.10 The Wali Songa as *wayang* puppet figures.

in Indonesia. People have been visiting his tomb at least since the seven-teenth century and in south-central Java he is the most prestigious holy person. Before the Indonesian government outlawed a popular lottery game (SDSP), Sunan Tembayat's secretary used to be asked for winning lottery numbers.[33] Sunan Tembayat's tomb is also a tourist destination for foreign and domestic tourists, who come to admire the architecture and the variety of 'cultural traditions' enacted by various groups of pilgrims.

Different types of visitors to Sunan Tembayat do so in accordance with their own understanding of their identities. Those who see him as a king replicate many rituals associated with the Mataram royal court, while those who see him as a pious holy man recite the Qur'an and supplicate God in an Islamic manner. Visitors needing healing literally see Sunan Tembayat as a doctor. Instead of money they bring flowers and incense; instead of a prescription they get *baraka* from him. The *baraka*-imbued flowers and water at the shrine are the medicine they take home. Others see Sunan Tembayat as a mediator between them and God, and hope for rewards from God. Other visitors ask for *baraka* directly from Sunan Tembayat and, through offerings of flowers and incense – and ideally an all-night vigil at his grave – they hope to receive as much as possible.[34]

Two major events at the shrine signal the end of one 'visiting year' and the beginning of the next visiting year. These are important markers for those who come on a yearly basis. The end of the visiting year occurs before the fasting month of Ramadan and is celebrated by changing the white cotton cloth that wraps Sunan Tembayat's tomb. This takes an entire day, with hundreds of people participating. Then the tomb is closed for Ramadan, because it is believed that one should not disturb Sunan Tembayat while he is fasting. After Ramadan there is a large feast in Javanese tradition with processions and horse and lion dances accompanied by music. The village chief, dressed in clothes of a Bayat king, then accompanies the eldest custodian to the tomb of Sunan Tembayat, as they inaugurate the start of the new visiting year.

The careful anthropological work of Jamhari demonstrates the diversity of perceptions of who Sunan Tembayat is and the corresponding rituals used when visiting him. When a mother asked her son what to do at the tomb of Sunan Tembayat, he replied:

[Y]ou should not ask for riches, long life and success in our trading. You only can ask such a thing to Allâh alone. If you do ask that to Sunan Tembayat, it means that you have done *syrk* [associating others with God]. We came here to remember him as a great *wali* [friend of God] and to recall again what his teachings are so we can follow them.[35]

Another who came with a group of 15 said:

[W]e [...] asked him [Sunan Tembayat] to guide us. This is because an ordinary man cannot convey the *tahlil* [saying that there is no god but God] to Allâh without the guidance of the *wali*. We believe that Sunan Tembayat is only sleeping and he can assist us.[36]

Lest we are tempted to think in black–white terms (Islamic versus non-Islamic practices), we are pleasantly reminded by a gentleman named Pak Dalang,

Actually I am a Moslem, although I do not do what Moslems usually do. Unlike Moslems who perform *ziarah* [shrine visitation] in the Islamic manner, such as reciting the Qur'ân, *tahlil* and so forth, I perform my *ziarah* based on Javanese beliefs. Therefore, I wear Javanese black dress with its accessories.[37]

Note the polyvalent nature of shrine visits in Indonesia. In this exquisite Indonesian example, the living representatives of the deceased welcome anyone, rich or poor, man or woman, Muslim or non-Muslim. No one community or group 'owns' the local or regional font of *baraka*. Just as the Qur'an declares Muhammad to be a mercy for the worlds (not just to Muslims), the heirs of the Prophet function in the same manner.

Dreams and shrines in Egypt

In this section we return again to what sufis call the imaginal realm, the dream-vision reality. This is also called the 'world of command', because what happens there, according to sufis and other contemplatives, affects the material world. Holy shrines provide concrete examples of the imaginal realm interacting with the physical realm through dreams. Amira Mittermaier has investigated four ways that dream visions and shrines are related:

1 Dreams move shrines from one location to another
2 Dreams influence people to visit shrines physically
3 Dreams can transport dreamers to visit shrines in a dream
4 Dreams are influenced by the buried person in a shrine.[38]

A fifth relationship is that of dreams causing shrines to be built (though Mittermaier was unable to interview any of the people involved to confirm what she had heard). In Egypt it is said that three consecutive presidents had dreams that led to building shrines. The shrine of Abu Hasan al-Shadhili (d. c.1258) is said to have been constructed after he appeared to President Gamal 'Abd al-Nasser in a dream. In another case, a student who had always prayed in al-Sayyid Badawi's mosque in Tanta appeared to President Anwar al-Sadat requesting to be buried inside his favourite mosque. Husni Mubarak is said to have initiated the building of a shrine for Shaykh Mutwalli Sha'rawi (d. 1998) in Daqadus, after the latter appeared to him in a dream.[39] Sayyidina Zaynab (the granddaughter of the Prophet) and Husayn (the grandson of the Prophet) have multiple gravesites in Egypt, but many of these do not claim to have actual bodies buried there. They are called 'vision-sites', because they have instructed people in dreams to build a tomb-shrine for them. One of the best known is the tomb of Sayyida Ruqayya (Zaynab's step-sister). In the twelfth century, she appeared in a dream to the Fatimid ruler al-Hafiz 'Abdulmajid, who subsequently built her a tomb in Cairo.

There are many logical reasons to doubt vision-sites – logical reasoning can be used to doubt anything, including this statement. Perhaps the real body is buried there, as many custodians of these sites claim; perhaps the people who had the dreams misunderstood them; or perhaps these shrines were built for other agendas. In the case of Zaynab and Husayn, it is generally recognized that the body of Zaynab was buried in Damascus and Husayn's body was buried in Karbala, where he was martyred. There is no way of verifying the authenticity of bodies buried in shrines. While Mittermaier was doing her fieldwork in Cairo, she met a woman who had a dream requesting her to donate food at Sayyidina Zaynab's shrine. This was just one of many instances in the course of her fieldwork where she met women who had met Zaynab in a dream and who then visited the shrine. Through dreams, many report that they have deeply personal relationships with Zaynab. The shrine is a physical node that connects to the infinity of the intermediary dream-vision world.

Sufis have been reported to choose their burial places by directing those escorting the body to where they want to be buried and sometimes they refuse to be moved from where they are buried. In al-Mansura, Egypt, they decided to demolish and rebuild the shrine of Shaykh Hasanayn. Four tractors broke down attempting to demolish his shrine and seven workers got sick enough to be taken to the hospital.[40] The report does not say who prevailed in that affair, but I have heard similar stories from people in Iran and Pakistan.[41] God knows best.

The holy dead are not exempt from governments seeking to exploit and tax them, and thus, shrines may become a part of the government's plans for tourist development. The tomb of the Seven Girls in the village of Al-Bahnasa, Egypt, now has a green iron fence around it and the area around the site has been 'cleaned up' (read: urban removal).[42] Since the 1960s, major shrines in Egypt have been under the control of the Ministry of Religious Endowments, which puts out locked donation boxes and keeps most of the donated money. There is increasing government interference in death anniversary celebrations at the larger sufi tombs in Egypt – either by controlling the distribution of market stalls or by a heavy-handed security presence. Some shrines now have a hospital, a secular school and a pharmacy attached to them. Although this sounds good in print, many people who have visited 'simple shrines' notice immediately that the combination of religious and civil space at shrines creates a different atmosphere than that of the openness of a traditional shrine. At the places of major sufi gatherings (like Sayyid Ahmad al-Badawi in Tanta), there are now permanent modern cafés adjacent to the shrine, with glittering shopping centres selling goods from India and China, and sufi music/remembrance rituals have been transformed into concerts.[43] Perhaps the affected holy deceased people will protest in a mass dream phenomenon and demand to be moved to more amenable surroundings. Stranger things have happened.

Conclusion

Holy tomb-shrines are like oases of divine grace in the desert of an increasingly rational-secular world. Desertification is gaining ground and it is a process very difficult to reverse. In pre-modern times, sufi lodges functioned as refuges across the Islamic world. Travellers and those who had hit bad times could always get a meal and a place to sleep on the floor. To some extent, shrines of the holy deceased do still continue to open their doors to those in need. One beauty of shrine environments is that they transcend religious and socio-economic boundaries. They bring people together in one place – not necessarily with the same rituals – and integrate local cultures into a larger one.

When visiting more popular sufi shrines, I used to feel disturbed by shrine caretakers crassly seeking to grab money. But over time I have seen that, for every victim in the radius of their grab, there are at least ten or more who have found solace in the shrine's nourishing atmosphere. There are not enough shrine caretakers to hassle everyone and they are easy to avoid. Now I have a very different perspective because I have learned to find places in the shrine away from the hustle and bustle. It is a different experience altogether and one that I hope you discover, whether as a tourist or a visitor. The only condition of entering this space is to respectfully follow the protocol, which is how we go about our everyday lives anyway.

One of the things that the post-modern perspective has contributed to our human repertoire is an appreciation of the incredible cultural diversity in each world religion. But not everyone is there yet. Modernist/ Wahhabi groups in the Islamic world cannot tolerate the ambiguity of simultaneous 'Islamic' and what they arbitrarily declare 'non-Islamic practices', religious and secular behaviour, and local and trans-local identities, all joyously happening in one place. If these modernist groups had their way they would level every Islamic graveyard and tomb-shrine in the world, as has been done in the Jannat al-Baqi' graveyard, adjacent to the Prophet's tomb in Medina. Literally, it looks like a dirt car park. This chapter has shown that the so-called dead retain a potential to connect to the living.

4

SUFI AUTHORITY
AND POLITICS

There was once a mighty king who decided to befriend a beggar outside his palace. The beggar was brought to the king, who asked him what he desired. The beggar replied that only God almighty could manage that and added that the king would not even be able to fill his begging bowl. So the king ordered the bowl to be filled with precious jewels, but whatever was put in the bowl simply vanished. The astounded king asked what kind of a bowl this was. The beggar, who was a realized sufi, answered that this is the desire bowl of the ego, which can never be satisfied. If you understand this, then you become a king; otherwise you are a beggar.

A WHILE AGO I was asked why Afghan Naqshbandi shaykhs frequently led resistance against invaders. The short answer was that their leadership might have been related to sufism and ethical training, but there is nothing special about the Naqshbandiyya per se, in a political sense, to distinguish them from other sufi groups. Functionally sufis have long been mediators and, to be mediators, they need to have credibility; and credibility is about acting ethically and in a trustworthy manner, which also gives one authority. Influential Qadiri sufi leaders in the Pushtun areas of Afghanistan organized resistance against the Russians, just like the Naqshbandis. If a sufi leader has many initiated followers, these can function as an army, especially in a tribal environment (e.g. Pir Pagaro below). The principle is that the *function* of sufis as mediators in society makes them the natural resistance leaders when their territory is invaded because they can mobilize more people under one banner.

Previously, we have noticed the support of the ruling elite in building sufi lodges and tomb-shrines. In turn sufis legitimized rulers, and in theory, had opportunities to counsel them – though it is doubtful that they listened. The trend, from Mughal and Ottoman times to the present day, has been for the ruling elite to co-opt and control sufi activity. In the contemporary political scene, sufi groups support certain political factions (e.g. Turkey and Pakistan) and tomb-shrines bring in considerable revenue (often siphoned off by governments, e.g. in Egypt and Pakistan).

The quest throughout this chapter is to reveal the extent to which sufis are applying principles of sufism in any kind of political activity. As explained in the introduction, the label 'sufi' has a wide application. Many well-known 'sufis', whose fathers were sufis, simply had the *baraka* of the lineage passed on to them – with no pretentions of undertaking any kind of sufi practice. For example, the famous Algerian 'Abdulqadir (d. 1883, Damascus) was a Qadiri through a hereditary link from his father, but apparently taught the Shadhili-Fasi practices in Damascus instead.[1] When he fought against the French in Algeria, he did so as a military leader, not as a sufi shaykh leading his followers into battle. From the secondary sources available, we do not know what Syrian Naqshbandi Ahmad Kuftaro (d. 2004, Damascus), Grand Mufti for the Asad regime for 40 years, had to do to become a shaykh or how Kuftaro trained his followers. Was it simply the *baraka* of his father passed down, or did he go through the rigorous transformational process of a committed seeker and complete the training? How did his being a sufi make any difference in how he conducted his affairs as a mufti?

Almost all of those writing about the intersection of politics with modern sufism focus on the outer political aspects. Academics appear to be unaware of the differences between a sufi talking politics over a cup of tea, a father taking a future sufi as a child to visit a sufi shaykh for *baraka* and yet a third scenario, of a person completing sufi training successfully. All these activities are 'associating with sufis', but there is a qualitative difference between the first two types of association and the third. It is like talking about books or visiting a library, versus actually reading books and writing a thesis. All of these activities involve books, but the actual reading and application of understanding is the metaphorical, if not literal, 'transformative' activity of applying intangible ideas in the books. For someone who cannot read, it is all just 'associating with books'. Recognizing sufi activity requires a bit of discernment and that leads us to the difference between authority and power.

Authority versus power

Authority and power are related to what is called inner/greater jihad and outer/lesser jihad respectively. Instead of jihad as war – the newspaper version of jihad – sufis stress the inner struggling (*jihad*) in the path of God, controlling the desires and ignorance of one's egoic self. Ignored by those utilizing religion for their own personal agendas, there is a hadith that Muhammad is said to have related after the Muslims gained a military victory against a much larger force at the Battle of Badr. He mentioned to the returning warriors that now they were returning from the 'lesser jihad' of fighting others to the 'greater jihad' of fighting their ego-selves. The vast majority of people discussing the relationship of sufism and political action seem to focus on the outer political events (the small jihad), without considering the kind of inner jihad that involves taming the ego (though this is exceedingly difficult to verify).

There is no contradiction for a sufi shaykh or shrine caretaker to be involved in larger social action. The term friend of God (*wali*) has an overlapping meaning of being close to God and having an authority that goes beyond his circle of students, giving him a role in society on the basis of non-ego-based authority. The political enactment of both authority and power can look identical. Authority is non-egoic, comes from the heart and sets a beautiful example that others *by themselves* want to imitate. Power is an ego – often a charismatic one – coercing other egos to behave or do something in a certain way. Authority manifests without attachment to the outcome, because there is no egoic actor. Power is control over subordinates to enforce what is no longer a request, but an order. Authority is to power what wisdom is to knowledge. Authority has the sweetness of love; power has a coldness of a steel blade. To the outside observer, those using the cold blade of steel in a non-ego-centred fashion to wage lesser jihad appear no different to other power-hungry individuals. It is difficult to determine who is who. One outer indication of authority is demonstrating the highest ethical standard through one's actions.

Politics, sufi lodges and shrines: Governments seek to control

The previous two chapters have mentioned in passing how the ruling elite and notable sufis worked together in agricultural societies before the modern period. Nile Green has attributed the popularity of prominent sufi lodges and shrines to a process of 'sanctification'.[2] By applying the Roman Catholic model and vocabulary of sanctification to sufi tombs, he proposes that the Muslim ruling elite patronized sufi lodges and tomb-shrines first and then common people followed their lead. The Christian parallel would be a papal committee deciding on who is a saint through official sanctification. Green's perspective balances my hypothesis, in the previous chapter, that it was people's shared experiences that made sufi lodges and shrines popular, which then pointed the rulers towards institutions worth patronizing.

Erik Ohlander's work on the early Suhrawardiyya confirms both perspectives. Abu Hafs al-Suhrawardi (d. 1234, Baghdad) was able to consolidate an effective form of institutionalized sufism, positioning his version of sufism among competing groups vying for religious authority, as the most authoritative. In addition to acting as a personal diplomat and mediator for the Caliph, Suhrawardi was able to successfully defend and legitimize the Caliph's regime. In this case Suhrawardi, with government support, was able to create a set of institutions that were robust enough to spread the Suhrawardiyya throughout the Muslim world after the Mongol devastation of Baghdad in 1258. There are fewer sources on Suhrawardi's activities before the Caliph became his patron, but evidence indicates that 'he made a name for himself as a preacher [...] drawing large crowds and achieving great fame among both the élites and the commoners'.[3] Perhaps this is what brought Suhrawardi to the Caliph's attention in the first place. If sufis functioned to legitimize rulers – as they still do – then a popular sufi would be a logical choice, although many have declined such invitations.

In defence of the top-down model, rulers had disproportionate influence. In many cases a ruler's military victory was attributed to sufis mobilizing unseen forces to do battle. If sufis could do this for rulers, just think what they could do for the common person's relatively minor problems. Rulers also had much to do with the magnificent shrine architecture we see today. The Ottoman sultan Bayazid II (r. 1481–1512) restored Rumi's tomb and sufi lodge in Konya, Turkey. After arranging for the Bektashi sufis to become officially recognized, Bayazid II restored Haci Bektash's tomb and his sufi lodge (see figs 4.1 and 4.2). Bektashi shaykhs also advised the Janissary corps of the Ottoman army until 1826. Perhaps these two tombs and systems of sufi lodges became more popular because of architectural renovations. Most likely, both government support and the popularity of certain lodges and shrines worked in tandem, along with resulting miracle stories, for certain sufi lodges and tomb-shrines to become prominent.

There has been frequent rhetoric in sufi sources about refusing royal patronage. For example, in India the Chishtis claimed to avoid rulers and their patronage, but their own archives and other sources indicate a much closer relationship than Chishti sources would lead one to believe. By the sixteenth century, Ottoman and Mughal rulers regularly donated funds and gave land grants to sufi shaykhs and caretakers of sufi shrines. Often it was the rulers who chose the successor to the presiding shaykh or shrine custodian. When individual sufis with large numbers of followers could not be co-opted, they were banished. The Mughal emperor Jahangir forced Naqshbandi shaykh Adam Banuri, who had a large band of supposedly 10,000 Pushtun followers, to leave Mughal territory in 1642.[4] Later, at the turn of the twentieth century, French colonial authorities in West Africa exiled sufis like Amadu Bamba for allegedly creating 'a state within a state'.[5]

FIGURE 4.1 Haci Bektash Vali, who talked with deer and rode on lions.

FIGURE 4.2 Haci Bektash Vali's tomb in Haci Bektash, Turkey.

In modern times, Pir Pagaro and his private army of 6,000 devotees (Hurrs) were the bane of the British in their occupation of the Sind Province in pre-partition India. Pir Pagaro set up an alternative government that collected taxes and administered justice. The British unsuccessfully tried to arrest most of the army and ended up executing the current Pir Pagaro, Sibghatullah II, in 1943.[6] After independence the Pakistani government confirmed Pir Pagaro's son's limited sovereignty. Under direct command of the Pakistani army, in 1965 the Hurrs were used in the war against India, and in 1983, to quell civil disturbances in Sind.

Rulers still seek to co-opt sufi authority and use it for their political and economic advantage. Pakistani Prime Minister Ayub Khan used sufi shrines as a vehicle to modernize agricultural techniques. In 1959 the government took over many of the largest and most lucrative shrines in Pakistan, namely Data Ganj Bakhsh in Lahore, Shah 'Abdulatif, La'l Shahbaz Qalandar, Bulleh Shah and Baba Farid, and ended up taxing the dead like their counterparts in Egypt. Mihr 'Ali Shah's shrine (mentioned in Chapter 3) was also targeted, but after a year of litigation the caretakers were able to keep the shrine out of the government's clutches. These take-overs were an attempt to undercut the politico-economic power of the caretakers, as the government endeavoured unsuccessfully to present 'sufi shaykhs' as social reformers rather than miracle workers.

Shrine custodians (aka 'sufi shaykhs') have been prominent in Pakistani politics. Seventeen members of the West Pakistan Legislative Assembly (dissolved in 1958) were shrine custodians or their close relatives. Secularist Prime Minister Zulifikar 'Ali Bhutto – the father of Benazir Bhutto – linked himself to sufi shrines as a way to legitimize his political power. When his officials went to the death anniversary ceremonies at Data Ganj Bakhsh's shrine, they proclaimed that the deceased eleventh-century sufi 'preached egalitarianism and visualized a classless society based on the equality of Muhammad'.[7] The next prime minister, Zia al-Haqq, then called together a convention of 'sufi shaykhs' (mostly shrine custodians), the first of its kind in Pakistan. With the intent of co-opting them, as he had attempted to do with religious scholars at a similar conference, he said that: '[B]y accepting the invitation for this convention, the shaykhs had demonstrated that they regarded the present government as the servant of Islam.' He went on to seek their advice, saying that they were the best group to counsel the government since '[the] majority of the population is not only under your influence but in a way under your command'.[8] This was to become more of a concrete reality after Zia al-Haqq appointed the paramount shaykh of the Suhrawardi lineage to be Governor of Panjab, the wealthiest province in Pakistan.

The Ottomans were more organized in controlling sufis than the Mughals had been. In 1854 the Meclis-i Vala, the supreme legal authority in the Ottoman Empire, decided to control sufi lodges by financing their operations and by appointing its nominees to head these lodges. By 1860 it even tried to regulate the people visiting a sufi lodge, by requiring sufis to make a record of those staying there.[9] This control over organized sufism went much further in 1866 with the formation of the Council of Shaykhs, whose mandate was to closely supervise sufi activity in the Ottoman Empire. Essentially, sufi lodges not only lost their independence, but also their privileges of having lodges built at government expense and exemptions from taxes. Now, when a shaykh died, there were bureaucratic procedures to follow. The sufi lodge submitted the names of candidates for the head sufi shaykh of the lodge. These candidates then had to take examinations that tested their knowledge of Islam and the history and practices of the specific lineage.[10] In a similar move, the Egyptian government has created a regulatory body, the High Council for Sufi Lineages, to mandate what 'proper sufism' should be. This council is responsible for the government presence at sufi-shrine festivals detailed in the previous chapter. Egyptian government supervision of sufi lineages facilitates deals between political parties (who get votes) and sufi groups, who receive enhanced national prestige and other benefits in return.

The general theme in these examples is that rulers attempt to co-opt any authority that subordinates or neutralizes their power. In many cases the government uses force to confiscate sufi resources, because it can. On the other hand, sufi authority expresses itself in the ability to mobilize people and resources, which can offset these political power plays. Sometimes sufis just play the political game like any other group of citizens – no need to pretend that there is 'sufi authority' involved. If a sufi has a large following, he has the potential to exert influence on the rulers, unless they have already co-opted him.

The myth of a pan-USSR militant Naqshbandi threat

Soviet Orientalists invented a non-existent pervasive Naqshbandi network, stretching from the Caucasus to Central Asia that was (incorrectly) notorious for 'political militancy'. Whenever anything happened in the mountain fastness of Daghistan, or Soviet ideologues complained about the 'subversive' activities of shrine visitation at Baha'uddin Naqshband's tomb in Uzbekistan, the Russian public was reminded of this Naqshbandi bogeyman, rearing its head once again. In the West, those reporting on the Soviet Union frequently warned against 'militant sufi brotherhoods' that could upset Russian hegemony in majority Muslim areas. Some self-proclaimed experts went so far as to say that the Naqshbandiyya was 'the only organized political opposition to the USSR'.[11] As it turned out, Naqshbandis in the former Soviet Union did not initiate any political unrest. If they had tried to do so, it would have been a massive uphill struggle for them to get support. In a 1991 referendum, 80 to 90 per cent of Central Asians preferred to stay within a reformed Soviet Union.[12] Nor had Naqshbandi shaykhs organized resistance to the Russians during the nineteenth century (though they may have participated), except during the short-lived rebellion in Andijan (in Uzbekistan and Kyrgystan) by a Naqshbandi shaykh Dukchi Ishan in 1898.[13] The 1877 rebellion in Chechnya and Daghistan turns out to have been initiated by local Muslim elites, instead of Naqshbandis. If we look at the entire USSR, we find that Naqshbandis accommodated Russian rule from Central Asia to the Volga–Urals almost all of the time. In Central Asia most of the sufis and religious scholars of the state-controlled Islamic Spiritual Board were Naqshbandi shaykhs or students of Naqshbandis.

The 'shaykh' who was never a Naqshbandi shaykh: Imam Shamil

What about the well-known Shaykh Shamil, the famous Naqshbandi example of sufi leadership, heroically fighting against the Russians? The general consensus (until recently) has repeatedly affirmed that Naqshbandi–Khalidi teachings were a major factor in 'Shaykh' Shamil's anti-colonial resistance to the Russians in Daghistan and Chechnya. The looming problem with this consensus is that there was never any mention of sufism during the ongoing conflict between roughly 1830 and 1859 (when Shamil surrendered to the Russians).

> [T]he Arabic sources of the jihad period reveal that Shamil did not claim sufi leadership for himself and that he did not call himself a shaykh, nor did he try to compete with other sufi shaykhs. His correspondence and other sources show that Shamil treated other sufi masters of the North Caucasus with utmost respect and tried to win them and their followers over to his own cause.[14]

So what happened? The conflict against the Russians apparently began with Ghazi Muhammad fighting against other Muslims over the role of customary law in Daghistani villages. Although Ghazi Muhammad's Naqshbandi shaykh opposed this action, Ghazi Muhammad appealed this decision to his shaykh's shaykh, who supposedly gave him permission to go to war in around 1830. As soon as they attacked a chief affiliated with the Russians, Ghazi Muhammad ended up fighting the Russians. In the 29 years of fighting, local political leaders, the Imams, made the military and political decisions. To get people to sacrifice their lives and fight, they needed the moral authority of a Naqshbandi shaykh. Neither Ghazi Muhammad nor Shamil had teaching certificates from their shaykhs (they were students among hundreds of others). After the Imam of Daghistan was assassinated, religious scholars and other military leaders supported Shamil as the new Imam of Daghistan, but no Arabic sources from Daghistan ever mention Imam Shamil as a shaykh. Indeed, 'There is no indication at all that Shâmil had acted as a shaykh, or that he had had educated Sufi murids [seekers]; even today there is no *silsila* [chain] among the Daghestani Khâlidis that would include Shâmil as one of its links.'[15]

The misperception of Shamil's military action being connected with sufism began with the Russians taking his vocabulary literally. Shamil redefined a sufi aspirant or seeker (*murid*) as a 'devoted fighter for Islam'.[16] This had the Russian colonial authorities define the anti-colonialism movement as 'Muridism'. The only Naqshbandi sufi shaykh in this Daghistani affair was Shamil's shaykh, Jamaluddin, who never stopped thinking that the best course of action would have been to make peace with the Russians (though his shaykh apparently gave Ghazi Muhammad the permission to fight). It appears that the Russian misunderstanding of one word propelled Shamil into the position of a sufi shaykh – a militant Naqshbandi shaykh. Even if Shamil had been an authorized Naqshbandi shaykh, how would we know that he used sufi principles in his rebellion against the Russians? Where would he have found these principles? Sufis have never written books for warfare like Sun Tzu's *Art of War*.

Naqshbandis in recent Turkish politics?

Over the past 20 years, it has been fascinating to watch the momentous changes that are propelling Turkey into a potential leadership role in the Middle East and Central Asia. Modern sufism in Turkey – and the demise of traditional Ottoman sufism – began on 30 November 1925 when law 677 was passed. This meant the closing of all sufi lodges and sufi tomb-shrines and prohibition of all sufi lineages, the use of the titles 'shaykh' and 'disciple', the performance of sufi functions and the wearing of special costumes. Anyone violating these prohibitions was to serve a minimum of three months' prison term and a fine of not less than 50 lira. Immediately after the law was passed, 773 sufi lodges and 905 sufi-tombs were closed and their resources confiscated by the government. This law mostly affected the Mevlevis and Bektashis, because their elaborate rituals required sufi lodges. Naqshbandis and many Qadiris, whose contemplative practices did not depend on sufi lodges, just went underground. A huge number of people became 'displaced', since before this edict *one out of every eight men* in Istanbul was associated with a sufi lodge.[17] In the Naqshbandi case, it is ironic that the lineage having the most sufi lodges in Istanbul was the one best able to dispense with them.[18]

Naqshbandi groups in Turkey have had a 'diversified and dynamic positioning in regard to politics'.[19] There are many Naqshbandi groups in Turkey and here we will discuss the political involvement of one Naqshbandi–Khalidi sub-lineage, now known as the Iskenderpaşa community. Continuing the lineage of Ziyaettin Gümüşanevi (d. 1893), Mehmet Zahit Kotku (d. 1980) headed the Iskenderpaşa group. Together with two other Naqshbandi–Khalidi shaykhs, Mahmut Sami Ramazanoğlu (d. 1984) and Mahmut Ustaosmanoğlu, he established the National Salvation Party (NSP) headed by Necmeddin Erbakan (d. 2011) in 1972. The Iskenderpaşa community, many of whom had small- and medium-sized businesses, rallied behind the NSP after it had been endorsed by Kotku. In an eloquent Turkish fashion, Kotku rephrased the sufi expression, 'one bite of food, one cloak' to 'one bite of food, one cloak, and a Mazda', to express economic aspirations.[20] Things deteriorated in 1980, when Erbakan was charged and arrested for working against the principle of secularism. Later in his life, Kotku admitted that the best way to make the world a better place was 'through education and spiritual enlightenment'.[21] He had realized that a head of state could not avoid oppressing others, and declared that an ideal Muslim should distance himself from government.[22]

Liberalizing the Turkish economy under Turgut Özal (both Turkish president 1983–9 and prime minister 1989–93) seems to have been the pivotal change that paved the way for Turkey's future economic boom. In

1983 Özal became the successful leader of the Motherland Party, which the Iskenderpaşa community supported. This support disappeared as soon as Özal's government championed Turkey's full membership in the European Union. Such an economic alliance would have made many small Turkish businesses unviable. Özal had previously associated with Kotku, who had died before Özal became president. It is not clear if there was a committed shaykh–seeker relationship or whether the connection was purely social. Did they just drink tea together a few times? How this undocumented relationship impacted on Özal's future economic policies is uncertain. In any case, what in sufi teaching could translate to economic policies? No sufi has written a book applying sufi principles to modern economic policy.

Kotku's successor, Esad Coşan (d. 2001), applied his teacher's economic ideals and established Server Holding, a conglomerate of 38 diversified companies. This holding company is the main contributor to the Iskenderpaşa conglomerate of charitable organizations, the Hakyol Foundation, which oversees schools, clinics, publishing houses, radio stations and hundreds of voluntary charitable organizations. Coşan has justified political involvement in these terms:

> [W]e must be interested in politics. We cannot afford to leave the administration of Turkey to incompetent, immoral liars, or stubborn corrupted politicians. We must not be simple-minded party supporters or partisons, we must not be divided into factions, we must stand for honest, political life.[23]

This and other statements by Coşan dealing with politics and economics do not mean that Coşan had forgotten about a larger context:

> We want all to be free from oppression, from discrimination, from injustice, from all kinds of sins generated by the enslavement to the *lower self*. Therefore we want to serve all with love, with forgiveness, with patience without discriminating against any individual, any nation.[24]

Erbakan, a political survivor, surfaced again in 1990, as the head of the Welfare Party. He decided that he could act as he desired, even to the point of criticizing sufi groups, which caused an open public split between him and Coşan (did Erbakan recognize Coşan as Kotku's successor?).[25] The Naqshbandi–Mujaddidi followers of Süleyman Hilmi Tunahan (d. 1959) and various Naqshbandi–Khalidi groups all campaigned for Erbakan's short-lived Welfare Party in 1996. The following year Erbakan (Turkish Prime Minister in 1996–7) was 'asked' to step down from the government by the military and his political party banned (once again). It was a government crackdown on what was seen as the 'menace of Islamism'.

Tayyip Erdoğan (the present Turkish prime minister, as of late 2015) was elected Mayor of Istanbul in 1994 and was applauded, even by his political opponents, for his effective administration. This came to a close in 1997, when he recited some lines of Turkish nationalist poet Ziya Gökalp (d. 1924), 'Minarets are our bayonets, domes are our helmets, mosques are our barracks, believers are our soldiers.'[26] The government put him in jail for four months (religious freedom for Muslims has improved since then in Turkey). In 2001 Erdoğan's new Justice and Development Party (JDP) won an overwhelming number of votes, which enabled the JDP to form a single-party government, the first in 19 years. People have asked Erdoğan about authors who may have influenced him in his life and he answers in very vague terms, as befits an astute politician.[27] It does not appear that Naqshbandi sufi principles and/or transformational practice (if any) have anything to do with the policies of these politicians (Özal, Erbakan, Erdoğan). There is no evidence.

With the formation of the Independent Businessmen Association in 1990, which now operates in 47 countries and contributes to 15 per cent of Turkey's GNP, a huge network of like-minded businessmen was created, most of whom would like to see more religious freedom for Muslims in Turkey. This increasing economic power is expressed in the rapid rise of a Gülen empire,[28] in addition to numerous transnational business organizations often called 'holding companies' (like Coşan's Server Holding). According to Coşan, the most effective way to shape society is 'engaging in (foreign) trade and commerce'.[29] On the other hand, Erbakan had seen capitalism as a 'Zionist conspiracy', and promoted state ownership of businesses. It is hard to see how any of these economic policies might have come out of Naqshbandi or any other kind of sufi teachings. The primary domain of sufism is avoiding a major deficit of inner peace when the ego is in control and promoting a surplus of inner peace by keeping the ego tranquil. It is questionable to assume that everything a politician says or does in any area of life can be attributed to his (supposed) sufi background – and what does a sufi background mean?

If one looks at how Erdoğan uses language to acclaim JDP achievements, the word 'service' (*hizmet*) occurs very often. This is also a key principle in Fethullah Gülen's group – sometimes even used to name his organization. Therefore, the JDP reminds the voters of its service to the Turkish people in terms of fast trains, new airports and other government projects. The latest (as of early 2014) announcement is the completion of the Marmaray tunnel under the Bosphorus, communicated in Istanbul by large strategically placed billboards with Erdoğan's picture. Service to others is implicit in sufi teaching. Yet service is an attribute of open-hearted behaviour that is not a monopoly of sufis or any other group.

Whether sufi teachings have influenced Erdoğan personally or in his political roles is anyone's guess. I am reminded of Suhrawardi's previous comment about spiritual paths, 'Others pursue a path of serving people by carrying firewood and hemp on their backs and selling it in the market, being honest in its price.' Perhaps these Turkish leaders have learned ego-less service at the hands of their Naqshbandi teachers (if they considered them teachers at all). Yet I wonder if these alleged sufi connections are more a way of networking and getting votes than indicating a shaykh–seeker relationship.

Again, this section has been only a very brief snapshot of the Iskenderpaşa community, one out of many Naqshbandi groups. It is impossible to define a standard Naqshbandi approach to politics just by looking at Kotku and Coşan's pragmatic involvement. Followers of Mujaddidi Süleyman Efendi had no affiliation with Özal and a very short-lived association with Erbakan, only supporting Erdoğan when he ran for mayor of Istanbul in 1994. Specific Naqshbandi shaykhs seem to have supported the establishment of political parties. Afterwards their involvement seemed to have waned, because soon these parties took on a life of their own as they evolved into loose coalitions of socially conservative groups independent of any particular Naqshbandi group.

Amadu Bamba: The sufi who was banished from home by politics

West African sufi Amadu Bamba never participated in armed warfare or promoted the idea for others to do so. Because of the multi-perspectival research of Anta Babou, we have a remarkable picture of Amadu Bamba that demonstrates the relationship between inner sufi education and social and political developments. Repeatedly, Amadu Bamba (founder of the Muridiyya, d. 1927) stressed a type of sufi training (*tarbiyya*) that focused on ethics and taming of the ego. 'The warrior in the path of God is not who takes his enemies' life, but the one who combats his nafs [ego] to achieve spiritual perfection.'[30] Note the paraphrase of the hadith of lesser and greater jihad.

Amadu Bamba appears to have had an aura of holiness that few other African sufis can match. The French colonists of Senegal contributed to this aura by exiling him for long periods and forcing him to suffer like a martyr. As with many other notable sufis, his authority came from being a learned religious scholar, in addition to people perceiving him as a friend of God. If we look back to the earlier part of his life, the first indication of Bamba's future greatness happened at his father's funeral, when he was asked to continue working for the local ruler as his father's heir. In the local Wolof culture, this was just assumed; the question was a mere formality. Bamba replied, 'I do not have the habit of mingling with rulers, and I do not expect any help from them. I only seek honor from the Supreme Lord (God).'[31] Such an honest response endeared him to no one. Bamba's fellow religious scholars, who worked for the rulers, saw him as being unnecessarily rigid, while the common people thought he was crazy, because he was passing up wealth. The rulers saw someone whom they could not easily control.

Bamba's next rise in unpopularity occurred when he returned to his school in Kajoor, Senegal, from a study trip in Mauritania, declaring that he was going to concentrate on training egos instead of scholarly religious knowledge. Most of his students left and the rest of his supporters in the scholarly establishment resented what he was doing. Bamba's focus on sufi ascetic exercises and embodied piety did not conform to their understanding of education, particularly when combined with what they considered an excessive devotion to the shaykh. The rulers of Kajoor went to their French overlords, accusing the Murids (students of Amadu Bamba) of preparing for war.[32] This forced Bamba to move to another area in Senegal in 1895.

Bamba had no intention or desire for material success, much less political power. He did, however, want to improve society by transforming people's egos through sufi training. The rulers in the new area quickly took a dislike to Bamba, because he behaved as their equal. They believed he was interested in usurping power and therefore posed a threat to their security. They had never seen a teacher so revered, and in their view, his followers acted more like slaves than students. Within four months, the French had exiled Bamba to Gabon. In an attempt to get their shaykh back to Senegal, Murids used their financial resources from peanut cultivation to finance the election campaign of François Carpot for a French National Assembly seat in 1902. On his election, Carpot worked on Bamba's release, which he successfully accomplished, demonstrating that, like any other group, sufis are able to work the political system to achieve their goals.

We do not have anthropological studies outlining what Murid training actually involves. There are litanies that are repeated, but I suspect most of the training is by example of the shaykhs. Because of the Wolof social structure, the mantle of sufi shaykhhood (and its *baraka*) is almost always passed down from father to son, mirroring the hereditary succession involved with tomb-shrines. Any *baraka* of a Murid shaykh after 1927 is seen to be a function of Amadu Bamba's *baraka*, just as the shrine custodian's *baraka* is a function of the deceased sufi's *baraka*.[33] There are, however, three kinds of Murid shaykhs: those who teach the Qur'an and religious sciences (religious scholars), those who do sufi training of the ego (sufis), and those who recruit and organize (marketing and administration). Bamba often criticized the latter group, though necessary in the Murid organization, for 'their excesses in the pursuit of material wealth and of their rivalries.'[34] These are very important distinctions, demonstrating that one cannot just talk about generic Murid shaykhs.

It is ironic to see how superficial accounts of Bamba have stereotyped him until relatively recently. If one had only read French colonial records, one would think that Bamba was seeking to rule Senegal and therefore was preparing for armed jihad, by first creating a Murid state within a state. Why did the French think this? First, because their North African experience, as they interpreted it, had impressed upon them that colonial resistance had been perpetrated by sufi leaders. Secondly, they probably knew about Shamil's resistance against the Russians by imagined sufi armies of 'murids'. The die was cast when African chiefs portrayed Bamba as a primary threat to French rule.

In 1910, Bamba wrote that 'he was neither a friend nor an enemy to the French'.[35] Since Muslims could practice their religion under French rule, and fared better with the peaceful French regime than they had under their own violent warring kings, he saw no reason to resist the French. However, it was hard for the French to reconcile these statements with his considerable authority (in their perception, power) over growing numbers of Murids, most of whom unquestionably followed his every command. As it turned out, sufficient mutual understanding and acceptance between the Murids and French did allow both to pursue their separate goals.

From sufi activity in politics to the dynamics of the shaykh–seeker relationship

This chapter has provided examples of sufis (or purported sufis) inter-acting outside the domain of their circle of students and sufi lodge-shrines. Connections between sufism and politics are not all that easy to document, yet popular sufis and caretakers of shrines (even small ones like Abu Bakr's) have found it hard to avoid some kind of political involvement. Any large group or institution will show up on the government radar screen – whether as a source of taxes or a potential security threat. Some sufis will have very self-aggrandizing agendas; others, like Amadu Bamba, will uphold the highest principles with dignity; and the rest, the majority, will fall between these extremes.

Yet in many cultures there are political expectations in the shaykh–seeker relationship, which radiate out to business contacts, marriage candidates and local and regional politics. Seekers expect their shaykh to help them directly with marriage, education, work and general prosperity. In some cases it is not certain where ego-training comes on the priority list; for example, in Senegal (where I have not been), people say, 'You have a good shaykh' when something good happens to someone. They say this, half seriously, implying that the relationship with one's shaykh has a direct connection to one's lot in life.[36] In theory, a Murid shaykh should have qualities that include Islamic learning, the ability to heal and being a protégé of God. In practice, however, the status of a shaykh, in addition to his being a descendant of Amadu Bamba, is directly a function of the number of his followers.

There is a circular effect, in that the greater number of followers a Murid shaykh has, the greater political power and influence he has, which in turn attracts more followers. Thus if one has a good personal relationship with an influential shaykh, then 'one has a good shaykh'; expected material rewards are more likely to follow.[37] This set of cultural expectations creates an environment of competitive sufism. A well-known Tijani shaykh, Abdul Aziz Sy (d. 1997), noted a certain one-upmanship between Senegalese sufi shaykhs, as they all go around proclaiming, 'I am the champion, I am the best, I am the only one.'[38] These kinds of dynamics should not be surprising when 90 per cent of the Senegalese are associated with the Murid sufi lineage and it rules the country. The next chapter will focus on the psychological and ethical dynamics in the shaykh–seeker relationship. It will be assumed that the primary activity is for the seeker to develop character and train the ego – just as in Amadu Bamba's school.

5

THE RELATIONSHIP BETWEEN THE SHAYKH AND THE SEEKER[1]

Choose a shaykh, for without a shaykh the journey is one of sadness, fear, and danger. Without a guide you are bewildered so do not travel alone on a road you have never seen nor turn away from the guide.

RUMI, 1.160[2]

SUFI TRANSFORMATIVE PRACTICES are supposed to be performed in the context of the shaykh–seeker relationship. Through the dynamics of this relationship, the sufi shaykh is able to model sincere inward character and beautiful outward behaviour. Sufi shaykhs do not have a monopoly on this process. Religious scholars and other members of the educated elite have emphasized the study of the Prophet's role model communicated through the hadith to facilitate inner character changes that later become reflected in outer ethical behaviour.

To a large extent the principal crucible for facilitating ethical behaviour has been the sufi shaykh–seeker relationship. It is one way to define what sufism is, namely an ethico-heart endeavour whose pedagogy is intimately related to the dynamics occurring in the relationship between the shaykh and the seeker. It is through living exemplars, usually associated – but not limited to – sufi shaykhs, that Islamic ethical values were transmitted and preserved in what became Islamic societies. Islamization is not simply about people proclaiming that there is no god but God and Muhammad is God's messenger and praying in mosques. It also includes inculcating the ethical values and beautiful behaviour of the Prophet in everyday life. Thus, individual practice of sufism radiates out from the one-on-one relationship with the shaykh to one's fellow seekers and to others in society.

Sufi shaykhs have been heirs of the Prophet to the extent that they provided the human behavioural and ethical-heart model exemplified by the Qur'an and Muhammad's example. The process of an ethico-spiritual training environment in the context of the shaykh–seeker relationship literally gave life to the historically and geographically distant ideals of the Prophet. This is why honouring and respecting an authentic shaykh is honouring and respecting Muhammad, which in turn is a reverence for God. Authenticity here is a circular system. One becomes authentic through inner sincerity – often developed through sufi practice. This is reflected in one's behaviour, which corresponds to that of the Prophet's actions. In turn, transformative change and ethical development are facilitated (the litmus test of authenticity).

Behaving in accordance with the inner and outer model of the Prophet is directly related to transforming one's ego-self. An example is not lying, which is following the general principles of moral behaviour. But as one's ego is transformed, there is less and less inclination to lie in the first place. From a sufi perspective, if the inclination not to lie comes with difficulty, then one still is on the path to control the ego. If this inclination not to lie is effortless, then that is a sign of a transformed ego. In this way, inner character development completes and perfects the outer behaviour of the Prophet. Inner work needs to come first. How can people be truthful or honest if they do not know what truth or honesty is? If individuals are not in touch with the love in their hearts, where will the compassion come from? It would therefore be hypocrisy to put on outward appearances of truthfulness or honesty without inner preparation. In sufi terms, there is no way for change to come from the outside to the inside. By changing the inner, the outer changes automatically. This is actual transformation and facilitating these kinds of transformations is the *primary* activity of a practising sufi. This is what the West African shaykh Amadu Bamba meant by training.

Developing a deep respect for others and a reverence for God requires a shift in egoic consciousness to God consciousness. Nobility of character, involving compassion, gratitude and sincerity, depends on reining in and transforming the unruly ego-self. It is these and other ethico-heart values that are the norms in the shaykh–seeker relationship and in the sufi group, which then are communicated through one's beautiful behaviour in society. The training of one's heart becomes translated into harmonious behaviour with others. This is in accordance with the Prophetic hadith stating that if the heart is sound, then the entire body is sound. As one has a more intimate realization of God, then a greater compassion towards God's creation follows naturally.

As Sa'di Shirazi (d. 1292), one of the great Persian poets, has noted, 'There is no worship without service to humanity.'[3] The active principle of submitting to God (*islam*), both individually and socially, is to live in an upright manner at the highest level of ethical integrity, i.e. according to the human example of the Prophet. The shaykh–seeker relationship – whether the shaykh is a religious scholar, a sufi or both – has been the pedagogical centre of radical ego transformation. This time-tested methodology, however, has come under attack in recent decades. Whether it is 'guru bashing' in the West or mistaking the sanctity of this relationship to involve 'associating partners with God' (*shirk*) among those in the Muslim community, many are seriously questioning the need for the shaykh–seeker relationship in the modern world.

The necessity of the shaykh–seeker relationship for transformative development

> There is truth [in] that position [that a shaykh is not necessary] because following the Qur'an and the example of the Prophet is sufficient, but it is the lowest position of the beginners among the pious ones [...] The highest level is knowing God in actions, characteristics, names

and essence in complete witnessing [...] This position is not obtained solely by exoteric knowledge and the study of books! The truth is that the noble Qur'an is the guide of the community and the shaykh of the Sunnis – But it is not the nature of everyone to obtain exalted states and divine perfections solely by following the Qur'an without a perfected guide. ('Ömer el-Fu'adi (d. 1636), a Turkish Sha'bani shaykh)[4]

If a metaphor for the seeker's growth is a journey, then the shaykh is the guide for the perilous trip through unknown territory and the teacher of the exercises necessary to proceed safely on the voyage. From another perspective, almost everyone is required to enter the teaching environment of the shaykh–seeker relationship, because very few can deal with the wily ego-self without assistance. The task is not destroying the ego, but transforming it. Humans develop egos to become healthy functioning adults, because we need an ego to survive in the world. Adults who do not have appropriately developed egos have difficulty living in the world and are therefore diagnosed as mentally ill. In addition, the ego is a series of psychological constructs that create our sense of separateness from others, our I-ness (poorly translated from the German *das ich* as 'ego'). The ego becomes formed from the age of three and is imprinted with impressions and distinctions formulated outside of our conscious awareness.

Difficulties arise when we identify who we really are with the ego's constructs of who we are. For the ego to survive, it goes about trying to control and manipulate everything it can. Anything that threatens the ego's dominance is seen as an attempt to kill the ego. In this sense the shaykh is trying to help the seeker metaphorically ride the donkey of the ego, rather than the donkey riding the seeker. Like a donkey, seekers' egos often flare up at the teacher, hollering and kicking. Most often, the ego will be much more subtle, using anything to maintain its autonomy. An external teacher is necessary to deal with these ruses that few can see themselves. A shape-shifting ego will transform everything to reinforce its domination, from the most material to the most sublime.

Instead of seeing ego-self dominance as a major difficulty, we see the ego-self as literally who we are. Therefore, when the shaykh threatens the ego-self, it automatically reacts, because seekers unconsciously feel that their entire identity is threatened. Many times this is the reason for seekers leaving the practice, because they cannot differentiate between the shaykh being the *ego*'s enemy and the shaykh being the *seeker*'s enemy. One of the hallmarks of good shaykhs is that they often use skilful means to trick the ego rather than confronting it head-on.

We put trust in all kinds of people in modern life: car mechanics, dentists, doctors, plumbers and electricians. We choose them after trying to ascertain their reliability, but then we trust their ability. For a lot of reasons, in the modern West we do not trust spiritual teachers in general, mostly because of media reports of abuse. This is part of an engrained secular-materialist attitude of dismissing anyone who takes religious or transformative practice seriously. A non-discerning mental skepticism for sufi shaykhs in the modern world is the cover for an ego ruse to prevent us from seeing the most precious pearl, even if it is right in front of us. Rumi asks:

> How long will you run around in circles? One needs a master to learn a trade and to do business. When you seek knowledge in China [referring to a Prophetic saying] do not disgrace yourself. Seek a shaykh and keep company with him. Whatever the Plato of the age tells you to do, give up your ego-self and act accordingly (6:486).

At the same time, quacks and questionable credentials exist in every area of expertise. Some questionable shaykhs start out being groomed from childhood and end up being the shaykh's successor with a full repertoire of subtle manipulative ego moves and a smooth 'sufi rap' (instead of heartfelt words). Being treated as an 'exalted personage' from childhood is hardly the optimal training for a future sufi shaykh. Another deviation from upright behaviour is the outward appearance of being humble, with a talent for telling people what they want to hear. Rumi says in a prelude to a section of poetry:

> [This is] a description of the cowardice and weakness of a spoiled sufi who has never struggled with the ego-self or experienced the pain and anguish of divine love. He has been deluded by the homage and

hand-kissing of people who venerate him, declaring that he is the most
famous contemporary sufi (5:224).

But the existence of malpractice is no reason to deny the guidance of the
shaykh and the efficacy of the shaykh–seeker relationship. After ascertaining
that a shaykh is appropriate, seekers need to trust their shaykh, or there will
not be any transmission between them. If one wants to learn something,
then one has to accept the authority of the teacher. This does not mean that
the shaykh is infallible or all knowing – trust comes over time and the seeker
loses out if he does not follow the shaykh's instructions. It is not really about
obedience per se – it is like a blind person choosing not to follow the advice
of someone who can see. How can one awaken from ego slumber if one does
not follow the advice of the teacher? The only thing that will transform us
is our *own experience*. How can we have our own experience, if we do not
follow the instructions of the teacher? How can someone be nourished, if
they refuse to eat the food that is offered? If a shaykh's behaviour or conditions are too much to handle, then it is better to leave. There has to be trust
in the ultimate goodness of the shaykh.

Many in the West who are used to participative learning and so-called
democratic-equal relationships view the hierarchical (and predominantly
male) shaykh–seeker system as outdated. They may not understand that one
of the closest analogues of the shaykh is a physician – they probably would
not want to have an operation performed by a surgeon who was trained
using Wikipedia for references. There is a great difference between abusive
hierarchy and a transformative and healthy hierarchy. Hierarchy is a fact of
life, one that necessarily exists in a teaching environment, and in all systems
from atoms to galaxies, cells to humans.[5] For the vast majority of people, it
will take them much more time than they will be alive in this physical life
to find their way in what may seem to be a pathless desert without the help
of a shaykh. Objecting to healthy hierarchies is yet another of the ego's ruses
and assures that one will continue being ruled by the ego.

Others contend that one's inner teacher can suffice and an external shaykh
is unnecessary, but whose voice is speaking in the name of the inner teacher?
What the majority of people think is their inner teacher is most likely to be
their ego in robes and a turban. There is such a thing as an inner teacher – in

my understanding and experience – but only spiritual Einsteins are able to access this guidance and dispense with a live shaykh. The rest of us have the ego pretending to be an inner teacher and need an *external* teacher to give us feedback in ways that are sometimes uncomfortably sudden wake-up calls. The sufi shaykh confronts seekers' egos with actual life trials if need be.

It is easy to be complacent and proud, while worshipping a transcendent God or venerating the Prophet. Those who believe they are submitting to God on the basis of memorizing the Qur'an and hadith reject any need for *personal* guidance. They are using intellectual knowledge to avoid disciplining their egos. A sufi shaykh will not allow seekers to hide – even if they try hiding behind the Qur'an. The shaykh's circle is intended to be a replication of the Prophet and his companions, guided by the letter and spirit of the Qur'an and Muhammad's example. It is what sufis call heart-to-heart companionship.

Self-deception is found around every corner in transformative practice, including all but the most advanced shaykhs – this is what determines an advanced shaykh. One has to rely on the living shaykh until one can discern the real from the false. The shaykh will let a person know when someone is at this point of discernment, because seekers cannot make that determination themselves. We cannot judge where we are on the path – only the person who has gone on the path and knows the territory can make that call. The shaykh reveals to students the incredible gap between who persons think they are and the way they truly are. Whatever people think themselves to be, they are not. Until the ego steps down from its pedestal of domination, it is safe to say that we are continually lying to ourselves. We are outsourcing our consciousness to the ego. Think about it.

The ego contrives innumerable defences. If seekers trace the resistance against the authority of a spiritual teacher – unless they have unresolved issues with their father or mother – they usually discover that it is the ego at the root of the situation. Rejecting an authentic shaykh is the natural course of action for the ego. The *last thing* the ego wants is to be dethroned from its hegemonic position. This may also explain why so many seekers over the centuries have ended up with charlatans as shaykhs. It is easy to outwardly imitate a so-called enlightened shaykh, who has the beard and exotic dress and even the lineage certificate or hereditary descent from a recognized shaykh. Whatever occurs in the world of con artists can be replicated in spiritual teachers. But as Rumi says, 'Seekers are deceived by their need for imposters and imagine them to be qualified shaykhs who are one with God. They do not know the difference between genuine and counterfeit and between what is contrived and what is innate' (1.123).

The seeker

The most famous transformative encounter between two people in the history of sufism is when Rumi, the erudite religious scholar, met his paramount shaykh, Shamsuddin Tabrizi.[6] There is an oft-repeated oral story explaining how Mawlana Rumi was sitting with Shams when someone rushed in with a note from a nearby village requesting Rumi to send them a shaykh. He exclaimed to Shams, 'Whew, that was a close one. If they had asked for a seeker one of us would have had to go.' Another variant of this story has Shams saying to Mawlana that shaykhs are a dime a dozen, but authentic seekers are really hard to find.

Although most of the discussion on shaykhs and seekers usually centres on shaykhs and proper behaviour in their presence, almost all shaykhs have been seekers themselves and continue to be seekers their entire lives. A beginning seeker is in a catch-22 situation. Too much discernment in choosing a shaykh has one safe, but without a shaykh, because no one is good enough. Too little discernment finds one in situations of compromised integrity. It is not wise to just use the mind and a list to pick a shaykh, any more than it is a viable way to pick one's spouse. Using mental boxes as the sole criterion to evaluate a non-linear living process is not a formula for success. If seekers include, but then move beyond mental understanding, they realize that no concept is a substitute for the mysterious and paradoxical situation that they are in. How can one in a lesser awareness evaluate one who is in a higher degree of awareness? People have all kinds of preconceptions about who a shaykh should be, typically a creation of their egoic minds. No one can teach a person who is already full of preconceptions and who lacks receptivity. They say that in the end it is the desire for God that propels one to God, no matter how many mistakes one makes.

The seeker, as is evident from the word, is looking for something and wants something. A more productive stance is to focus on what the shaykh expects. The seeker may want to pause and consider that shaykhs are taking time out of their own lives to get to know them so that they, the seekers, can be provided with guidance – which these same seekers will most likely ignore the first and second time around. In most actual training environments there are minimum qualifications for a seeker, who is expected to be fully functioning in society. This means psychologically that a person has a healthy ego. A person with a weakened ego structure cannot realistically have a healthy relationship with anyone, much less a sufi teacher. Even people with well functioning egos may come to shaykhs with a lack of self-esteem and, instead of motivation to refine their egos, they participate in sufi practices to receive love, acceptance and approval from the shaykh, all of which is unhealthy for everyone.

There are all kinds of motivations that thwart the search for a suitable shaykh. With an underlying fear of death, the prospective seeker looks for a path that will underline an eternal life of the ego. Often seekers confuse a search for transformation with the ego's desire to be needed, to have a goal, to provide meaning and have a higher purpose. Searching for a sufi teacher is often a search for power, fame, prestige – which is why charismatic teachers are so popular. An ambitious person is likely to have ambition in the sufi world. Rumi says, 'The heart leads you to the people of heart's realm; the body leads you to a prison of clay' (1.41). As an authority figure, the shaykh very often becomes a surrogate father or mother, along with all the unresolved issues a lot of people have with their parents. Thus, seekers proceed in the same way with their sufi teacher as they do with their other intimate relationships and often behave in a manner they think will get the teacher to love them. This is not a healthy way to begin the sufi path.

There are many other considerations. Someone who is a very qualified shaykh may not be right for some people – literally he is too far ahead. A person in kindergarten, which is where just about everyone is, does not need an expert with a Ph.D. Ahmad Sirhindi mentions how lesser 'ecstatic' shaykhs are usually more effective with beginners.[7] It is good for the shaykh to let his students know that he is still in the process of growing too. This in no way detracts from his being an invaluable living example of the Prophet Muhammad.

Obstacles of one sort or another continue to confront seekers. One of the more modern versions is the instant virtual reality of digital networking, which does not create habits for heart relationships and for activities that require years of daily effort with occasional unexpected rewards. In pre-modern times, people stayed with their teachers for three or four decades if they could. Now a decade seems like a lifetime. A continuing theme is the difficulty of enacting deep change by abandoning old habits and creating new behaviours. It is usually a new experience for a seeker to honour the shaykh in his function as a physician of the heart rather than as a father figure, lover substitute or friend. To review, the ego-self does not want to find an authentic teacher. Unqualified seekers often want a shaykh from whom they can obtain things easily and with no effort – one whom will not demand they change their ego-burdened lives. They desire a shaykh who is like them. One either says 'yes' to the ego or 'yes' to God. The former involves no change and the latter opens up the path to God.

Part of the responsibility of the seeker is learning to behave in a beautiful manner in the presence of the shaykh. This cultivation of beautiful behaviour complements the seeker's imitating the shaykh inwardly and outwardly. Throughout the Persianate world there has been an elaborate code of behaviour taken from Persian court etiquette. The shaykh sat on a cushion slightly higher than everyone else, the equivalent to a king's throne. No one used the shaykh's water container for ablutions, did ablutions in his special place, stepped on where he usually prayed, talked to him in anything but a subdued tone of voice or looked him straight in the eye. When the shaykh stood up, everyone stood up and, when he came in or left the assembly, everyone used to stand (at the time of the Prophet this was standard for every tribesman entering and leaving, not just for the Prophet). No person's shadow should touch the shaykh, nor should the soles of one's feet face towards where he sits even when he is absent. One left the presence of a shaykh, whether living or deceased, by backing up until one reached the door and put one's shoes on. One still finds these behavioural norms in more traditional settings in areas where Persianate culture used to or still predominates. Today, particularly in the West, behaviour is usually much more informal, even though some seekers coming back from majority Islamic countries have decided to imitate some of these customs (sometimes in very silly ways). It is sincere respect and obedience that is the hallmark of a conscious seeker's behaviour – the outer aspect of which augments the inner heartfelt multi-levelled resonance with the shaykh. This may or may not coincide with imitating customs from another time and place. One cannot ascertain solely by outward behaviour what is in the heart of the seeker – or for that matter, the shaykh or anyone else.

The shaykh

> Who is the shaykh? An old man with white hair. But do you know the meaning of white hair O deceived one? The black hair is his attachment to ego-self. He is not old [a shaykh] until there is no more attachment to ego-self. When there is no more ego attachment then he is old [a shaykh], whether he is black-haired or white-haired [...] If his hair is white and he is still attached to the ego then he is not a shaykh and not of God's elect (Rumi 3.100).

As we have seen, an authentic shaykh cannot be ascertained solely by a list of mental criteria. Some sufis, such as Shah Waliullah (d. 1762), made ideal checklists to ascertain who was a proper shaykh, but this is not practically useful because few shaykhs of any era could satisfy all the criteria.[8] If companionship with the shaykh does not instil a love of God, while decreasing attraction to worldly affairs, then there will be little transformation in the shaykh's circle. Yet if there is one criterion that is universally agreed upon, it is that the shaykh lives ethically. In Islamic terms, this means following the guidelines mandated by the Qur'an and hadith. There are also cases of prospective students judging a shaykh by how well he conforms to the minutiae of Islamic practice – in ritual prayer for example. This is an example of jumping to conclusions about external behavioural details, when it is the inner character that cannot be seen at first (or second) glance that makes the difference. One cannot rely on appearances. The same apparent behaviour in two individuals can be very different – one acting out of ego and one not acting out of ego. The shaykh is expected to follow the ethical guidelines of the inner character of the Prophet. Having a beard and other outer trappings of seventh-century Arab culture are not the touchstones of inner character. This does not imply that blameworthy behaviour is a desideratum either. Aware behaviour, that is, acting in the best interests of the seeker, may involve the shaykh cajoling and having great empathy, or his severely reprimanding the seeker, depending on the circumstances. Compassionate behaviour is the appropriate behaviour to call the ego to task in that moment, not the feel-good preconceptions people may have.

Here is a good place to discuss 'charisma', a term to describe a quality that differentiates certain shaykhs from others, but overlooks the contemplative context. Charisma fools people. In an ego-based world, the flashier the shaykh and the bigger the entourage, the better the shaykh. In extreme cases, brilliant psychopaths can be charismatic in a pathological way, though many only sense the charisma and are oblivious to the pathology. Charisma is probably more of a disqualifying characteristic and, at minimum, not very useful for finding a shaykh. Markers of ego, like flaunting power and intellectual cleverness, attract like-minded seekers. The shaykh who arrives in a gathering with a large entourage of bearded and turbaned seekers, who all stand up when he stands up and all wait for him to sit down, impresses many people. This is how some shaykhs accumulate thousands of adoring followers. Many very admired shaykhs have later been shown to be other than what their admirers thought them to be. Another scenario is a charismatic shaykh with his group, who experience blissful altered states of consciousness around him. His students interpret these altered states to be signs of his advanced awareness, an identification providing yet another obstacle to further transformation – blissful states are not the main fare of ego training. There are also shaykhs appearing to be blissed out and smiling a lot, looking very benevolent – the stereotype of the holy man. Maybe holy, maybe not so holy. Again, ego-based bliss and non-egoic bliss look the same.

If attainment on the sufi path is not being dominated by the ego, then at best ecstatic states are only the beginning of the path. Ecstatic states are great, and perhaps for some even necessary. To represent such altered states as the entire path is misleading, because it is a transcendental escape with no ethical grounding in the seeker's actual daily life. Authority is not about charisma and being able to corral thousands of blindly obedient students by facilitating ecstatic experiences. It is more about the ability to facilitate a person's turning towards God by working heart-to-heart, overcoming life-long obstacles. That is real authority – one just cannot question it. Although the results are palpable, ultimately the process is in the realm of mystery, from a seeker's point of view. To be in awe of this mystery shows that the seeker has started to learn something. That usually happens after the learning process is well under way. It takes a while before the fruit appears and ripens. As Rumi says, 'If you desire poverty of spirit, it depends on companionship with the shaykh – it is not about writing or speech. The spirit receives [this kind of] knowledge from spirit, not from a book or verbal conversation' (5:59).

Humans make errors and it is good for seekers to remember that their shaykhs are human. To project perfection on to them is not indicative of a healthy shaykh–seeker relationship. Perhaps, in the beginning, this kind of projection can be useful, but the shaykh needs to break the seeker of this habit and see it for what it is. In a sense the projection phase of the shaykh–seeker relationship can often be similar to falling in love, when the relationship may be based on a fair amount of delusion. Sufi work can start once this kind of psychological debris is cleared out of the way and trust is built upon the actual experience of the shaykh's compassion and heartfelt intentions for the seeker's benefit.

It is appropriate that shaykhs acknowledge their flaws and limitations. I have seen too many sufi shaykhs who have tried to cover up their flaws – this is an occupational hazard when too many around a shaykh see him as infallible. Although this can be a red flag to a student, the other extreme to projecting perfection on the shaykh is for them suddenly to find all the faults in their imagined perfect guide. Muhammad never proclaimed himself infallible – he constantly reminded his companions that he was a human being like them.

Especially in a modern globalized environment of diversity and high rate of change, it is a worthwhile pedagogy for shaykhs to be constantly confirming whether their way of practising is working for each of their students. One of the signs of good teaching is how it is very nuanced and tailored for each person. There are sufi groups where the shaykh has over 100,000 students. Even with 1,000 authorized shaykhs (is there a diploma mill here?) imparting the practices and giving their students individual attention, this situation could still feel like an assembly line to many seekers. It is difficult for me to comprehend how 'ego management' can be achieved without a close system of checks and balances, with the shaykh having a manageable number of seekers. How can a shaykh, often a globetrotting teacher with thousands of seekers, give personal guidance on an ongoing basis? Perhaps the best students can figure out what to do, but the rest will be lost without regular personal guidance.

Yet there are shaykhs with groups around the world that are able to personally provide heart-to-heart companionship on a regular basis. One scenario is a shaykh who is assisted by a team of subsidiary teachers, with whom he keeps closely in touch. In addition, the shaykh regularly visits each group (not more than 30). Some shaykhs now have online 'spiritual companionship' once a week and others even promote online initiation. Others do workshops around the globe, where there is no commitment other than to pay the entrance fee. The litmus test here is the effectiveness with which a shaykh can help each seeker deal with the wily ego. I find myself sceptical of certain types of sufi activity, but I keep reminding myself that appearances are deceiving and divine grace works in mysterious ways.

Another set of questions involves the qualifications of the shaykh. It is useful to observe the shaykh and the advanced seekers around him, but this can give one only an outsider's glimpse into the group. Typically a shaykh is in a lineage and has been given permission to teach, which is either conditional or unconditional. This chain of initiation and permission goes back through the founder-figure and then to the Prophet. If everyone had kept up high qualification standards, then this system would work as a quality-control mechanism. Unfortunately, like educational and medical institutions that have become more like business organizations, a teaching certificate from a sufi shaykh too often has little value. As soon as unqualified people begin to teach, the transmission is lost and the former transformative practices are usually replaced with the recitation of litanies and an exaggerated emphasis on the shaykh. There are other possibilities in the transmission of teachings that do not involve teaching certificates, e.g.

the previously discussed phenomenon of Uways al-Qarani, who is said to have met the Prophet in a visionary experience without ever having seen him in corporeal form. Again, one cannot rely on external criteria alone to assess the qualifications of a shaykh.

A qualified shaykh never ceases to be a seeker, because there is an ongoing connection to the lineage. This is the stabilizing influence that goes beyond any one human being. The shaykh–seeker relationship is only the latest link in a long chain of sufis, going back to the Prophet. The shaykh is only representing this chain of masters – that is, if he is heart-connected to the lineage. In reality the seeker is submitting one's ego to this chain of transmitters, who in turn are submitting any homage and respect they are given to God. The lineage's practices and expected behaviour are integral to the lineage, because the lineage and the teacher, along with the transmitted practices, constitute a protective container for the student.

The shaykh–seeker relationship

The shaykh also has every right to test the seeker. Indeed, the shaykh has to choose the people who are ready and who are compatible with him. He will give seekers tasks to make it clear to them if they are not ready. It is a blessing to have a shaykh who selflessly takes care of the seekers as their egos blast away, kicking and fighting, to protect ego autonomy. The shaykh is aware of our unconscious mechanical way of being and the suggestions offered may seem onerous, but this is the medicine that facilitates transformation. The bottom line is that a qualified shaykh has a deep compassion, an essential kindness that undergirds everything he does. 'Companionship with a person of God makes you one of them' (Rumi 1.41).

Some find their shaykh in a dream, while others request God to guide them (*istikhara*). One cannot assume that the shaykh will accept everyone as a bona fide seeker. Some shaykhs have been given the mandate to accept anyone who asks, resulting in thousands of seekers, while other shaykhs may only have a handful of seekers in their circles. Nizamuddin Awliya (d. 1325) was asked why he initiated just about everyone who came requesting his *baraka*.[9] He replied that he had permission to do so from his shaykh and that he had heard that his initiates had become practising Muslims and better people. Akhundzada Sayfurrahman (d. 2010), when living in Qanduz, Afghanistan, only accepted seekers who had seen him in a dream. After 1979, when living in Pakistan, he accepted any seekers who were practising Muslims and who adhered to the creed of the rightly guided Sunni mainstream.[10]

Initiation with a sufi shaykh, with a two-handed handclasp, is following the prophetic precedent of the companions pledging their allegiance to Muhammad at Hudaybiya in 628. By clasping the shaykh's hand, one is symbolically shaking the hand of all the previous shaykhs, and therefore ultimately clasping Muhammad's hand. Typically there are three types of initiation. The first is repenting from sins and swearing on the Prophet and the rest of the lineage that one will perform the ritual duties expected of an adult Muslim and avoid major sins. The second kind is an affiliation of blessedness, with the intention of receiving the blessings transmitted through the lineage from Muhammad. In the past, the shaykh often gave a sufi robe on this occasion. Sometimes this type of affiliation is one in which the shaykh becomes an intermediary between the believer and God (like the function of shrine-caretakers). Multiple sufi affiliations, after finishing the exercises of the primary lineage, often are of this type. What is usually understood to be initiation is the third type, where the performance of transformative practices is added to the prerequisites of the first two. This involves a much more committed seeker, who necessarily needs to obey the shaykh. Such is the beginning of a very close heart-to-heart companionship. God wants people to find the way and the shaykh tries to help the seeker clear the way, so God can guide the seeker back. The shaykh–seeker relationship is heart-to-heart resuscitation.

Becoming a formal seeker involves becoming part of a lineage that existed long before we were born and will exist long after we die. Part of the seeker's responsibility is to become a conscious seeker, instead of an unconscious seeker. In pre-modern cultures, the authoritarian teacher–student relationship was part of the culture, beginning with family relationships and subsequent teachers – it fitted into the prevalent ego structure at that time (i.e. expectations were culturally compatible with the ego). This mode of learning promotes culturally programmed responses to behave respectfully, but it discourages questioning and engagement with the teachings. Cultures are changing worldwide and this authoritarian model is being phased out in many places all over the modern world. On the flip side, questioning the shaykh's authority, as an undiscerning skeptic, is as mechanical as blind acceptance. A seeker who sincerely and respectfully accepts the shaykh's real authority, while keeping a probing, questioning and engaging stance with the teachings, is more likely to transform. This is the difference between blind following and striving to understand what is actually being communicated.

Psychologically there is a spectrum from those on one hand, who are blind followers, to those on the other hand who are skeptical of any kind of authority. Individually, for example, there are personality types that get ego gratification from being dependent on serving others. Some seekers are looking for a parent figure, to avoid taking responsibility, and others want the security of a group that will take care of them if they do what they are told. Likewise, what often is an ego expression of a person's apparent resistance and anger with the shaykh can be the cover story for something else. The ego is quite wily and, in the shaykh–seeker relationship, appearances do not always accurately reflect what is happening. A seeker's top priority is to become responsible, simply because the shaykh–seeker relationship demands a higher level of responsibility. In the modern world, it is often an effective teaching strategy to let the new seeker question and challenge for a while. When the seeker is ready to learn, he eventually comes to wholehearted confidence in the shaykh's abilities from his own experience, instead of acting out of blind trust.

In the context of ego training, there are many reasons for the seeker to put the shaykh above himself. In a sense, honouring this difference between the shaykh and the seeker is the middle path between resistance and blind obedience. Sincere humbleness and submission of the ego are qualities that are constantly being cultivated. Blind obedience, the hallmark of an un-conscious student, hinders this process. One aspect of conscious obedience, however, is seeking to foster an increased awareness, responsibly facilitating a genuine heart-to-heart companionship. In this sacred crucible of companionship there will be non-linear fumbling, with abrupt starts and stops, punctuated once in a while by incredible insights and deep love. The work is continually the responsibility of the student. One could say that the relationship of sufi companionship is a workshop for seekers to experiment and figure out how to perceive the affairs of the world within a larger perspective, not the consensus reality of the ego and society. One is reminded of the Prophetic supplication to God, 'Remove from our eyes the veil of ignorance, and show us things as they really are.'[11] Although the shaykh is indispensable in the learning process, there is only so much a lineage and a shaykh can do. It is the seeker who 'walks the path'.

Typically the seeker has only one sufi shaykh, so that the shaykh can get to know the personal manifestation of each seeker's ego resistance, which enables both of them to work more effectively. This extended contact also provides an opportunity for the transmission of the lineage to penetrate the ego defences. If the seekers happen to be with a shaykh other than their own, any benefit resulting from that exchange should be regarded as coming from their own shaykh. There are cases where the seeker outgrows the shaykh. It is the responsibility of a qualified shaykh to alert the seeker to this. Sometimes a seeker is sent to another shaykh for a while. Shaykhs also die and people move to different locales. Many things can happen and changes are often quite difficult and painful. Here again, it is useful to remember why a conscious seeker is preferable to a blindly obedient one. Even though there are power and consciousness differentials, each adult seeker has a responsibility and cannot whine about being an innocent victim. The shaykh has a responsibility not to exploit and the seeker's responsibility is not to be exploited.

The connection with the shaykh is more important than recollecting God, because one cannot derive full benefit from the latter without the former (which is why this chapter precedes the chapter on actual contemplative practices). Connecting with the lineage also means a shaykh is able to transmit divine grace, hastening the inner transformation of the seeker. This is one of the underlying reasons the seeker has to have a comfortable, receptive, respectful attitude toward the shaykh. It allows the seeker to become attuned with the shaykh, which in turn allows this energy to be shared. As this process proceeds, there is annihilation in the shaykh, before annihilation in the Prophet and eventually annihilation in God. It is natural for the seeker to cultivate a love for the shaykh, as one is cultivating a love of the Prophet and ultimately a love for God. This multi-dimensional resonance between the shaykh and the seeker is one aspect of 'being in the hands of the shaykh as a corpse is in the hands of the corpsewasher'.[12] The intent is not for the seeker to be a blindly obedient robot.

In addition to psychological and emotional bonding with the shaykh, the seeker's learning involves conscious behavioural modification and unconscious modelling of the shaykh. The shaykh instructs through example and personal contact, as the seeker cultivates a loving desire to be like the shaykh. This modelling process is a very powerful one. Humans are programmed to model their parents and other adults as young children. That is how they largely acquire their pre-adolescent way of being in the world, before the peer pressure of adolescence. As an example of how powerful this modelling process can be, some undergraduates enrolled in an experiment in the mid-1970s to imitate the behaviour of the master medical hypnotist of the twentieth century, Milton Erickson. One young man was so good at it that he was able to imitate Erickson's special presence, much to the surprise of those who knew Erickson. Unfortunately this gifted young man had to leave the experiment because the left side of his body was becoming paralysed like Erickson's. It is still unclear how this modelling process exactly works, but it is very potent.[13] In the sufi environment, when there is rapport between the seeker and the shaykh, reinforced by modelling the shaykh's inner and outer behaviour (sometimes including visualization), amazing transformations can occur. This is a direct connection to Muhammad and God, and it explains why many seekers have called their shaykhs 'the *qibla*' (the direction to the Ka'ba in Mecca). Rumi says:

> God made the *qibla* manifest so stop searching [...] If you forget this *qibla* for a moment, you will be distracted by every whim of desire. Showing ingratitude to the shaykh who gives you discernment will have you ceasing to recognize the *qibla* (6:403).

From the guide to the practices

After finishing a public talk about sufism I am sometimes asked to recommend a shaykh. My honest response is that I cannot help in that regard. When people are ready, their teacher will find them. Only one person ever has asked how she could get ready, but I tell people anyway, by communicating what Rumi once said, 'If you do not have a shaykh, then everyone is your shaykh.' A corollary comes to mind. A Tibetan monk once said to me that a student should consider his spiritual preceptor to be enlightened, without any doubt whatsoever. When I asked about a person who sincerely considers everyone to be enlightened, he replied that a person who can treat everyone as if he were enlightened is enlightened himself. Up to now, transformative practice has been mentioned many times and in the next chapter we will be approaching the root of the tree of sufism. The foundation of these sufi transformative practices is always a deep heart-to-heart relationship with the shaykh.

6

SUFI VARIETIES OF TRANSFORMATIVE PRACTICE: TRANSFORMATION OF THE EGO-SELF

WHY IS TRANSFORMATIVE practice so important? Think back to when you were 15. Would you have preferred at that time to be five years old? Think back to when you were in your mid-twenties. Would you have preferred to be 15? The sum total of physical, emotional, mental and spiritual development as we grow up is called human consciousness development. If we look at our own lives, we can see that, as our own development unfolded, entirely new and wonderful dimensions in life became available for us to explore. There may also have been painful transitions. The technology of transformative practice is about conscious evolution beyond the mental-cognitive realms. If and when the critical mass of transformation occurs, life will never be the same again.

The early part of this chapter emphasises the critical importance of being aware of our own consciousness development, a taboo subject in modern educational institutions. Academics are used to treating the subjects they teach as conceptual objects, having no relationship to who we are as human beings, living real lives in the world. This is how we learned our subjects and were taught to teach. Nor has it changed since I started my graduate work in 1985. It is an academic taboo to discuss sufism – or any other subject – as if it were transformatively *real*. But exploring sufism is all about 'self-help'. Ask any sufi, sufi practitioner or visitor needing to go to a sufi shrine. Seriously, what *else* could sufi practice possibly be about? Look back at the Rumi quotes of the previous chapter. He is continually addressing *you* – something that happens occasionally in this chapter, because there are subjects where it is appropriate to get *real*.

The other significant aspect of transformative contemplative practice is that it is one of the most effective ways we know how to consciously evolve beyond what becomes our developmental (cognitive) threshold – usually reached in our late twenties. Hardly anyone cares to go beyond this threshold. It is not because of the lack of information. We have thousands of years of human experience recorded by those who have transformed themselves, aka 'mystics', that communicate marvellous insights verifying their transformative methodologies. For the first time in human history, these books have been translated into languages we can read and are publically available. But we usually disregard this accumulated wisdom, just as we ignore the knowledge that in a very short period of time we will no longer be walking on this earth. It astounded the Buddha-to-be that people lived their lives pretending that they were never going to die. After becoming enlightened, he found a methodology and was able to say, 'Even death is not to be feared by one who has lived wisely.'[1] In a subsequent statement, revealing the methodology of how to live wisely, Muhammad confided with the well-known sufi hadith, 'Die before you die.'[2] This meant that the domination of the ego should die – not by killing the ego but by transforming it.

It is easy to see why transformative practice has not become a mainstream item, when the wisdom of the Buddha – and of thousands of others since his time – has been so completely ignored in the past 2,500 years. What the vast majority of people think is happiness is only a temporary, lower level of pain, relieving us of the greater ongoing pain of our lives. Without consciously evolving, we miss whole areas of knowledge and being. All of us have magnificent homes (our inner being), but how many of us spend our lives idling under the streetlight looking for the key to our house? Transformative practice can have long-term implications for a person's life and forms the very root of the tree of sufism.

The methodology of contemplative practices

For most contemplative paths the preliminary exercise is to still the mind. The senses and the rational mind are to be transcended if one wants to rend the veil and perceive the inner realms. If you have a minute (literally), find a watch with a second hand and look at the second hand rotating, without any thoughts. Keep track of how long it takes for a thought to arise. The vast majority of people cannot focus, even for a minute, without thoughts arising. Where do these thoughts come from? It is clear that one of the most powerful tools we have, the mind, is totally out of control. It took us many years to learn to control our bodies and emotions, at least most of the time, but most of us have never learned to control our minds. If the sufi path of transformation is a journey, then the wayfarer on this journey cannot even begin to travel until the mind is rendered free from thought. Ramana Maharshi (d. 1950, Tiruvannamalai, Tamil Nadu, India) succinctly summarized the situation: 'The mind is only a bundle of thoughts. The thoughts arise because there is the thinker. The thinker is the ego.'[3] Mind is the contents of consciousness and it identifies itself with these contents. This is part of the ego-self, the prison of identifying with the stuff of the mind. Sufi practice, developed over the centuries, has been designed to transform the ego – and remind us that we are not the mind/ego-self.

A typical concentration exercise introducing sufi practice is the remembrance of God (*dhikr*), with the seeker repeating 'Allah', aloud or silently. The advantage of the silent mode is that one can practice it anywhere. By focusing on this word, the mind is stilled – although there is more to it than its simply being a mantra. More advanced recollection exercises (see the Naqshbandi section below), called 'meditation' and 'contemplation', require solitude and a quiet place. In a very generalized sense, there are three stages to transformative practice: concentration, meditation and contemplation. Concentrating the mind is like sharpening a pencil; meditation is like learning to form letters; and contemplation is like writing words and sentences. The transition from concentration to meditation often begins in the heart. Sufis have repeatedly stressed that the foundation of remembrance of God rests in the heart, just as the profession of faith (there is no god but God and Muhammad is God's messenger) involves the tongue and the heart simultaneously. There are many practices in the sufi repertoire and what they share in common is a methodology that allows human beings to find out who they really are.

The methodology of listening to chanted verse and music to facilitate altered states

In sufism and other transformative practices, altered states of consciousness are part of the experiential terrain. At one extreme, this perceived 'attraction to God' in altered states can cause people to barely function in everyday life (as mentioned in the introduction). One of these 'attracted-to-God' persons touched one of the sufis I worked with in Peshawar, Pakistan, and he was then not able to write for about six months, because his arms continued to shake so much.

Naqshbandis are supposedly a 'sober' group – admittedly in many places they are, but my impetus to study the Naqshbandi–Mujaddidis happened after witnessing the most 'drunken', ecstatically out of control group of people I had ever seen. The Mujaddidi shaykh sat in front of about 100 people, transmitting what I later discovered to be a subtle energy that activated their subtle centres (explained below). This phenomenon was also called 'attraction to God'. When the subtle energy exceeded the capacity of their subtle centres, people stood up and started moving around; some in circles, some running back and forth crashing into walls and some rolling on the ground. It was mayhem. The audio portion of the session included crying out and screams. I was one of the very few people who remained quite sober, sitting on the floor. As I later discovered, this happened regularly every Thursday evening and was a way of 'working out' the subtle centres, so that seekers could better develop them in their much more sedate and sober contemplative practices.

When I read the Chishti accounts of what goes on in their listening sessions, it appears very similar to what I witnessed with the transmission of spiritual energy. (However, this is comparing my interpretation of a text with an experience, which may not be a valid comparison.) Chanted verse and music in the Chishti context is supposed to facilitate greater intimacy between the human lover and the Beloved.[4] Perhaps this is the same as increasing one's attraction to God through the use of more poetic language.

Chishti practice of listening to chanted verse and music has had a strict set of rules and an accompanying discipline of ego training. In the case of Nizamuddin Awliya (d. 1325), each listening session began and ended with recitation of the Qur'an; everyone had to be in a state of ritual purity (a requirement before Islamic prayer); and there was no chewing of betel nut allowed. Instead of explaining the altered states of consciousness during listening to chanted verse and music in terms of subtle centres, one of Nizamuddin's pupils, Burhanuddin Gharib (d. 1337, Khuldabad, Maharashtra, India), explained it in terms of longing for God (or not). If the listener is totally longing for God, with very little, if any, longing for the world, then listening to music in sufi assemblies is permitted. If there is more longing for the world than for God, then listening to music is not permitted. Nizamuddin described three kinds of ecstasy:

1 Empathetic ecstasy of the uninitiated, seen by a voluntary movement of a listener
2 Momentary ecstasy of a sufi seeker, who listens through his current state of awareness
3 Durative ecstasy of an advanced sufi, who hears the music via a direct connection to God.[5]

This activity has continued to prove controversial since the ninth century, partly due to occcurences of abuse in letting all and sundry listen to music in a sufi context.

My sense, looking from afar at Mevlevi and Chishti practices of listening to 'chanted verse', where altered states are the goal, is that they do assist somehow in the other meditation—contemplation practices. In the Mevlevi case, it started with Rumi having spontaneous ecstatic experiences.

Subsequent development of Mevlevi practice – like the whirling ritual – came into being as a way to consciously experience these states – and surely to keep them within ritual limits. Chishti sources do not discuss how spontaneous altered states became institutionalized into what we now know as the Chishti ritual of chanted verse and music. Reading the sufi literature on listening to music, one would imagine that it was the 'be-all and end-all' of sufism as it opens up 'the heart's understanding of realities, becoming aware of God's meditations and the divine speech and will, [and] opening up of the tongue of conscience to God'.[6] This may well be the case, particularly with gifted individuals. On the other hand, an anonymous eleventh-century shaykh remarked, 'A time will come when this music will be no more to you than the croaking of a raven. The influence of music only lasts so long as there is no contemplation, and as soon as contemplation is attained music has no power.'[7]

Varieties of sufi practice

The methodologies employed across the world by sufi shaykhs are almost as varied as the number of practising shaykhs, or so it appears. Here are a few brief contemporary examples. The Egyptian Rifa'i shaykh, Zahir Abu Zaghlal begins the remembrance session at 9 p.m. (The Rifa'i lineage is named after Ahmad Rifa'i, d. 1182, Iraq.) After a meal, the men stand in a circle, inclining to the right saying 'la ilaha' (there is no god), then straightening their bodies in the centre, to then incline to the left and say 'illa Allah' (but God). The shaykh is part of the circle, but it is the singer leading the session through repetition of names of God or verses of poetry who determines the tone of the session, in subtle harmony with the shaykh. The remembrance gathering goes through half-hour segments, with the tempo increasing throughout, until it peaks at around midnight. Two generations ago, they stopped using musical instruments and, more recently, Abu Zaghlal abolished the Rifa'i practice of passing iron skewers through throats and stomachs, because he thought it was just showing off.[8]

In Herzegovina, Hisham, a Naqshbandi shaykh, conducts a one-hour remembrance session in a small lodge at the source of the Buna River. The men sit in a circle in one room and women sit in rows in another. After reciting from the Qur'an, sitting sufi aspirants repeat various names of God, followed by '*la ilaha illa Allah*'. Sometimes the repeating of names is done in the heart and other times articulated while breathing quickly at four breaths per second. There is some movement right and left. Further Qur'an recitation and praising of the Prophet finish the session.[9] These Naqshbandi–Khalidi practices bear no resemblance to any I have seen in Afghan, Turkish or Indo-Pakistani Naqshbandi groups.

In Macedonia the Halvetis are the most popular sufi lineage. One sub-lineage (Hayati) no longer practices a rotating movement while standing in a circle nor uses musical instruments. The men sit in a circle, wearing the long caps that Mevlevis wear, and gently move their heads to the right and left and forward and backward repeating '*la ilaha illa Allah*', '*hu*' and '*hayy*'. The shaykh also gives everyone special exercises to do before and after the Islamic morning prayer, as part of their ego training. Most of the seekers in this group are sons of those already in the group. Women can watch the remembrance sessions, but not participate.[10]

Historically, there was also considerable variety in sufi practice. Chishti Nizamuddin Awrangabadi (d. 1730, Awarangabad, Maharashtra, India) wrote a compendium of meditation and contemplation methods in his Persian treatise, *The Order of Hearts*. These included ways to remember God by repeating 'Allah', '*la ilaha illa Allah*', or other names of God, visualizing letters or words, using various methods of breath control and moving a name or formula from the lower to the upper part of the body. One practice was to recite a given formula, while only breathing 2,000 breaths in a 24-hour period. He also incorporated Qadiri and Naqshbandi techniques, e.g. visualizing 'Abdulqadir Jilani and practising some of the 26 Naqshbandi contemplations. Yoga contemplative technology, adapted harmoniously to an Islamic context, expanded the repertoire even further.[11]

A Naqshbandi–Mujaddidi system

The beginning, 'concentration phase', of Naqshbandi practice begins with repeating the word 'Allah' and simultaneously involves an activation of the heart 'subtle centre', part of a subtle realm associated with the human body. There are what I call 'subtle bodies', which are expressed in the literature as *latifa*s, literally, 'subtleties'. Two of these are located in the world of creation – the physical frame and the ego-self; and the other five are located in the world of command – heart, spirit, mystery, arcane and super-arcane. In a training environment, where aspirants need specifics, these subtle bodies are given locations on the body and are called 'subtle centres', with colours associated with them.[12]

Of all the subtle centres, the heart subtle centre is primary; it is the inner catalyst that enables other subtle centres to become active. This is not the physical heart, though its location is described by Naqshbandis as overlapping the part of the physical heart that has a shape of an inverted pine cone. One way Naqshbandi shaykhs activate the heart subtle centre is by putting the four fingers of the right hand on the place of the heart subtle centre (sometimes called the 'mouth' of the heart) and saying 'Allah' three or more times, while delivering a blast of subtle energy to the seeker's heart. This often happens during initiation, depending on the shaykh's practice. For initiating women, either their husband practitioners initiate them or the woman holds a metre-long piece of cloth at the heart and the shaykh holds the other end of the cloth.

Naqshbandi shaykhs have explained that, by imparting the name of God, they are establishing God's imprint (*naqsh*) on the heart. One definition of a 'Naqshband' is 'a person whose heart is impressed with God's name'. Usually the seeker is instructed to spend time each day being aware of the heart, constantly repeating 'Allah', until the heart repeats it all the time. Although this is silent recollection of God, as opposed to vocal recollection, technically speaking, it is recollection of the heart. The advantage of this type of recollection is that it can be performed in any circumstance *and* it begins to activate the human system of subtle centres. A cross-legged body posture, with the hands down on the knees, is the same for all Mujaddidi practices.

The shaykh's subtle centres transmit a subtle energy – an enabling energy – that apparently connects the macrocosm with the human microcosm and facilitates the development of subtle centres. Sometimes Naqshbandis describe the actual flow of energy as spiritual attention. For this process to work properly, there needs to be an attunement between the shaykh and the seeker. It is this concept of divinely emanating energy that is used to explain how sufi shaykhs positively influence people's behaviour or cure others of undesirable conditions and illnesses. Sometimes this subtle energy – often perceived as divine grace – can be transmitted through the breath, like blowing in a glass of water, through a handshake, or by touching the head or places on the chest. But when 'hearts are near', this process can occur with no physical contact whatsoever.

When all of the subtle centres are reciting 'Allah', the seeker proceeds to 'the recollection of negation and affirmation'. The negation is, 'There is no god' and the affirmation is, 'but God'. Holding the breath below the navel, the seeker brings the word '*la*' from below the navel to the point between the middle of the eyes.[13] Then the word '*ilaha*' is mentally conveyed from the middle of the forehead to the right shoulder, ending with the final forceful mental motion that 'hits' the heart from the right shoulder with '*illa Allah*'. This can be loosely called the meditation stage of Naqshbandi practice. When seekers are proficient in this exercise, they are ready to travel towards God in the contemplations, the progressively more subtle cosmo-logical levels. Contemplation in Naqshbandi terms is waiting in stillness as the subtle centres attract subtle energy, turning away from states and attributes, and being immersed in an ineffable beauty and love. There are 26 separate Mujaddidi contemplations, each with its special intention to guide one closer and closer to God, visiting various prophets on the way.

Exactly where Naqshbandis go in their subtle travelling is not easy to determine. There is the precedent of the Prophet's journey through the seven heavens, but Naqshbandis seldom, if ever, speak in those terms. Wherever this journey takes place, it is certainly not in the normal waking mind, which is why the concentration exercises come first. It is impos-sible with our current understanding to know what part of the human being actually travels in these other realms, but there is the possibility that Naqshbandi practice is the creation/activation of latent, more subtle bodies. One can then travel in the corresponding subtle realms with these subtle-body vehicles. Picture a ferry carrying a car with people in it. The ferry is the vehicle for water, as the car is the vehicle for land. When one gets out of the car to enter a building, the body is the vehicle, and in dreams yet another vehicle operates. Four realms corresponding to four vehicles.

From this perspective perhaps Naqshbandi practice is simply developing vehicles, learning how to move between them at will to experience different ontological realities. Whether this hypothetical model corresponds to how things actually work or not, access to various realms of the non-physical cosmos is inside each of us. Sufis report that the inner universe, accessed through the heart, is seven times larger than the physical universe. The experiences described earlier – of contact with deceased sufis and Uwaysi initiations – or even seeing and communicating with a shaykh in dreams – could be explained as instances of interactions between subtle bodies.

The fourfold cyclical path to God (see fig. 6.1)

Before beginning the sufi path, an ordinary person living in consensus reality is in a state of abiding in ignorance. The world preoccupies him both on the inside and the outside. This is known as the 'first abiding'. The Naqshbandi–Mujaddidi cyclical fourfold path begins by wayfaring to God in the world of command, the shadows of God's names and attributes. The first mode of wayfaring occurs in the outer world, going further and further, followed by inner wayfaring, moving closer and closer. Finishing the latter mode roughly coincides with the completion of wayfaring to God. Many sufis get stuck at this stage of wayfaring to God, because of frequent ecstatic experiences. Sometimes one is given conditional permission to teach at this point. Here the aspirant experiences God on the outside and the world on the inside. The end of ascent in the 'lesser intimacy of God' is associated with 'the unity of contemplative witnessing'.

The next part of the journey involves a descent 'returning to the world of creation for God and by means of God'. This is the beginning of greater intimacy with God, where one begins to purify the spirit from the ego-self. The journey culminates in the fourth and last cycle: to live as an extraordinarily ordinary person in the created world. Although one experiences the multiplicity of the world, it is experienced as a mirror of the One. Here unity is experienced in the multiplicity, and multiplicity is experienced as a unity. This is the place where one is with God on the inside and with the world on the outside. It is the 'best of both worlds', where one can see with

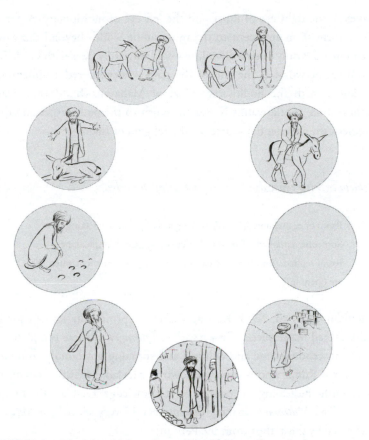

FIGURE 6.1 The Mujaddidi path, moving clockwise from the bottom picture: 1. Nasruddin in the bazaar [the first abiding]; 2. Nasruddin looking for his donkey [starting to deal with the ego-self]; 3. Nasruddin finding footprints of the donkey [starting to work on the subtle centres]; 4. Nasruddin finding the donkey [more awareness of the ego-self – the beginning of wayfaring to God]; 5. Nasruddin catches his donkey, although the donkey is recalcitrant [grappling full-on with the ego-self]; 6. The donkey is calmly following Nasruddin [the beginning of a tranquil ego-self]; 7. Nasruddin riding the donkey [a tranquil ego-self – the beginning of wayfaring in God]; 8. An empty image [beginning of separation of the spirit and ego-self from the heart – complete ascent and an experience of annihilation of the ego]; 9. Nasruddin walking back to town without the donkey [returning to the world of creation for God and by means of God]; 10. The same image as no. 1 [the second abiding – extraordinarily ordinary], Nasruddin in the bazaar.

two eyes: the right eye of unity and the left eye of multiplicity. A person who returns from an ascent to the most subtle worlds beyond the world of command is only outwardly in the world. Inwardly he is with God. This return to the world as the end of the path was pioneered a millennium previously, with the bodhisattva ideal of Mahayana Buddhism. Travel in these more subtle realms is also to return to the paths experienced by prophets, the experiential sources of the religion of Islam.

Mevlevi turning towards God: 'The whirling dervishes'

> Rumi once exclaimed, 'Music is the gates of paradise creaking.'
> Someone remarked, 'The sound of creaking gates is unpleasant.'
> Rumi replied: 'You hear the gates closing, but I hear them when they are opening!'

Jalaluddin Rumi (d. 1273, Konya, Turkey) is principally known for his multi-layered masterpiece of poetry, the *Mathnawi*. If there is a planetary poet, transcending time and cultures and speaking profoundly to human hearts, it is Rumi, who is usually known as Mevlana in Turkic languages, an honorific indicating a person of great knowledge. Here are the first 18 verses of the *Mathnawi*, making the number 18 very special for Mevlevis (translated by the author from the Persian):

> Listen to the lament of the reed flute, of being separated, but not mute.
> Since I was cut from the reed bed, my notes have made people lament.
> I can only share this pain with a heart that is split like a broken window-pane.
> Anyone pulled from the primal source yearns to return.
> Grieving in the crowd, amongst the happy and those who yearn.
> They became my friend for their own sake; none sought the secrets within me that they could not take.
> The secrets of sadness are in the song that no one hears, no ears.
> Body is not hidden from soul, nor soul from body; alas no one sees the soul.

The reed flute is played with fire, not breath – without this burning, only death.

Love's fire exhales the reed's notes as love so fine dissolves in wine.

The reed is a friend of those forced apart as it lifts the veils of the heart.

It's a poison and cure like the beloved and the longing lover, one inside the other.

The reed leaves a bloody trail pouring from the heart as one madly in love falls apart.

Propelled beyond the senses on the reed song if one can hear, otherwise it is just the ear.

In grief day after day, burning aches and pains never leaving the fray.

Let these days go without concern; remain with the One who makes the heart burn.

Only fish are relieved of thirst, but without daily bread the stomach hurts.

The raw are far from being ripe so best to cut this short and say goodnight.

The story of the reed flute expresses the plaintive longing of humanity. Just as humans are lifeless without the merciful breath of God, the flute can only cry when someone breathes into it. The flute, cut off from its homeland in the reed bed, is akin to human beings who are separated from realizing their real home of deep and exalted being. It is this separation, ironically, that allows the reed flute to exclaim its longing to return.

When Rumi was alive, he first held group sessions of listening to music and turning, at Karatay, the school where he taught, then at other schools and gardens, and even at the governor's palace. This ritual of turning – not a dance – developed to train those who did not have spontaneous ecstatic states, in order to to cultivate these altered states of consciousness.

It is likely that many contemporary observers of this ritual – mostly tourists in Turkey – do not realize the profundity of worship that used to exist before it became a whirling tourist attraction. They just buy their tickets and sit down to watch. In practising Mevlevi teacher Kabir Helminski's words, the turning ritual of facing towards God is 'honoring and reverencing our relationship with the Divine'. It is also a meditative practice in motion; a much more challenging type of meditation, because the moment a person loses focus and presence, it will immediately affect the equilibrium of their turning. One is returning closer to the Source inside, but also connecting to a series of relationships. In Helminski's words:

> You have to be aware not only of yourself but of your position and distance from the other turners and inwardly aware through the heart of your connection to the shaikh who is leading the ceremony, holding the transmission of the lineage. There's a continuum that connects to a transmission back to the shaykh, back to Mevlana. So the ceremony is elegant; it's disciplined; it's sober; it's ecstatic; it's creative; it's holy; it's all these things.[14]

In traditional Mevlevi sufi lodges, some of which are now open for 'performances', there is a special octagonal assembly hall where this ritual turning takes place. Coming through the entrance, one faces the prayer niche in the opposite wall, indicating the *qibla* (the direction towards Mecca which Muslims face when they pray). In front of this prayer niche, the presiding shaykh sits on a red-dyed sheepskin. The area is divided into two symmetrical halves by an imaginary centre line, starting from the sheepskin and extending to the entrance, and representing the shortest path to God; dervishes must never step on this line.[15] The musicians are seated by the entrance. A typical ensemble often includes musicians playing the reed flute, a small double kettledrum, a zither-like instrument, with 72 strings, and a lute. Mevlevi attire includes a long white robe worn over a short, tight-fitting jacket, open in front and a conical-shaped hat. High-ranking dervishes have a turban wound around the hat (see figs 6.2, 6.3, 6.4, 6.5 and 6.6).

The dervishes enter and sit with their legs folded underneath. When the shaykh sits on his sheepskin, the ritual begins. Verses from the Qur'an are recited, followed by praises to the Prophet Muhammad and to Mevlana. The drum bangs four times, announcing an improvisation on the reed flute that symbolizes the breath of compassion breathing the universes into existence. The eulogy to the Prophet precedes the creation of the universes, because of the holy hadith (where God is speaking in the first person) stating, 'If it hadn't been for Muhammad I would not have created the universes.'

The next part of the ritual, the prelude, is in honour of Rumi's son, Sultan Walad. After the reed flute solo, the dervishes stand up, led by the shaykh, and begin to walk slowly around the hall counter-clockwise – just as pilgrims circle around the Ka'ba in Mecca. The shaykh takes his place at the left of his sheepskin. He bows and walks to a point on the right side of his sheepskin. The master of ceremonies (*semazen*), who is behind him, takes his place to the left of the sheepskin. They bow to each other and then each of the dervishes bows to the shaykh. Step by step, slowly and deliberately, they all circle the hall three times counter-clockwise. After this third rotation, the shaykh takes his place on the sheepskin, and the prelude music ends. A flute improvisation concludes the first part of the ritual.

The second and main part of the ritual, the whirling, is divided into four salutations. The dervishes are simultaneously anchored to the ground yet 'flying inside' to become closer to God. Each of the four salutations has a different tempo and type of music. With the exception of the master of ceremonies and the shaykh, the dervishes lay aside their outer black robes (symbolizing death), leaving a white undergarment (grave shrouds) and their skirt. The master of ceremonies kisses the shaykh's hand and the

FIGURE 6.2 Three Mevlevi conical hats. These were made of two layers of felt. The middle one (a *dal sikke*) was for students and affiliates (*muhibbs*), without the sash. The ones on either side, with wound sashes, were worn by those authorized to teach, a green sash being reserved for a descendant of the Prophet and a purple sash for heads of sufi lodges.

FIGURE 6.3 Three turbans on tombstones. The turban on the left is a four-banded 'crown-hat', bound at the rim with thick cloth, located in the cemetery adjacent to Sünbül Efendi's (d. 1529) shrine in Istanbul. The middle one is an Adhami (named after Ibrahim ibn Adham, d. *c*.777) four-banded crown-hat from Kastamonu, and the turban on the right is on the tombstone of Ahmed Efendi, a Naqshbandi-Khalidi shaykh buried in Kastamonu.

FIGURE 6.4 A Shamsi crown-hat, said to be like that of Shams-i Tabrizi, which can be traced back to Central Asia. The words *la ilaha ila Allah* (there is no god but God) are sewn on the cotton part of the hat.

FIGURE 6.5 Early twentieth-century photo of Mevlevi dervishes in front of a water fountain alongside the Galata Mevlevi sufi lodge in Istanbul.

shaykh, in turn, kisses his hand. This means the shaykh gives his authorization and blessing for the ritual. Each dervish pauses in front of the shaykh, bows and kisses his right hand, while the shaykh kisses each dervish's hat. When a dervish reaches the shaykh's sheepskin, he turns around and bows to the dervish following him in the ritual, both looking into each other's eyes.

Holding their arms crossed in front of the chest with hands on opposite shoulders, each dervish bends his head towards one shoulder with downcast eyes. Then the dervishes start to whirl, forming a circle, one by one. The whirling is done by pivoting around on the left foot with the right foot crossing over the top of the left instep to keep up the motion. As the speed of the spinning increases, the arms are raised, with the right palm turned upward and the left hand lowered with the palm turned downward. Sometimes one arm is outstretched and the other pressed against the heart. As they quicken their rotation, the long white skirts become fully expanded in open circles. The master of ceremony indicates which dervishes should turn in the outer orbit, while others remain in the inner orbit.

FIGURE 6.6 Interlaced letters 'Ya Hazret-i Mevlânâ' (O holy presence of Mevlana), forming a conical hat. The hyacinth bouquets are the symbol of the Sünbüli branch of the Helveti lineage.

This is repeated three times. Kissing the hand of the shaykh is only done in the first stage of salutation. After that, each period between the salutations is broken by a pause in the music when the dervishes cross their arms on their chests, putting their hands over their shoulders. The salutation is done by bowing slightly while standing with the right toe over the left toe and the right hand on the heart. As the music picks up again, they begin to turn. This pause allows the dervishes to step back from the brink of ecstasy to affirm servanthood and then re-enter the ritual. Through the first three salutations, the music keeps building and building. The third salutation is the most energetic, most ecstatic part of the ritual, where one comes into the closest intimacy with God.

The fourth and final salutation is different, because the master of ceremonies keeps everybody in the outer circle. The shaykh takes part by whirling to the centre – both of the centre line and the hall – the axis point and the space symbolically reserved for Rumi, as he radiates the *baraka* of the lineage. The singing of the music part of the ritual finishes as the dervishes are still moving. The *whoosh* of the dervishes' robes and their leather-slippered feet fall silent, as a single reed flute starts playing and the dervishes stop, standing wherever they are. When the shaykh spins back to his sheepskin, the flute improvisation and the whole ritual abruptly end. A Qur'an reciter then starts, often picking the verses, 'The east and the west are God's and wherever you turn is the face of God' (Q. 2:115). 'God needs only to say "be" and it is.' (Q. 2:117). The dervishes go quickly back to their sheepskins and kneel, putting on their outer garments. After this recitation, the master of ceremonies stands up and makes a supplication for Muhammad, Mevlana and the lineage, before the dervishes follow the shaykh out of the door.

People observing this amazing ritual have become a historical part of the Mevlevi ritual itself. There has typically been a place for guests, either around the hall itself or in a gallery above the ground floor. The sacred space of the ritual in a Mevlevi sufi lodge is intentionally designed to share the *baraka*, again underlying the notion of service to others.

You can see from this brief description that Ataturk's law, in 1925, affected Mevlevis quite adversely. With the clothing, rank and the ritual itself outlawed, along with the Mevlevi lodges being confiscated, one would not have expected the Mevlevis to have survived to the present day. In fact, clandestine ceremonies continued to be held and, in 1953, the Turkish government allowed the first public turning ceremony to be held, in a Konya cinema, for Rumi's death anniversary on 17 December. This festival has continued annually, although many Mevlevi teachers in Konya do not consider this to be a positive development. In 1967, a senior Mevlevi teacher resigned from the association that organized the annual festival in Konya, arguing that the authenticity of the ceremony was severely compromised, having been debased into a tourist show.[16] Scholars writing about Mevlevi activities in Turkey, which for them are synonymous with the turning ritual, are under the impression that the Mevlevis as a sufi lineage are defunct, only 'going through the motions' in the whirling ritual. When I ask why this is the case, they say it is because the rigorous 1001-day retreat training to become a qualified dervish is no longer possible, since there are no longer any functioning Mevlevi sufi lodges.

The 1001-day Mevlevi retreat: Intensive sufi training in the lodge

By the seventeenth century, the turning ritual had been formalized along the lines we know today, together with the formal 1001-day Mevlevi retreat. Both activities continued to evolve over the centuries. Primary Mevlevi sufi lodges were designed and authorized for the 1001-day sufi training. There were an estimated 140 in the Ottoman Empire at the beginning of the twentieth century. Numerous subsidiary Mevlevi lodges existed throughout the empire, but they were not equipped for training of aspirants (see figs 6.7–6.12).

Whoever decided to do the retreat and become a Mevlevi 'elder' had to have parental permission, be at least 18 years old, unmarried and of worthy character. After a vow of repentance, there was a three-day trial period, during which the aspirant could observe the Mevlevi way of life from a designated place in the kitchen. The sheepskin of the water-carrier was then placed on a bench to the left of the entrance to kitchen, the busiest place in the lodge. Here the aspirant ate, prayed and slept in the same spot. No one spoke to him, nor was he allowed to read anything. He was closely observed. If he decided to stay and if he was found suitable, the chief of the cauldron assigned him an 18-day course of physical and mental tasks around the lodge. He still wore his own clothing for this 18-day trial period. After this second trial period the chief of the cauldron conferred with the head of the kitchen, who then gave him a cap to wear and 'service clothing', which he wore with a long-sleeved shirt. Then he began 18 different menial tasks, each supervised by an individual dervish, e.g. washing the dishes and laundry, sweeping floors, making beds, serving food and cleaning the toilets. Mevlevi sufi training was explicitly based on training the ego through discipline and rules of conduct, overseen by the chief of the cauldron. The novice was slowly cooked over the 1001 days.

In Mevlana's kitchen, the room designated for 'cooking' novices, the aspirant learned to whirl by placing two toes of his left foot around a knob on a metre-square wooden board covered with salt. To learn to do the turning ritual well enough to participate in the formal ritual with the other dervishes, it took anywhere from three months to a year. Mevlana's kitchen was the special room where aspirants learned to beautifully recite the Qur'an, to sing praises to Muhammad and to learn the basic religious sciences. Depending on his skills and inclination, the aspirant

FIGURE 6.7 Front entrance to the Galata Mevlevi sufi lodge, early twentieth century.

FIGURE 6.8 The Mevlevi-presiding shaykh, sitting on the sheepskin with the dervishes on his left. The large picture in the background is a depiction of Mevlana Jalaluddin Rumi.

FIGURE 6.9 A seventeenth-century artist's depiction of the Galata Mevlevi sufi lodge, with dervishes 'turning towards God'. The *mihrab* (indicating the direction to the Ka'ba) has been displaced by the artist and hidden behind pillars. Instead, it should be directly in front of the entrance, where the wooden seat, a low *minbar*, is located.

could also learn to play an instrument or sing the vocals used in the Mevlevi ritual turning ceremony. In many lodges there were opportunities to learn miniature painting, wood engraving and calligraphy.

After both the dawn prayer and the evening prayer, the dervishes gathered in the mosque space to repeat aloud 'Allah' together, the well-known Mevlevi meditative practice of the 'majestic remembrance of God'. Every aspirant had to ask permission of his supervising dervish to imprint 'Allah' in his heart. Alone in his cell, the seeker repeated 'Allah' 3,000 times each day. When he reached the point where the tongue of the heart automatically repeated 'Allah', he no longer needed to do vocal remembrance of God alone in his cell.

Once the aspirant successfully finished the 1001-day retreat, there was a celebration with candles, desserts, special sheepskins and a prayer, blessing the chain of shaykhs in the Mevlevi lineage. The head of Mevlana's kitchen assigned the new dervish a cell, where he remained for three days with

FIGURE 6.10 A contemporary view of the ceremony of turning towards God, seen from above. The Mevlevi dervishes are all whirling in white, with the musicians on top in black and the shaykh to the left.

FIGURE 6.11 A miniature painting depicting Rumi's ecstatic encounter with Salahuddin Zarkub, a goldsmith and Rumi's future son-in-law, as he was beating the gold. Their astonishment is indicated by the forefingers pointing towards their mouths.

FIGURE 6.12 'Ya Hazret-i Mevlânâ, quddus Allah sirrahu' (O holy presence of Mevlana, may God bless his inner heart). A nineteenth-century depiction of three Mevlevi conical hats inside each other. The coiling sash is green, signifying the wearer to be a descendant of the Prophet.

the door shut. Each of the elders of the lodge came to his cell with gifts, congratulations, food and coffee. Except for prayer and using the toilet, he was not permitted to leave. After three days, the head of Mevlana's kitchen would come, ask permission to enter and take the dervish to the shaykh for a formal initiation, where he was given a robe. The final test was an 18-day period when he could not leave the lodge – one can look at this period as a seal of the dervish's new rank as an elder.

After this final 18-day period had ended, the temporary ritual attire that the aspirant had used to learn the turning ritual was replaced by another set of clothing. There was a celebratory meal in the evening when an 18-branch candelabra was lit, symbolizing the various kinds of tasks he had performed. After the meal, there was a special ceremony in which the new dervish was crowned with his own felt wool hat, approximately 45–50 cm high, made of two layers of felted wool. In a very real sense, this hat was a badge of rank for the new dervish. (The most serious punishment for a wayward Mevlevi was to have his hat confiscated.) Then the new dervish was either given a small room in that lodge with a window, small fireplace, a bed and a chair for visitors, or transferred to another Mevlevi lodge. In any case he received a small stipend from the income of the lodge. Some returned to their families and began careers, often as musicians at the Ottoman court. There was no contradiction in working in the world while continuing one's sufi practices.

Today newly appointed Mevlevi teachers are expected to do an 18-day retreat in the Konya lodge. Ibrahim Gamard,[17] who kindly clarified many questions I had concerning the 1001-day retreat, was given verbal authorization by the hereditary head of the Mevlevi lineage, Faruk Chelebi Efendi. Ibrahim then did a modified retreat in a hotel in Konya for 18 days, had daily contact with a friend of his, who was a Mevlevi teacher, and was allowed to do some symbolic acts of service at Mevlana's Mausoleum. Some time later in Istanbul there was a ceremony of Mevlevi prayers, followed by a new shaykh's turban being placed on his head. Then he was given a written authorization to teach, written in Ottoman calligraphy and signed by Chelebi Efendi.

What happened to the 1001-day retreat? The retreat now is the retreat of one's daily life, the integration of Mevlevi ethics and character practised in everyday life combined with communal Mevlevi meditation and ritual turning ceremonies, according to what is possible in each person's particular circumstances. Here we have a textbook example of a major change in contemplative practice in less than a century. Ataturk had this to say to Abdulhalim Chelebi of Konya and Vice President of the First House of Representatives:

> You, the Mevlevis have made a great difference by combating ignorance and religious fundamentalism for centuries, as well as making contributions to science and the arts. However we are obliged not to make any exceptions and must include Mevlevi tekkes [sufi lodges]. Nonetheless, the ideas and teaching of Mevlana will not only exist forever, but they will emerge even more powerfully in the future.[18]

Ataturk may very well have been correct in his prediction. Until proper anthropological research is done, which would potentially be illegal, it seems premature to categorize Mevlevi activities in one way or the other. Perhaps the best way to protect Mevlevi practice in Turkey is to pretend that it does not happen any more; it is simply one more cultural-educational organization registered with the government.

7

TWO CONTEMPORARY
WOMEN SUFI TEACHERS

When a wild lion comes out of the forest, nobody asks if it is male or
female.

NIZAMUDDIN AWLIYA'

WOMEN HAVE BEEN involved with sufi practice from the beginning,
although this is not immediately obvious from the written historical sources,
where they have only sporadically shown up. As anecdotal evidence, in
every sufi group I have visited, there have always been women practitioners,
though often one has to inquire, since they are not usually in the sufi lodge
with the men. In sufi biographical compendia, information on women sufis
is located at the end of the book. In the case of this book, it has been delib-
erate to save these two fascinating interviews to the end.

Sultan Valid's daughter (Rumi's granddaughter), Sefer Hatun, taught
men and women, as did Mevlevi shaykhas for a couple more generations. In
the seventeenth century Destina Hatun, the great-granddaughter of Divane
Mehmet Çelebi (d. after 1544), was initiated as a Mevlevi shaykha, as was
Küçük Mehmet Çelebi's daughter Güneşhan. We know that women participated in the turning ritual – separately from the men it seems – because

there were separate entrances for them (not only as observers) to the main hall, where the turning ritual took place. This is continuing today.[1]

Let me now introduce two notable sufi women from other sufi lineages.

Cemalnur Sargut

Cemalnur Sargut (see fig. 7.1) is currently a sufi teacher in Istanbul who has a background of Rifa'i teachers (the Rifa'i lineage is named after Ahmad Rifa'i, d. 1182, Iraq) in the sub-lineage of Kenan Rifa'i (d. 1950). It is said that numerous people, including an unnamed Qadiri shaykh, had dreams that indicated Samiha Ayverdi to be Kenan Rifa'i's principal successor. Cemalnur was a student of Samiha Ayverdi (d. 1993), who requested Cemalnur to teach Rumi's *Mathnawi* when she was in her early twenties. Since 1996, Cemalnur has been the President of the Turkish Women's Cultural Association (TURKKAD), founded by Samiha Ayverdi. TURKKAD organizes international symposia, seeking to apply sufi principles to contemporary problems. Cemalnur has been active in sharing her experience with sufism around the world and has lectured in universities in the United States and Germany. She is the author of a dozen books in Turkish, ranging from transcribed radio talks to subtle commentaries on the Qur'an.

Interview with Cemalnur Sargut (recorded 15 November 2010, Istanbul)

ARTHUR: As I have explained, this book introducing sufism will be attempting to communicate how the experience of the sufis, their inspirations and transformative practices, are the centre and starting point of sufism. Without this there is nothing. Let me begin by asking about your Rifa'i background and practices.

CEMALNUR: I was born as a Rifa'i, because I was born into a Rifa'i family and I'd never questioned being a Rifa'i all throughout my life – but I didn't want to learn the things that my parents wanted to teach me. My family didn't

FIGURE 7.1 Cemalnur Sargut.

force me at all in this respect. I started to get interested in philosophy, but [...] at the same time I was studying chemical engineering. Then philosophy led me into depression, because philosophers were saying so many good things. But when I observed their lives, I realized that none of them were happy in their own lives. So I turned to my mother [Meşküre Sargut, who was also a student of Kenan Rifa'i and a sufi teacher]. I said to her, 'Show me and give me someone that has actually lived in accordance with goodness and high ideals.' Then she gave me [Jalaluddin Rumi's] *Mathnawi*. So I got to know the *Mathnawi* when I was 21 years old. Now I'm 59 years old, approaching 60, so I've been together with the *Mathnawi* for a while now.

When I was 23 years old, Kenan Rifa'i's student, Samiha Ayverdi, was also my spiritual guide and she told me that I had to teach the *Mathnawi*. I got so surprised, because I said to her that I didn't know anything. She said to me that those who say that they don't know anything are able to teach. Then she told me a story from the *Mathnawi*. A child climbs up on the roof of a house and the mother goes to Hazrat 'Ali and asks him to please rescue her son because he's on the roof. Hazrat 'Ali sent another child to that child. Hazrat 'Ali said that he actually knew what to say, but he sent another child, because he knew that other child would know what to do. I understood from that [story] what she wanted me to do, and that she will talk through me. I am a child and I must take children to that.

That's how I started teaching. In the fifth year of my teaching, my teacher sent me to another teacher of the *Mathnawi* and together with her we studied for six years all the commentaries of the *Mathnawi* and *The Discourses of Rumi*. The new teacher was a teacher of literature and was an expert on the *Mathnawi*. She showed me how to work and how to study in an academic way. Then I formed groups with my students to work on the other great sufis [lit. 'completed human beings'], especially Ibn al-'Arabi [d. 1240], 'Abdulkarim al-Jili [d. c.1428], Ahmad Rifa'i, 'Abdulqadir al-Jilani [d. 1166], Hajji Bayram [d. 1430] and Bayazid Bistami [d. 874]. [Ibn al-'Arabi (d. 1240, Damascus) had multiple visions showing him to be the Seal of God's Friends. He is deservedly one of the most well-known sufis and has made a vast contribution to the disciplined exposition of post-rational human consciousness without, however, elucidating a methodology so that others can achieve these realizations.]

They are so interrelated. In order to know Ibn al-ʿArabi, one should also know Daʾud Qaysari [d. 1350] [an interpreter of Ibn al-ʿArabi]. Then we started working on the Qurʾan and I started writing interpretations and commentaries of Qurʾanic verses by various completed human beings. So our commentary, our interpretation, was arranging their commentaries. The reason why I chose to start with the sura [chapter] of Yasin was [because of what happened] 15 years ago when I first went on ʿumra [a visit to Mecca and Medina outside the time of hajj]. On that trip, I said that the sura that is going to be recited will be for us, and then they recited sura Yasin. It's very interesting because they never recite Yasin in the mosque, so it was like a miracle. After studying Yasin for ten years, I started writing. Now we have finished the [longest] sura of al-Baqara. There are only ten verses in one book. We are now preparing the second 20 verses for the second book. *Inshallah*! *Inshallah*! [If God wills! If God wills!]

And then I began to write about [Ibn al-ʿArabi's] *The Bezels of Wisdom*, because I had been given lessons about it for nearly ten years. [For information about translations of Ibn al-ʿArabi's texts, see Suggested Reading.] I began with the prophet Adam and wrote that part as a book this year. *Inshallah*, I will go on to the other prophets. Now I am studying about the Prophet Muhammad. I will finish in Bayram [the celebration after hajj], *inshallah*.

A: So it sounds as if your sufi training was through all of these great sufis [completed human beings] and through your [living] teachers. Do I understand correctly?

C: Yes, you understand very well, because my vision, *inshallah*, my intention, my mission is to unite all the sufi paths, not in form but in meaning, and to let them work together towards the Muhammadan path.

A: Well I have another question to ask, and I would like you to explain. It's something that I don't understand myself – the Naqshbandis quote Bayazid Bistami.

C: Yes, because he is in their lineage.

A: Yes! So they relate that Bayazid Bistami said, 'You take your knowledge from books but we get our knowledge from the hearts.' That is my understanding. Now I understand that Allah works in many different ways. And so, why not through books?

C: Bayazid Bistami is really correct, because if I had not had the benefit [lit. the eyeglasses] of my teacher Kenan Rifa'i I would not have been able to understand any of Ibn al-'Arabi, because it's very hard to understand. It's very hard to understand and teach Ibn al-'Arabi, but Ibn al-'Arabi gave permission to me because I used my teacher's eyeglasses. I think Ibn al-'Arabi likes my teacher very much and because of this I understand [Ibn al-'Arabi].

A: There is an Ibn al-'Arabi scholar who says that all you need to do is get five of your friends who want to read Ibn al-'Arabi, and you get together in a group with the translations you can find. Then you will be guided by Ibn al-'Arabi. So this is kind of like learning by democracy. What's your opinion on this, how do you see this?

C: One should really be able to see Ibn al-'Arabi or any other great sufi [completed human being]. Without seeing the great sufi himself in reality and *really* seeing, you won't be able to understand their knowledge. So those who *really* see will have a very different experience.

[The people of] Turkey are very open and able to understand Ibn al-'Arabi. When Ibn al-'Arabi was going around the Ka'ba in Mecca, as he describes in his *Meccan Revelations*, the Prophet told Ibn al-'Arabi to go to Anatolia, because it was the only place where his knowledge could be understood. This is very interesting, because our NGO sponsored the first international symposium on Ibn al-'Arabi in Turkey. Even in Turkish households, people read Ibn al-'Arabi. Ottoman sultans knew about Ibn al-'Arabi.

A: This is shining a lot of light [on the subject]. Now please let me change the same question a little bit to focus on your students. Do you call the people that you teach students or seekers?

C: My beloveds.

A: Now that you're the teacher, do you teach them in the way that you learned or have you found different ways?

C: I thank you very much for your question. First of all a teacher should know that being a teacher doesn't mean anything for Allah. This is a job assigned like any other job is assigned in this world and such a job has no value, no validity, in the other world. I'm responsible for my own deeds and my own actions and for my own love of Allah. Since none of my students resemble each other, we call it personal guidance. In the general system they all have the same training, but when we talk privately it is personalized [lit. we actually behave differently]. Some students like strict teachers, some people like more flexible teachers.

A: Everyone's different. So it's a very personalised teaching. Everyone has her own perspective, created from the mind.

C: It's their perception of their own [version of] Allah. These perceptions are created in their minds. We're trying to make them get rid of these [mind] forms, these movies that they've created. We're trying to have them realize that Allah has this endless, limitless capacity.

In the oneness of being, there are people who are at the level of an eye or at the level of the heart, or the level of the intestines. And we're also letting them know that if there were no intestines, then the body wouldn't work.

A: There is a question that comes from one of the conversations that Shamsuddin Tabrizi had with Mevlana. [To paraphrase] Shams said, shaykhs are a dime a dozen, but where are the seekers like Mevlana?

C: My teachers have said that they have never had the pleasure of being a spiritual guide as they have had from being a seeker. It's more pleasing for me to be a seeker actually than being a spiritual guide. Allah says that each seeker should know that one should obey only those who don't ask anything in return. We don't expect anything from our students. We're just human beings; we have been inside and we just declare. The best gift I could be given is a student who knows how to feel thankful, grateful and a student who is not very badly influenced by what's happening [in the world].

A: What's the biggest obstacle for most seekers that prevents them from feeling this appreciation?

C: A student should be obedient with no doubt, and should trust. That's why I just wait or I make him wait when a seeker comes to me and says he is fully sure [that I am the right guide for him]. That may be true. I mean that a person may be on the path of Allah, but I may not be his or her spiritual guide. That seeker should be sure. That is the first thing. The second thing is submission. The submission is, God forbid, not to me. It is submitting to what I say that comes from Allah.

A: Abu Saʿid al-Kharraz [d. 899] once said that one who believes that God can be reached by human exertion will encounter endless torment and one who believes nearness to God can be attained without exertions will encounter an endless wishful dream.

C: It's true. Thank God I've been dealing with sufis for 40 to 45 years nearly and never have I been to a conference or gone to a lesson without working in advance. Yet I don't remember speaking from the things that I've worked on and studied. Working means praying to Allah, asking Allah to please talk through me. So without any effort you cannot reach Allah. The Prophet taught this in his ascension. The Prophet ascended through his own effort. His effort increased Allah's mercy and Allah descended towards him.

A: What is the relationship between the performing of the injunctions of Islam [the *sharia*], the sufi path and Reality? Are these concepts that you use in your teaching?

C: I'm not doing anything special, but we start out by saying that there is no sufi path without performing the sharia injunctions. Mevlana explains this very nicely. He says the Prophet led us to the way, and sometimes there were very, very dangerous risky places. So he first walked through and put out signs indicating not to enter this area and not to do this or that. This is sharia. He did it for us so we can be safe. We're just obeying. We're doing our ritual prayer. In our group there is not anyone who does not do the ritual prayer. I don't insist anyone do the ritual prayer. I don't force anyone to do it. But they start because, when they do ritual prayer, they know that they make me feel happy. It's also such a blessing for me. From my talks on TV I know that there are lots of people who started performing their ritual prayers. People have learned that praying ritual prayer is not something that is outside of life.

We're also performing the other pillars of Islam. We generally go once or twice on *'umra* [visiting Mecca and Medina outside of the pilgrimage season] every year. When I ask my children [students] if we should go to Edirne [a city close to Istanbul]. They say, 'Well, we don't have any way to get there.' Then I say, 'How about we all go on *'umra*?' They say, 'Well, OK.' [Laughter.] One of the things that really makes me very happy is that young people are so willing to go on *'umra*. We actually consider *'umra* not as a form of worship only, but also a journey of love.

What I like in my children most is that they have increased their voluntary worship practices. So they're trying to fight against their ego-self. But our group is trying to live actively in both the spiritual world and the material world. When there was this big earthquake in Adapazarı [17 August 1999], my students and I went there over the following year to help people. We had 75 tents there. After doing that we tried to go to a place to have lunch or dinner together in a very beautiful place, so that we could balance that negative energy with positive. Sharia is like the skin, the complexion of the body. If there were no sharia, no skin, then the flesh would not be preserved or protected. Without the sharia there would be no sufi path or realization of Reality.

A: What would you say, for the readers of this book, the goal of sufi practice is?

C: The goal is to wear or to acquire the character traits of Muhammad, because the character of the prophets is the character of God. So that's what we're trying to live. There are actually two things in sufism; one is prophetic revelation [*wahy* as opposed to non-prophetic inspiration *ilham*]. As you know, prophetic revelation is only for prophets, but my teacher actually commented on prophetic revelation – it is something that people perceive without the help of the five physical senses. You don't use those five senses. So the first step is Allah's touching someone. So that person revives, and

A: Wakes up!

C: Wakes up, exactly, yes wakes up. That is the first step. The second step is following the Prophetic example [sunna]. If we just stop at the place where we comprehend these things, then we wouldn't be able to have the character of Muhammad. So we should follow the sunna; we should be doing what the Prophet did and we shouldn't be doing what he didn't do. Otherwise we wouldn't be able to live a life of sufism.

A: What are the most important things about sufism that you have not mentioned that would be important for someone who doesn't know very much about sufism?

C: My teacher Kenan Rifa'i said that there are three different kinds of eyeglasses. The first one is the one that sees the mirror. Shortsighted and dimly lit politicians put on such glasses. So this is the pair of glasses that shows one as two, which is for cross-eyed people. The second type is the pair that I'm wearing. Notice how nice these are [touching her glasses].

A: Can I look through those? [Laughter.]

C: These are for those who wander in the other world and fly. The third one is the most advanced one, and that's the type that sees both together as one. When those who wear this third type of glasses look at this world, they ask whether Allah is content with him or her. So those who always wear such glasses are always in heaven.

A: You've worked reading the Qur'an over decades. There are also many who would like to learn something from the Qur'an, and so, without a teacher what can they do? You've already explained about the books and that one needs a teacher. Is there any hope for someone who can't find a teacher – specifically for the Qur'an?

C: It's a hard question. Of course the Qur'an cannot be learned without a spiritual guide, but there are those who directly meet with a guide and those who actually live the teachings of a spiritual guide. For example, many [non-Muslims] here in this world are acting according to the Muhammadan way, but they call themselves Christian. So, many are actually living like the Prophet or practising what he does in terms of knowledge, but they are not aware that their guide is the Prophet.

A: Thank you. Now, the last question that I have is about the future, but no one knows the future.

C: I know that I see the future, because Allah says that the deeds that you perform now are the outcomes of your past deeds. And the deeds that you will see in the future are the outcomes of what we do now. So if I know that, if I'm happy now, then I know that I will be happy in the future as well.

I'd like to add one more thing. The key to happiness is in heaven, you know, as Allah told us, but it's not the heaven that we think it is. Heaven is the place that consists of four different kinds of rivers: water, milk, wine and honey. Perhaps I might just drink water, because I did not like the other three. Then, when I heard about these things, I said I wouldn't want to go to heaven because I don't like the other three, I only like water. But then I learned that water means modesty or humbleness. Milk is Allah's knowledge. Wine means Allah's love. Honey is the unification of Allah. So if one person holds all those four, then that person is in heaven; that person is heaven himself. And if you can drink from these four rivers, then things get very easy. When I said easy and simple, I just remembered once [Sadruddin] Qunavi [the main successor to Ibn al-'Arabi] and Mevlana [Jalaluddin Rumi] met each other. Mevlana asked Qunavi how he could explain such a simple thing in such a difficult way. Qunavi asked Mevlana how he could explain such a difficult thing in such a simple way. Everything is simplicity actually.

Nahid Angha

Nahid Angha, Ph.D. (see fig. 7.2) is the co-director and co-founder of the International Association of Sufism (IAS), founder of the International Sufi Women Organization, the executive editor of the journal, *Sufism: An Inquiry* and the main representative of the IAS to the United Nations Department of Public Information, NGO section. An internationally published scholar, she is a sufi teacher, scholar and translator of sufi literature today, with over 15 published books. She has lectured throughout the world, including the UN, the Parliament of the World's Religions in Cape Town (1999) and Barcelona (2004), and at the Smithsonian Institution. She was among the distinguished Muslim leaders and scholars invited to gather for the first annual Shakir World Encounters, an Islamic conference of peace in Marrakech, Morocco, and is the first Muslim woman inducted to the Marin Women's Hall of Fame (Marin County, California). Her latest book is a translation of 'Abdullah Ansari's *One Hundred Fields*.

Interview with Nahid Angha (recorded 9 December 2010, San Rafael, California)

ARTHUR: So how did you become a teacher?

NAHID: I began in my twenties. My father [Shah Maqsud Sadiq 'Anqa, d. 1980, of the Uwaysi lineage], who was a sufi master, held his gatherings on Mondays and Thursdays. Thursdays were for men followers and Mondays were for women followers. After everyone had listened to him talk and had done some sufi meditation [*dhikr*], food was served to those present and also taken to be shared with the needy.

A: Where was this?

N: In Iran, first in Tehran. Then, in the mid-1970s, we moved to Sufiabad [the abode of sufis], a few miles north of Tehran, and gatherings were held there in his sufi lodge in Sufiabad, a big complex. It was in Tehran that my father asked and appointed me to teach women's Monday gatherings, and I continued in Sufiabad. On Mondays, my father used to teach first. Then he asked me to talk and share what I had learned from him.

A: What happened before you started to teach? There was a period before your twenties.

N: My father was open-minded. He never asked us [Nahid and her siblings] to become spiritual followers or anything. It was during my childhood, when I became very interested in 'what he knew'. He was generous in teaching me, encouraging me on my way and discussing such matters of importance in a language that I, a small child, could understand. Meditation became a part

FIGURE 7.2 Nahid Angha.

of my life from a very early age, so that the path of spirituality came to me very gently and smoothly. As I grew older and my teen years began, that yearning to know, to learn, to become did not stop. So I was born a sufi and I remained one.

A: Were there any kind of notable, spiritual experiences that transformed you in this early part of your life?

N: I used to sit at night and meditate, according to my father's instructions. During one of those nights, an unexpected spiritual opening, an unexplainable illumination, entered into my heart and transformed me entirely. It transformed my understanding of meditation. After that experience, I found a deeper longing in my heart and began to understand the notion of 'sufi love' as a fundamental principle, a longing that consumes and transforms one's entire being. It guides you towards the direction of unity. After that experience, I heard and understood my father's words and teachings differently. I remember asking myself why, because his teachings were exactly the same as before. It was I who had changed and transformed.

A: What kind of transformation happened through teaching? Because that was, all of a sudden, a whole new arena for you.

N: On the spiritual path, I see two roads emerging side by side. One road is the personal pursuit, your own heart's longing. The second is teaching, which is not only the heart's mission, but it also involves your mind and your intellectual ability. As an intellectual seeker, the teachings must make sense to you. So you study and expand your knowledge. Those teachings encourage you to become a traveller on the path, to begin your own personal spiritual and inner journey. It is here that your personal experience, if accurate, becomes a vehicle of transformation. It is here that your intellectual capability becomes confident in your heart's pursuit, and the two poles of love and logic find a common ground.

A: What does it mean to become more of a traveller?

N: Travellers journey towards a destination, according to a map, a knowledge that helps them to come closer to the desired destination. Many may take this journey towards understanding the divine reality, but not everyone becomes knowledgeable of the path, the direction and the goal. With every step you take, you know that there is much more that you don't know. Yet if your heart is set to learn, you will continue. If you are truthful in your quest, truth is what you will find.

A: When you were teaching on Mondays, how many women usually showed up?

N: There were about 100 when we lived in Tehran. Then it grew to about 300–400 people in Sufiabad. I continued teaching when we came to the United States, around the time of the revolution [in 1979]. We [Dr Kianfar and Nahid Angha] had our gatherings, and then we founded the International Association of Sufism [IAS].

A: How did that start?

N: It was the early 1980s that we, Dr Kianfar (my life's partner) and I, thought that it would be a great service for sufis around the world to come together. Why shouldn't sufis communicate with each other and all become a spiritual family? So we began a global effort to bring sufis together and the first international endeavour was the publication of the journal, *Sufism: An Inquiry*, in 1988.

A: This was before the internet.

N: Yes. IAS was founded in 1983, before global internet communications. We began classes and events, and the publication of *Sufism: An Inquiry*. We invited a great range of sufi scholars, artists, and leaders to send in their articles, essays, etc. Then I thought why not meet face to face, learn from each other, and start to establish a global spiritual family? That was the beginning of the Sufism Symposium in 1994.

A: Were Iranians the majority of your first students in the United States?

N: At the beginning many of the students were Iranians, with a few Americans. Then we began our teaching of American students in 1981, with a few Iranians. One of the good things I appreciate about American students is that they are honest in their quest; it is very refreshing. You don't need to deal with complexity; you are who you are. In the West I have found a certain eagerness and thirst for spirituality, even though Americans tend to expect spiritual development to be a quick process, which it is not.

A: When did the Sufi Women's Organization [SWO] come about?

N: The SWO came about one year before the Sufism Symposium in 1993. I asked sufi women to come together and create a sufi women's organization that supported and worked towards women's rights. One outcome of this effort manifested in the Sufi Symposium, when I ended up sitting in the centre circle of the *dhikr* session. The centre circle of the *dhikr* has always been reserved for men, but not women. Afterwards many people, including those leaders, appreciated my participation in that centre circle. In the following years we have always had women in the *dhikr* circle. I made sure that our sufi sisters and brothers stand side-by-side during the symposium. Through a respectful friendship, you can go a long way to change habits.

A: What are some other ways of doing things in a sufi way?

N: We have created different departments, projects and programmes. I became involved with interfaith movements and activities from the mid-1980s. IAS also became one of the recipients of the UNESCO's Culture of Peace and Non-Violence Award.

The practice of sufism is to serve, and share the blessings that one has received. If the service is whole-hearted and truthful, then one's service will become a worthwhile contribution and serve humanity. If it is not truthful, then perhaps it was meant to serve one's ego. In that case, serving one's ego is the outcome, nothing more.

Sufi psychology was another endeavour of IAS, promoting a dialogue between the ancient wisdom of sufism and the modern practice of Western psychology. Then we developed a sufi youth group called 'Voices for Justice' that became ambassadors for UNICEF. This group was devoted to the rights of children and contributed many services, including immunizations and after-school programmes.

A: Shifting gears a bit, what are the greatest obstacles to a student's progress on the sufi path?

N: The greatest obstacle is the overuse of mental faculties, our limited reasoning. What we are trying to understand is ultimate reality – whatever that reality means. To try to understand it through the limited mental faculty is an obstacle. You cannot explain something that is not explainable. You cannot go through the linear logic of one step at a time to understand something that has absolutely no beginning and no end. Sometimes, in our pursuit for spiritual understanding, we completely forget about the heart and even ignore it. We may think that everything is just like the hard drive of a computer, forgetting about the devotion of the one who has created that computer.

When we begin to discuss what is not explainable, we become philosophers; we debate. When the 'unexplainable' is expressed through the language of ideology and philosophy we take sides. Yet when the same 'unexplainable' is expressed through the language of poetry it mesmerizes us! What is this language of the heart that is universal? Our mental faculty is very much limited. Our logic and reasoning are mostly based on this limited mental faculty. It is a tool that cannot explain that which is outside of its limitations. It is here that heart, and thus the story of love, comes into the picture. What happens when you fall in love? What is that harmonious attraction? Even though science may tell us that our brain may act in certain ways when in love, still there must be something within the heart that communicates that emotion with our brain and affects the entire system. The Qur'an refers to 'the heart that sees'. So what is this heart?

A: So this is part of sufi practice.

N: Definitely *my* sufi practice. You have to locate the heart, the physical heart. We need to begin from there. That is all I have. My survival depends on the life of the heart and my quest is to understand how it can host my spiritual growth. How can it open a door towards understanding that reality, the reality that is entrusted to the human heart, according to Islam? It is worthwhile to go through long years of meditation to experience something similar to what those teachers, like the Prophet of Islam, have experienced. Revelation is not history; it is not something that happened to somebody else. It is an actual possibility. Spirituality or understanding divine reality is not a fantasy; it is not imagination. It is actual and factual. Some people are spiritual and some people are not. We cannot force people to become who they are not. We are unique in what and who we are. We see, hear and progress differently. There are possibilities, but nothing may be coerced. Everything works in harmony. Sometimes I think that I am a sufi because I was 'born into' sufism. I was born into an open space. Yet, the fact of the matter is that I 'was born' a sufi, being spiritual. Spirituality is woven in my entire being. If that longing were not born with me, then being born into a spiritual space would not have made me a sufi. It probably would have helped, but would not have me become a sufi.

A: Now, one of the chapters in the book is on sufism and politics. Do you have any thoughts on the relationship between sufism and politics?

N: Please tell me what you mean by politics, so we are on the same page.

A: I am conceiving of it as having power.

N: We like to be powerful and we follow power, no matter where it goes and how it is used. Power has charisma; it mesmerizes us. That being said, going back to the question of power and sufism, it all depends how power is used. Power itself is not a cause of corruption or a reason for valuable and ethical acts. How power is used changes it into something destructive or beneficial. So the moral question here is not the 'power' but the 'powerful'.

Let's think of 'prejudice'. It seems that prejudice and judgement are interlinked. We are creatures of judgement. Yet, as long as the judgement is not harmful to one's self and to other people, it is not harmful. As soon as it becomes harmful to you and to others it becomes prejudice. If prejudice does not benefit others, then who benefits from 'my' prejudice? If there is somebody who receives benefits from your (harmful) prejudice, then that somebody has the 'power'. The same reasoning may be applied to power. Power is not bad or good. We are the people who are seeking power and we like to equip ourselves with power. As soon as 'power' becomes harmful to you and other people, we have to ask if that power does not benefit the human family, then who benefits from this power? Whoever benefits from that power is not a friend to the human family. Honest and illuminated spiritual leaders will not demand blind obedience from their students. But if students desire to behave with blind obedience, then, according to the rule of harmony, those students receive what they desire! I have made a personal rule from the very beginning of my journey. If a teacher's authority does not benefit humanity and does not serve creation with humility, compassion and respect, that person is unable to lead me on the path of spiritual quest and towards understanding.

Nobody has the right to stop somebody from this journey. The road from the human being to that ultimate reality is a straight road. Nobody can stop any truthful seeker from that journey. The only one that can stop that road is oneself. So I have to take responsibility for everything that I do, whether I am in a state of power or I am in a state of powerlessness. I have to take responsibility and that is one of the missions of sufis. Sufis have been active in politics, served in governments and even ruled nations. Spiritual seekers meditate and reflect. At the same time they must serve, provide help and assistance, and share blessings with others. Whatever blessings you receive from this generous universe you have to share.

A: Yes. A more traditional way of looking at sufism involves a threefold schema: the injunctions of Islam (sharia), the sufi path and Reality. How are these related?

N: Well, there are many writings about and opinions regarding these terms. In my humble opinion, as you know, 'sharia' comes from *shar'*, which means road. A road connects you from one destination to another. Without a road we cannot embark on a journey. Sharia, the law, becomes the road. I am not talking about the laws of sharia that are made arbitrarily by people. Some set out a road for people that they themselves do not follow. I am talking about the teacher who actually began this story [Muhammad]. I am not talking about his followers. Sharia is like a highway. You have to go on this highway to arrive at a destination. The path is like signposts on the road, signs that you see. So sharia, the road and the signs, help me to stay on the road. They work together to bring me to Reality. Some people think that sharia is the only thing we need. Some people think that road signs are all that there is. Some people say there is only the Reality. If they do not work together ...

A: No one arrives at the destination.

N: I have seen some people who fall into following the injunctions of Islam [sharia] as if there were no tomorrow. Of course, there is the road, but you need to walk the road, you need to follow signs to make sure you arrive at your destination. I have seen people fall into the sufi path as if there were no road. There are people who say that there is only Reality. What does that mean? You have to start from somewhere in order to arrive at a destination in the human world. There is a destination, a road leads to that destination and there are signs on the road telling me if I am going towards the desired destination. All these three need to work together.

A: Now that you've mentioned arriving, what would you call the goal of sufism?

N: The goal of sufism is knowing and having an understanding of the reality of God or the Divine. I am not talking about the ultimate reality of God, because that is beyond human perception. When I am in the physical form with this mental faculty, I am in a four-dimensional world. When we talk about God we are talking about a reality that goes beyond those dimensions. Within the four-dimensional world, what we refer to as God is only God's attributes and not God's essence. The Essence has no definition. Any definition is limited. Yet within this existence or this universe of seen and unseen, I do exist and have occupied space and time. This space and time is entrusted to me. What an incredible generosity! I have to understand that which pertains to me and who is this 'I' that exists in space and time. In my understanding, the goal of sufism is to understand what is within and without, to understand this 'I' in its deepest and truest meaning.

Nothing is outside my being. In reality, outside does not exist. There is no other. Everything is within the seen and the unseen. So this reality is not going to just disappear because I am in a four-dimensional universe. I, as a spiritual traveller, need to shed away that which is not the very essence of this core and discover the self [the connecting point] that is connected to that ultimate Self. That is what religion, spirituality or whatever we call this endeavour, should offer me. Somebody else's knowledge may help me to find a way, but that knowledge does not belong to me. Those humble, knowledgeable and generous teachers are not telling us to become them, but teaching us to find our own way. Muhammad does not tell me to become Muhammad. He tells me that I too am capable of understanding and finding the way. This does not begin with religion, nor does it end with religion.

A: You've done many translations. I would like to ask you about your latest translation, especially since I arrived on the day when you got your first copies. In Persian, it is entitled *One Hundred Fields*. How did you come to choose this book [by 'Abdulla Ansari of Herat (d. 1088)] to translate?

N: When I was in my teens I began reading his *Intimate Prayers* and memorized it. I really like him. So this is a very short answer to why I translated *One Hundred Fields*.

A: Sometimes when people translate, particularly something of a sufi nature, sometimes they feel like they are actually in communication with the deceased author.

N: Yes, yes I believe so. I remember quite a long time ago when I was translating my grandfather's book. *From Eternity to Eternity*, when I came across one statement that did not make sense to me. I was stuck on just one sentence for almost two days. I did not want to continue translating before solving this puzzle! So one night (night times are my best time writing or translating) I was sitting and I thinking (and as if I was talking to him),

'What is this puzzling statement, I have no idea what you are saying.' And, to my surprise, I had an experience as if someone was reading that very sentence to me, in a tone that I could understand. A voice actually read that statement in a way that I could understand. So the puzzle was solved. Once, when I was a teenager, I asked my father, 'Can I hear the voice of the Prophet?' He said, 'Nothing in this universe disappears; you have to develop a harmonious tool for understanding.' Nothing vanishes in this world.

A: What about the future of sufism. I know none of us can see the future, but how do you see sufism manifesting in a way suitable for the modern world or the post-modern world?

N: I personally think that organized and institutional religion is losing ground. The younger generation is not very attracted to the old and punishing figures in religion. Dogmatic religion is limiting and demanding. Religion is power and so many things that have nothing to do with the ordinary human. Nowadays, we talk about 'spirituality', but not so much about 'religion', however, the mysticisms of religions are somehow more appealing. They are personal and honour individual human beings. They celebrate a person. I actually see and have great hopes for sufism. It is expanding. Rumi is becoming one of the most read poets in the West. These teachers tell us about the beauty of nature, of the endurance of human heart, of the divine presence in everything and of the value of human life. Their teachings spring from their own hearts and touch the hearts of their readers, students and beyond.

AFTERWORD:
FUTURE SCENARIOS FOR
SUFI PRACTICE – GUESSES
FOR THE TWENTY-FIRST
CENTURY

BEFORE EVEN LOOKING in the direction of the future, let's look briefly at the past history of changes in sufism. At the outer, institutional level, we have seen small informal groups developing into lineages to become institutionalized in sufi lodges. In the modern period there are significantly fewer sufi lodges in many places in the world (e.g. Turkey and the Arab world), as sufi practice occurs in more informal groups, adapting to structural changes in society. Yet in places like Pakistan, some sufi lodges are thriving more and more. It has always amazed me how the lodge complex had expanded each time I visited Mubarak Sahib's sufi lodge in Khyber Pakhtunkhwa (1986–2000). Increasing donations to the shaykh fuelled much of this visible change. Other colleagues around the world report similar developments. All it takes is a rich donor and the sufi shaykh has a beautiful house and 'retreat centre', the modern name for a sufi lodge. Turkish Naqshbandi groups are expanding globally through educational institutions funded by business conglomerates in Turkey.

Women will continue to have more prominence in sufi activity. In other cultural contexts, there will be more discreet manifestations of sufism, each led by a qualified master who manages to create a spiritual family. Visibility may be a low-profile internet site – though there are already numerous high-profile sufi sites. All this diverse institutional activity is happening now and is likely to continue, adapting to increasingly changing circumstances – a rate of change so fast that the now is the past.

Sufi shrine activity will continue to flourish. One cannot assume that changing from agricultural to industrial/information production (modernizing) will necessarily influence more people to adopt a scientific–materialist worldview. Forcing ideas that originate outside the culture – whether modernist Islamic ideas or scientific–materialist – does not work well, because shrine practices can be very ingrained in cultures. For example, the Soviet colonization of Central Asia did little to reduce activities around sufi shrines – especially for women, who communicated the value of these traditional practices to their children. Economic development over a few more generations could gradually change the contour of sufi shrine activities – or not. It depends on the culture – in Japan, shrines are doing quite well. People from all socio-economic strata of Indo-Pakistani society visit sufi shrines, including those who have had the best English-medium education. On the other hand, modernist/fundamentalist Islamic groups will continue to declare shrine visitation un-Islamic. As I am writing this (mid-2014), violent fringes of these modernist groups are bombing sufi shrines in Mali and Pakistan. One counter move is the large sums of money flowing out of Turkey to upgrade shrines around the Islamic world and in some Central Asian cases to lavishly restore them. Expect to see sufi shrines attracting the pious for the rest of your life.

Sufi practice is always a work in progress, because an effective shaykh and sincere seekers are also works in progress. In Muslim majority countries, many shaykhs have discontinued the use of musical instruments, perhaps because of the modernist/fundamentalist critiques of sufism. Sufism has survived Soviet and Turkish attempts to eliminate it, but those clumsy attempts have arguably made sufi practice stronger. What better way to promote something than to make it forbidden? The modernist/fundamentalist currents in Islam are potentially much more 'game changing', because they claim Islamic legitimacy in their denial of sufi practice. Making sufi practice non-Islamic trivializes it in a way that parallels the effects of a scientific-materialist education, which is now a middle-class worldwide phenomenon. Depending on the culture, sufi practice could be put even more on the defensive, because these modernist versions of Islam have an appeal to people overloaded by rapid change, such as villagers moving to cities. There is not enough data to spot a trend yet. When will the tipping point happen, to expose the flatland perspectives of scientific materialism, or the heartless form of modernist Islam funded by the Saudis that has been reduced to blindly following rules? It may happen sooner than we think. Sufi masters have found ways to facilitate ego training for a millennium. With that track record, it is likely that for the rest of your lifetime they will continue to do so.

The future will be radically different from anything people can imagine now. The ego-based focus on control – and therefore exploitation – of the environment, together with the focus on scientific and technological development – treating people as replaceable economic units – has produced a technological wonderland and increased life expectancy. This makes the scientific–materialist worldview an increasingly attractive ego option in the twenty-first century. Consider the X-Men films, comic-book superheroes with superpowers, and science-fiction accounts, ranging from gene-enhanced human capabilities to a post-human species (enter transhumanism). Soon we will be able to personalize these ego options to a greater and greater degree. There is little in mainstream culture, at least in economically developed countries, that promotes superhuman compassion, generosity and love for all sentient beings.

The increasing presence of virtual realities will not enhance these heart qualities either. The digital realm is the playground of control and manipulation, cleverly designed to work on satisfying our egos – you have 390 friend requests on Facebook today. When I look around, in New Zealand, it seems that more and more people's experience is shifting from physical reality to virtual reality. Preliminary studies show that our brains are becoming reconfigured as a result of our interfacing with digital/virtual realities. This is not likely to enhance conscious evolution in any kind of contemplative practice. If anything it will be another obstacle. Surfing the net, for example, is great for increasing the information going into our working memory, but it creates an exponential increase in cognitive load, which directly amplifies the distractedness we experience. Antonio Damasio has shown that the more distracted we become, the less able we are able to experience empathy and compassion.[1] Digital devices encourage multitasking, which is not only inefficient, but for most people it further destroys concentration. Just as the increasing use of machines has made humans more machine-like, humans adapting to digital realities will change accordingly. None of these changes appear to enhance people's greater self-knowledge or their SQ (spiritual quotient).

As Einstein noted, 'We cannot solve our problems with the same level of thinking that created them.' It amazes me that books dealing with global crises, climate change, population growth, distribution of wealth and proliferation of weapons, for example, never take into account this astute observation. There is very little concern about increasing awareness, so that people can consciously evolve out of the problems they have created.[2] The sufi shrines will be there, the sufi shaykhas will be there, but with more and more digital zombies and the exponential explosion of ego-attractors, where will the seekers be? The Infinite Context trumps all these silly games. Rumi articulates the human need to return to the Source. Even though one can temporarily divert this deep river of human existence and try to dam it up, eventually it reaches the ocean. It may even appear that the river has dried up, but eventually all the water does get to the ocean – look up at the clouds.

Last but not least, I am hoping that future developments will force sufi shaykhs out of their small isolated groups (no matter how many followers they have and how globalized they may appear) and academics out of their materialist disciplinary silos.[3] Neither sufis nor academics seem to be interested in our common human transpersonal developmental processes and the effectiveness of the methodology used – the transformative contemplative practices. With such apathy, we are far from even formulating a vocabulary of transpersonal development *that can be communicated cross-culturally to others*. Much to my dismay, the organized study of these methodologies has hardly begun. Sufis do not seem to be interested in talking about the dynamics of transformative practice with other sufis, much less academics. They, too often, uncritically replicate the practices that maybe worked in another time and place.

The overwhelming majority of scholars engaged in transpersonal psychology (as few as they are) do their work philosophizing in armchairs, without meaningfully engaging with contemplatives.[4] It was only in 2011 that scholars in the study of religion started to formally consider contemplative practice as an area of study. In the sufi case, one first step is to forge a common language to discuss sufi experience and practice in each sufi lineage. The second step is to understand how these practices work and why certain methods are superior to others. In the academic case, it is time to expose the cognocentrism (the narrowness of our cognitive experience) in academic studies and put it in the same bin as ethnocentrism (the narrowness of cultural experience).[5] How hard is it to imagine accelerating an increase in human awareness? I am reminded of the disparate systems of alchemy before the discipline of chemistry evolved, with one common table of elements and an articulation of how chemical processes worked. No wonder enlightenment is still an accident at the beginning of the twenty-first century. Not to worry. Recognizing sufism is tasting the nectar of the heart. Only the dominating ego stands between each of us and that nectar.

NOTES

Preface

1 For a short autobiography, see Annemarie Schimmel, 'A Life of Learning' (ACLS Occasional Paper no. 21, 1993). Available at www.acls.org/Publications/OP/Haskins/1993_AnnemarieSchimmel.pdf (accessed 26 October 2015).

2 The word 'ego' in this book means what Freud meant by the word *Ichheit*, namely 'I-ness'. The psychological identification with this I-ness, instead of our innate being, has much to do with our human suffering.

3 Carl Ernst, 'Sufism: History, Politics and Culture', *Sufi: Journal of Mystical Philosophy and Practice* (Winter 2014), p. 34.

Introduction: Sufism, Sufis and Transformation

1 Barry Windsor-Smith, *Opus, Volume Two* (Seattle, WA: Fantagraphics Books Inc., 2000), p. 21.

2 Walter Percy, *Lost in the Cosmos* (New York, NY: Farrar, Straus and Giroux, 1983), p. 7.

3 Though sufi texts often refer to this as a hadith, hadith specialists consider it to be a saying. For Ibn al-'Arabi's understandings of this phrase, see William C. Chittick, *The Sufi Path of Knowledge* (Albany, NY: State University of New York Press, 1989), pp. 344–6.

4 Alan Watts, *The Book: On the Taboo Against Knowing Who You Are* (New York: Vintage Books, 1989).

5 Warmly communicated to me by Shabda Kahn, a student of Sam Lewis (12 November 2012).

6 Carl W. Ernst, *Shambhala Guide to Sufism* (Boston, MA: Shambhala Publications, 1997), p. 1.

7 Ibid., pp. 8–18.

8 Annemarie Schimmel, *Mystical Dimensions of Islam* (Chapel Hill, NC: University of North Carolina Press, 1975), p. 31

9 Georges de Hongrie, *Des Turcs: Traité sur les moeurs, les coutumes et la perfidie des Turcs*, translated from Latin by Joël Schnapp (Toulouse, France: Anarcharsis Éditions, 2007), pp. 170–1. Thierry Zarcone kindly brought this to my attention.

10   Ahmet T. Karamustafa, *Sufism: The Formative Period* (Edinburgh: Edinburgh University Press, 2007), p. 51.

11   Kenneth Lee Honerkamp, 'Sufi foundations of the ethics of social life in Islam', in Virginia Gray Henry-Blakemore (ed.), *Voices of Islam*, 5 vols. (Westport, CT: Praeger Publishers, 2007), 3:182.

12   Arthur F. Buehler, *Revealed Grace: The Juristic Sufism of Ahmad Sirhindi (1564–1624)* (Louisville, KY: Fons Vitae, 2011), p. 227.

13   Honerkamp, 'Sufi foundations', 3:183.

14   William James, *A Pluralistic Universe*, ed. Fredson Bowers (Cambridge, MA: Harvard University Press, 1977), pp. 299–300.

15   Personal communication (20 December 2012).

16   Thomas Kuhn, *The Structure of Scientific Revolutions* (Chicago: University of Chicago Press, 1996).

17   On Majlis Dhikr, see Arif Zamhari, *Rituals of Islamic Spirituality: A Study of Majlis Dhikr Groups in East Java* (Canberra, Australia: ANU E Press, 2000).

18   Julia Day Howell, 'Urban heirs of Ibn al-'Arabi and the defence of religious pluralism in Indonesia', *Australian Religious Studies Review*, 18/2 (2005), pp. 201–4 [197–209]. Professor Howell kindly sent me a copy of this informative article.

19   Julia Day Howell, 'Sufism and Neo-Sufism in Indonesia today', *Review of Indonesian and Malaysian Affairs*, 46/2 (2012), pp. 10–11 [1–24]; and for ICNIS see her article, 'Sufism and the Indonesian Islamic revival', *The Journal of Asian Studies*, 60/3 (Aug., 2001), pp. 720–1 [701–29].

20   Zamhari, *Rituals of Islamic Spirituality*, pp. 17–20.

21   'Ali b. 'Uthman al-Hujwiri, *The Kashf al-Mahjub: The Oldest Persian Treatise on Sufism*, trans. Reynold A. Nicholson (London: Luzac, 1911), p. 44.

22   Carl W. Ernst and Bruce B. Lawrence, *Sufi Martyrs of Love* (New York: Palgrave, 2002), p. 13.

23   Paraphrasing Zen teacher Robert Aitken (d. 2010), 'Enlightenment is an accident, but practice makes you accident prone.' This expression appears to be falsely attributed to Shunryu Suzuki, Richard Baker, and other Zen teachers. See Crooked Cucumber: The Life and Zen Teaching of Shunryu Suzuki (8-07-13). Available at http://www.cuke.com/Cucumber%20Project/other/dc/dc-on-sr.htm (accessed 12 December 2014).

24   For one of the latest, though not necessarily reliable, accounts of Shah, see Yannis Toussulis, *Sufism and the Way of Blame: Hidden Sources of a Sacred Psychology* (Wheaton, IL: Quest Books, 2011), pp. 53–68. The classic exposé on Castaneda is Richard de Mille, *Castaneda's Journey: The Power and the Allegory* (Santa Barbara, CA: Capra Press, 1976).

25   Irina Tweedie, *Daughter of Fire: A Diary of a Spiritual Training with a Sufi Master* (Point Reyes, CA: Golden Sufi Center, 1995).

26   Muslim ibn al-Hajjaj, *Sahih Muslim*, trans. Nasiruddin al-Khattab, 7 vols. (Riyadh: Dar al-Salam, 2007), 6:432, no. 6542.

1 Qur'an, Transformative practices and the Discipline of Sufism: 700–1000

1   Martin Nguyen, *Sufi Master and Qur'an Scholar: Abu'l-Qasim al-Qushayri and the Lata'if al-Isharat* (Oxford: Oxford University Press, 2012), p. 123 (slightly reworded).

2   Arthur F. Buehler, *Sufi Heirs of the Prophet: The Indian Naqshbandiyya and the Rise of the Mediating Shaykh* (Columbia, SC: University of South Carolina Press, 1998), p. 6.

3 Nguyen, *Sufi Master*, p. 58 (comments in square brackets in original).
4 Paul Nwyia, *Exégèse coranique et langage mystique. Nouvel essai sur le lexique technique des mystiques musulmans* (Beirut: Dar al-Machreq, 1970), p. 358. One also has to consider that he did not suffer persecution because his sufi companions did not share in writing what he had said until he had passed away.
5 Louis Massignon, *Essay on the Origins of the Technical Language of Islamic Mysticism*, trans. Benjamin Clark (Notre Dame, IN: University of Notre Dame Press, 1997), p. 108.
6 Ibid.
7 Ibid.
8 Ask a Chinese person to point where the locus of the mind is located and she will point to the heart.
9 Leah Kinberg, 'What is Meant by *Zuhd*?', *Studia Islamica* 61 (1985), p. 30 [27–44]. The word *nafs* has been loosely translated as 'soul', but it is more accurate to translate it as 'ego-self', which I have substituted in the text to avoid confusion.
10 Ibid., p. 34.
11 Ibid., p. 31.
12 Ibid., p. 38.
13 Ibid., p. 41.
14 Annemarie Schimmel, *Mystical Dimensions of Islam* (Chapel Hill, NC: University of North Carolina Press, 1975), pp. 38, 53.
15 Nguyen, *Sufi Master*, p. 127.
16 Jacqueline Chabbi, 'Remarques sur le développement historique des mouvements ascétiques et mystiques au Khurasan: IIIe/IXe siècle–IVe/Xe siècle', *Studia Islamica*, 46 (1977), p. 54 [5–72].
17 Ahmet T. Karamustafa, *Sufism: The Formative Period* (Edinburgh: Edinburgh University Press, 2007), p. 65.
18 Ibid., p. 64.
19 Chabbi, 'Remarques sur le développement historique', p. 64. She does not specify which of Hakim Tirmidhi's publications she used to obtain these figures – yet another historical fragment in isolation.
20 Suleiman Mourad, *Early Islam between Myth and History: Al-Hasan al-Basri (d. 110H/728CE) and the Formation of his Legacy in Classical Islamic Scholarship* (Leiden: Brill, 2006), p. 67.
21 Massignon, *Essay on the Origins*, pp. 132–3.
22 Mourad, *Early Islam*, p. 66.
23 Massignon, *Essay on the Origins*, p. 132.
24 Mourad, *Early Islam*, p. 120.
25 Schimmel, *Mystical Dimensions*, p. 37.
26 Massignon, *Essay on the Origins*, p. 172.
27 Ibid., pp. 144–5. 'His' and 'He' in all quoted material is replaced by 'God's' and 'God'.
28 Alexander Knysh, *Islamic Mysticism: A Short History* (Leiden: Brill, 2000), p. 41.
29 Schimmel, *Mystical Dimensions*, p. 45.
30 Ibid., p. 44.
31 Gavin Picken, *Spiritual Purification in Islam: The Life and Works of Muhāsibī* (New York: Routledge, 2011), p. 192.
32 Michael Sells, *Early Islamic Mysticism* (Mahwah, NJ: Paulist Press, 1996), p. 112.
33 Ibid., p. 255.
34 Massignon, *Essay on the Origins*, p. 185.
35 Ibid., p. 186.

36 Ibid., p. 188.
37 Ibid., p. 34, fn 1.
38 Nasr Hamid Abu Zayd, 'Towards understanding the Qur'an's worldview', in Gabriel Said Reynolds (ed.), *New Perspectives on the Qur'ān: The Qur'ān in its Historical Context 2* (Oxford: Routledge, 2011), p. 51 [47–87].
39 Massignon, *Essay on the Origins*, pp. 34–6.
40 Farhana Mayer (trans.), *Spiritual Gems: The Mystical Qur'an Commentary Ascribed to Ja'far al-Sadiq as Contained in Sulami's Haqaiq al-Tafsir from the Text of Paul Nwyia* (Louisville, KY: Fons Vitae, 2011), p. 66.
41 Ibid., p. 49.
42 Gerhard Böwering, *The Mystical Vision of Existence in Classical Islam: The Qur'ānic Hermeneutics of the Ṣūfī Sahl At-Tustarī (d. 283/896)* (New York: Walter de Gruyter, 1980), p. 49.
43 Ibid., p. 136.
44 Sahl b. 'Abd Allāh al-Tustari, *Tafsīr al-Tustarī*, trans. Annabel and Ali Keeler (Louisville, KY: Fons Vitae, 2011), p. xxviii. I have taken out all the transliteration of Arabic words in parenthesis whenever quoting this source.
45 Ibid., p. 241 (italics added).
46 Ibid., p. 161.
47 Ibid., p. 199.
48 Jalaluddin Rumi, see A. J. Arberry (trans.), *The Discourses of Rumi* (London: Curzon Press, 1993), p. 22.
49 See Qur'an 6:125, 39:22, and 94:1 – all variations of *sharh al-sadr*.
50 Louis Massignon, *The Passion of al-Hallāj: Mystic and Martyr of Islam*, trans. Herbert Mason, trans., 4 vols. (Princeton: Princeton University Press, 1982): 3:16–17.
51 Knysh, *Islamic Mysticism*, p. 62.
52 See Rkia E. Cornell (trans.), *Early Sufi Women: Dhikr an-niswa al-muta 'abbidat as-sufiyyat* (Louisville, KY: Fons Vitae, 1999).
53 Sells, *Early Islamic Mysticism*, p. 162.
54 Schimmel, *Mystical Dimensions*, pp. 38–9.
55 Ibid., p. 51.
56 Knysh, *Islamic Mysticism*, p. 61.
57 Massignon, *The Passion of al-Hallāj*, 3:25.
58 Paul Nwyia, *Exégèse coranique*, p. 237.
59 Karamustafa, *Sufism*, p. 67. There is also an appendix in this book defining 155 sufi terms.
60 Often misspelled as Kalabadhi. See Anon., *'Ilm at-tasawwuf*, ed., Nasrollah Pourjavady and Mohammed Soori (Tehran: Iranian Institute of Philosophy, 2012), p. 5 in English introduction.
61 Knysh, *Islamic Mysticism*, p. 121.
62 Karamustafa, *Sufism*, p. 95.
63 Haydar Amuli, *Jilwah-i dildar: tarjamah-i Jami' al-asrar wa-manba' al-anwar*, translated from the Arabic by Yusuf Ibrahimian Amuli (Tehran: Nashr-i Risanish, 2009), p. 138, in Buehler, *Sufi Heirs*, p. 82 (without bibliographic attribution and mistranslated). This phrase is also attributed to Baha'uddin Naqshband (d. 1389), the founder-figure of the Naqshbandi sufi lineage.
64 Karamustafa, *Sufism*, p. 98.
65 Ibid., p. 102.
66 Some of his *Enlivening the Religious Sciences* has been translated into English.

2 Institutionalization of Sufi Practice

1   Arthur F. Buehler, *Sufi Heirs of the Prophet: The Indian Naqshbandiyya and the Rise of the Mediating Shaykh* (Columbia, SC: University of South Carolina Press, 1998), p. 29.

2   Vincent Crapanzano, *The Hamadsha: A Study in Moroccan Ethnopsychiatry* (Berkeley, CA: University of California Press, 1981), p. 179.

3   Richard W. Bulliet, *Conversion to Islam in the Medieval Period: An Essay in Quantitative History* (Cambridge, MA: Harvard University Press, 1979).

4   Mir Khurd, *Siyar al-awliya'* (Delhi: Muhibb-i Hind Press, 1885), p. 338, cited in M. Mujeeb, *The Indian Muslims* (London: George Allen and Unwin, 1967), p. 125.

5   Devin DeWeese, 'The legitimization of Bahā ad-Dīn Naqshband', *Asiatische Studien* 50/2 (2006), p. 267 [261–305].

6   See the quotation by Mirza Mazhar Jan-i Janan in Buehler, *Sufi Heirs*, pp. 16–17.

7   Valerie J. Hoffman, *Sufism, Mystics, and Saints in Modern Egypt* (Columbia, SC: University of South Carolina Press, 1995).

8   One exception is the Mevlevi lineage, which has been historically an 'order' with the grandshaykh in Konya, Turkey, administering a centralized organization appointing shaykhs to head Mevlevi lodges throughout the Ottoman Empire. Thierry Zarcone kindly confirmed this information for me.

9   Devin DeWeese, 'Spiritual practice and corporate identity in medieval sufi communities of Iran, Central Asia, and India: The Khalvatī/'Ishqī/Shaṭṭārī continuum', in Steven E. Lindquist (ed.), *Religion and Identity in South Asia and Beyond: Essays in Honor of Patrick Olivelle* (London: Anthem Press, 2011), pp. 252–99.

10 Ahmad Sirhindi has cogently explained that this authority over other sufi shaykhs was only for the sufis of 'Abdulqadir's time. See Arthur F. Buehler, *Revealed Grace: The Juristic Sufism of Ahmad Sirhindi (1564–1624)* (Louisville, KY: Fons Vitae, 2011), Letter 1:293.

11 Erik S. Ohlander, *Sufism in an Age of Transition: 'Umar al-Suhrawardi and the Rise of the Islamic Mystical Brotherhoods* (Leiden: Brill, 2008), p. 27 (hijri dates omitted in quote).

12 Ibid., p. 142.

13 Ibid., p. 147. (Arabic transliterations omitted).

14 Ibid., p. 189. (Arabic transliterations omitted).

15 Ibid.

16 Ibid., p. 311.

17 Ibid., p. 314.

18 Carl W. Ernst and Bruce B. Lawrence, *Sufi Martyrs of Love* (New York: Palgrave, 2002), p. 28.

19 Butrus Abu-Manneh, 'Khalwa and Râbita in the Khâlidî Suborder', in Marc Gaborieau, Alexandre Popovic and Thierry Zarcone (eds), *Naqshbandis: cheminements et situation actuelle d'un ordre mystique musulman* (Istanbul/Paris: Éditions Isis, 1990), pp. 291–3.

20 Shortened and paraphrased from Devin DeWeese, 'Succession protocols and the Early Khwajagani Schism in the *Maslak al-ārifīn*', *Journal of Islamic Studies* 22/1 (2011), pp. 25–6 [1–35].

21 Buehler, *Sufi Heirs*, pp. 44–5.

22 Victor Turner, *The Ritual Process: Structure and Anti-Structure* (Ithaca, NY: Cornell University Press, 1977).

23 Buehler, *Sufi Heirs*, pp. 51–2.

24 Muhammad Ibn-i Munawwar, *The Secrets of God's Mystical Oneness*, trans. John O'Kane (Costa Mesa, CA: Mazda Publishers, 1992), p. 493.

25 Paraphrased from Rashida Chih, 'What is a sufi order? Revisiting the concept through a

case study of the Khalwatiyya in contemporary Egypt', in Martin van Bruinessen and Julia Howell (eds), *Sufism and the 'Modern' in Islam* (London: I.B.Tauris, 2007), pp. 29–30 [21–38]. The existence of contemplative practices and transformational processes was not a concern for this author.

26 Ahmet T. Karamustafa, *God's Unruly Friends: Dervish Groups in the Islamic Later Middle Period, 1200–1550* (London: Oneworld, 2006), pp. 90–2.

27 Abu 'Abd al-Rahman al-Sulami, *A Collection of Sufi Rules of Conduct*, trans. Elena Biagi (Cambridge: Islamic Texts Society, 2010), p. 6.

3 Sufi Shrines: Down-to-earth, Day-to-day, Devotional Sufism for the Masses

1 Joseph Chelhod, 'La *baraka* chez les Arabes', *Revue de l'Histoire des Religions* 148/1 (1955), pp. 68–88.

2 For those unfamiliar with the 'evil eye', take a look at Rupert Sheldrake's *The Sense of Being Stared At: And Other Unexplained Powers of Human Minds* (Rochester, VT: Park Street Press, 2013).

3 See Ubaidullah Baig and A. A. K. Brohi, *Journey into Light: An Instant Guide to Devotional Tours* (Islamabad: Pakistan Tourism Development Corporation, 1985).

4 My heartfelt thanks go to Pak Bambang, then in Malang, who kindly invited me to participate in that incredible experience, and to my fellow pilgrims.

5 For insights concerning these modernist/Wahhabi groups see Khalid M. Abou El-Fadl, *The Great Theft: Wrestling Islam from the Extremists* (San Francisco: HarperCollins, 2005). The idea that the Prophet is dead contradicts what Muslims say in prayer many times a day, *'as-salamu 'alayka ya ayyuha an-nabi'*. The construct *'ya ayyuha'* in Arabic can only be used if a person is present.

6 Related by Anas b. Malik in Ibn Hajar's *Fath al-bari* 6:487; and Abu Da'ud, *Kitab al-manasik* #1745 respectively.

7 John J. Curry, *The Transformation of Muslim Mystical Thought in the Ottoman Empire: The Rise of the Halveti Order, 1350–1650* (Edinburgh: Edinburgh University Press, 2010), p. 230.

8 Ibid.

9 Jürgen Wasim Frembgen, *At the Shrine of the Red Sufi: Five Days and Nights on Pilgrimage in Pakistan* (Oxford: Oxford University Press, 2012), p. 52.

10 Ibid., p. 91.

11 Huub de Jonge, 'Pilgrimages and local Islam on Java', *Studia Islamika* 5/2 (1998), p. 6 [1–25].

12 I kindly thank the anonymous reviewer who provided this clarification.

13 The detailed information of shrines in the former Soviet Union is kindly provided by Michael Kemper, personal communication (25 February 2014).

14 Philip Lewis, *Pirs, Shrines and Pakistani Islam* (Rawalpindi: Christian Study Centre, 1985), pp. 11 and 19. Lewis writes about the 'shaykh' and 'disciples', which is probably the terminology used by the people at the shrine. I prefer to use the terms 'head custodian' and 'devotee' until there is evidence of transformative practice. In *Sufi Heirs*, I used the term 'mediating shaykh' for a person like the grandson of Mihr 'Ali Shah.

15 Ibid., p. 13.

16 Jamal J. Elias, *On Wings of Diesel: Trucks, Identity and Culture in Pakistan* (London: Oneworld Publications, 2011), p. 29.

17 Lewis, *Pirs, Shrines*, p. 14.
18 Ibid., p. 34.
19 Ibid., p. 183.
20 This passage is from an earlier version, edited to make it more readable. For the current rendition see http://khawajagharibnawaz.com/VowsMannat.html (accessed 27 Jan 2014), supposedly from the head custodian of the shrine. Inclusion in this volume does not imply endorsement of this fundraising website.
21 Kumkum Srivastava, *The Wandering Sufis: Qalandars and Their Path* (New Delhi: Aryan Books International, 2009). This research and the work done by Jamhari on Indonesian shrines in the following section clearly show both anthropologists to be more than casual visitors. In addition, they took the time to talk to visitors over a period of time and quoted them in their research. Both of these studies are refreshingly uncluttered by postmodern theoretical nonsense, which is a lot easier to concoct in a comfortable armchair than doing time-consuming fieldwork.
22 Ibid., pp. 124–5.
23 Ibid., pp. 178–9.
24 Ibid., p. 183.
25 Ibid., p. 187.
26 Ibid., p. 194
27 Ibid., pp. 196–7.
28 Ibid., p. 228.
29 James J. Fox, 'Wali: the first preachers of Islam in Java', in James J. Fox (ed.), *Indonesian Heritage*, 10 vols. (Singapore: Archipelago Press, 1996–8): 9:18–19.
30 Jamhari, 'The meaning interpreted: The concept of *Barakah* in *Ziarah*', *Studia Islamika* 8/1 (2001), p. 114 [87–128].
31 Ibid., p. 115.
32 Ibid., pp. 92–6.
33 Jamhari, 'In the center of meaning: *Ziarah* tradition in Java', *Studia Islamika* 7/1 (2000), p. 69 [54–90].
34 Ibid., pp. 70–3.
35 Ibid., p. 84.
36 Ibid.
37 Ibid.
38 Only some of these will be discussed here. Amira Mittermaier, '(Re)imagining space, dreams and saint shrines in Egypt', in Georg Stauth and Samuli Schielke (eds), *Dimensions of Locality: Muslim Saints, their Place and Space* (London: Transaction Publishers, 2008), p. 53 [47–66].
39 In the case of the Mutwalli shrine there are conflicting dream stories (the shaykh appeared to Mutwalli's son), but stories involving presidents demonstrate the power of righteousness over worldly power. Ibid., pp. 54–5.
40 Ahmed A. Zayed, 'Saints (*awliya*), public places and modernity in Egypt', in Georg Stauth and Samuli Schielke (eds), *Dimensions of Locality: Muslim Saints, their Place and Space* (London: Transaction Publishers, 2008), p. 115 [103–23].
41 Also documented in Afghanistan, see M. Homayun Sidky, 'Malang, Sufis, and Mystics: An ethnographic and historical study of Shamanism in Afghanistan', *Asian Folklore Studies* 49/2 (1990), pp. 275–301. Shamim Homayun kindly brought this to my attention.
42 Ibid., p. 119.
43 Ibid., pp. 119–121.

4 SUFI AUTHORITY AND POLITICS

1   Itzchak Weismann, *Taste of Modernity: Sufism, Salafiyya, and Arabism in Late Ottoman Damascus* (Leiden: Brill, 2001), p. 197. This situation is common. Ahmad Sirhindi had a hereditary link through his father and the Chishti lineage, but it was not until he met his Naqshbandi shaykh that he went through ego-transforming sufi training.

2   Nile Green, *Sufism: A Global History* (New York: Wiley-Blackwell, 2012), pp. 94–6.

3   Erik S. Ohlander, *Sufism in an Age of Transition: 'Umar al-Suhrawardi and the Rise of the Islamic Mystical Brotherhoods* (Leiden: Brill, 2008), p. 87.

4   Arthur F. Buehler, *Sufi Heirs of the Prophet: The Indian Naqshbandiyya and the Rise of the Mediating Shaykh* (Columbia, SC: University of South Carolina Press, 1998), p. 71.

5   Cheikh Anta Babou, *Fighting the Greater Jihad: Amadu Bamba and the Founding of the Muridiyya of Senegal, 1853–1913* (Athens, OH: Ohio University Press, 2007), pp. 105–50.

6   For a detailed description of the British perceptions of Pir Pagaro and his Hurrs, see Peter Mayne, *Saints of Sind* (London: J. Murray, 1956).

7   *The Pakistani Times*, 15 March 1974, cited in Philip Lewis, *Pirs, Shrines and Pakistani Islam* (Rawalpindi: Christian Study Centre, 1985), p. 53.

8   *The Pakistani Times*, 23 September 1980, cited in Lewis, *Pirs, Shrines*, p. 54.

9   E. Melek Cevahiroğlu Ömür, 'The sufi orders in a modernizing Empire: 1808–1876', *Tarih* 1/1 (2009), p. 81 [70–93].

10   Ibid., p. 84.

11   See Michael Kemper, *Studying Islam in the Soviet Union* (Amsterdam: Amsterdam University Press, 2009), pp. 8–9, 12 [1–27]. The latter quote is from Alexandre Bennigsen and Marie Broxup, *The Islamic Threat to the Soviet State* (London: Taylor and Francis, 1983), p. 147, cited in Kemper, *Studying Islam*, p. 12.

12   Kemper, *Studying Islam*, p. 9.

13   Ibid., p. 11.

14   Michael Kemper, 'The changing images of Jihad leaders: Shamil and Abd al-Qadir in Daghistani and Algerian historical writing', *Nova Religio: The Journal of Alternative and Emergent Religions* 11/2 (2007), p. 34 [28–58].

15   Michael Kemper, 'The North Caucasian Khâlidiyya: Historiographical problems', *Journal of the History of Sufism* 5 (2008), p. 165 [151–68].

16   Ibid., p. 166.

17   Carl Ernst, 'Sufism: History, Politics and Culture', *Sufi: Journal of Mystical Philosophy and Practice* (Winter 2014), p. 35.

18   Hamid Algar, 'Devotional practices of the Khâlidî Naqshbandîs of Ottoman Turkey', in Raymond Lifchez and Ayla Esen Algar (eds), *The Dervish Lodge: Architecture, Art, and Sufism in Ottoman Turkey* (Berkeley: University of California Press, 1992), p. 224 [209–227].

19   This is a phrase my friend Irfan Basik used when advising me about this subject.

20   Gülsen Devre, 'The roots of political activism and modernity within the Naqshbandi sufi order and its enduring ideological influence on contemporary political Islamists in Turkey' (MA Thesis, University of Amsterdam, 2012), p. 52.

21   Mehmed Zahid Kotku, *Nefsin Terbiyesi* (Istanbul: Seha Neşriyat, 1984), p. 128. Cited in Emin Yaşar Demirci, *Modernisation, Religion and Politics in Turkey: The Case of the Iskenderpaşa Community* (Istanbul: Insan Publications, 2008), p. 151.

22   Demirci, *Modernisation, Religion*, p. 157.

23   Halil Necatioğlu, 'Alimin Tarışılmaz Üstünlüğü', *Islam* 8/87 (1990), pp. 5–6. Cited in Demirci, *Modernisation, Religion*, p. 160. Coşan's pen-name is Halil Necatioğlu.

24   Mehmed Zahid Kotku, *Yeni Dönemde Yeni Görevler* (Istanbul: Seha Neşriyat, 1993), pp. 95–6. Cited in Demirci, *Modernisation, Religion*, p. 174.
25   Fulya Atacan, 'Explaining religious politics at the crossroad: AKP-SP', *Turkish Studies* 6/2 (2005), p. 191 [187–99].
26   Devre, 'The roots of political activism', p. 40, fn 263.
27   Ibid., p. 41.
28   As I edit this chapter, the Turkish government is seeking to extradite Fethullah Gülen from the United States as 'a leader of a criminal organization' (*Daily Sabah*, 29 December 2014). Available at http://www.dailysabah.com/politics/2014/12/29/first-step-taken-towards-securing-gulens-red-notice (accessed 6 December 2015). For more on the Gülen movement see M. Hakan Yavuz, *Toward an Islamic Enlightenment: The Gülen Movement* (Oxford: Oxford University Press, 2013).
29   Devre, 'The roots of political activism', p. 54.
30   Babou, *Fighting the Greater Jihad*, p. 5
31   Ibid., p. 59.
32   Ibid., p. 63.
33   Ibid., p. 100.
34   Ibid., p. 101. There are many instances where Bamba criticized his brother and many others of falling far short of proper behaviour.
35   Ibid., p. 154.
36   Leonardo A. Villalón, *Islamic Society and State Power in Senegal: Disciples and Citizens in Fatick* (Cambridge: Cambridge University Press, 1995), p. 121.
37   Ibid., p. 145.
38   Ibid., p. 146.

5 The Relationship between the Shaykh and the Seeker

1   *Shaykh* and *pir* have a root meaning of 'elder' in Arabic and Persian respectively. Shaykh is also used as a title for religious scholars.
2   The (book: verse) notations from Mawlana Jalaluddin Rumi's *Mathnawi* are from the Nicholson version, easily available in pdf online. The translations are by the author.
3   The next line reads, 'It is not about the rosary, prayer rug or sufi robe.' He is referring to the outwardly pious people who serve themselves more than they serve others. One English translation of Sa'di's *Bustan* is available at http://sadishenasi.ir/Upload/file/The%20Bustan%20of%20Sadi%5B1%5D.pdf (accessed 14 December 2014). This quote is on page 19 and I have re-translated parts of it.
4   John J. Curry, *The Transformation of Muslim Mystical Thought in the Ottoman Empire: The Rise of the Halveti Order, 1350–1650*. (Edinburgh: Edinburgh University Press, 2010), p. 241.
5   Technically holarchies.
6   For an in-depth rendition of this transformative meeting see Franklin D. Lewis, *Rumi: Past and Present, East and West: The Life, Teachings, and Poetry of Jalal al-Din Rumi* (Oxford: Oneworld Publications, 2000).
7   Arthur F. Buehler, *Revealed Grace: The Juristic Sufism of Ahmad Sirhindi (1564–1624)* (Louisville, KY: Fons Vitae, 2011), Letter 287.
8   Buehler, *Sufi Heirs of the Prophet: The Indian Naqshbandiyya and the Rise of the Mediating Shaykh* (Columbia, SC: University of South Carolina Press, 1998), p. 152.

9   For an excellent translation of the discourses of Nizamuddin see Bruce B. Lawrence, *Nizamuddin Auliya: Morals for the Heart* (Mahwah, NJ: Paulist Press, 1992).

10   From author's fieldwork, 1986–2000.

11   'Abd ur-Rahman Jami, *Lawa'ih, A Treatise On Sufism*, trans. E. H. Whinfield and M. M. Kazvini (London: Royal Asiatic Society, 1914), p. 2. In a more modern translation of Jami's *Lawa'ih* by William Chittick, 'Make these imaginal forms into the mirror of Your beauty's self-disclosures, not the cause of veiling and distance', in Sachiko Murata, *Chinese Gleams of Sufi Light: Wang Tai-Yu's Great Learning of the Pure and Real* (Albany, NY: State University of New York Press, 2000), p. 132. This latter translation is from the sufi vocabulary of Jami, not a supplication the Prophet would have made.

12   Buehler, *Sufi Heirs*, p. 2.

13   Ibid., p. 144, fn 67.

6 Sufi Varieties of Transformative Practice: Transformation of the Ego-Self

1   Jack Kornfield's paraphrase of the original Abhaya Sutta, 'And who is the person who, subject to death, is not afraid or in terror of death?'. Abhaya Sutta available at http://www.accesstoinsight.org/tipitaka/an/an04/an04.184.than.html (accessed 3 November 2015). Jack Kornfield, *Buddha's Little Instruction Book* (New York: Bantam Books, 1994), p. 88.

2   Badi' uz-Zaman Furuzanfar, *Ahadith-i Mathnawi*, 3rd edn (Tehran: Amir Kabir, 1983), p. 116.

3   Sri Mungala Venkataramiah, *Talks with Sri Ramana Maharshi*, 7th edn (Tiruvannamalai: Sri Ramanasramam, 1984), p. 160.

4   This useful nuance of 'chanted verse' comes from Bruce B. Lawrence, 'The early Chishti approach to Sama', in M. Israel and N. K. Wagle (eds), *Islamic Society and Culture: Essays in Honour of Professor Aziz Ahmad* (Delhi: Manohar, 1983), p. 72.

5   Carl W. Ernst and Bruce B. Lawrence, *Sufi Martyrs of Love* (New York: Palgrave, 2002), p. 37.

6   A quote from al-Qushayri (d. 1072) in Carl Ernst, 'The theory and practice of Sama' (listening to music) in the sufi circle of Burhan al-Din Gharib', in Proceedings of the 1987 Conference on Amir Khusrau. Available at www.http://aksa.us/akconference.html (accessed 22 October 2015). Unpaginated.

7   Ernst and Lawrence, *Sufi Martyrs of Love*, p. 38.

8   Nicolaas Biegman, *Living Sufism: Sufi Rituals in the Middle East and the Balkans* (Cairo: American University in Cairo Press, 2009), pp. 34–6. This book has many colour photos of sufis doing various forms of remembrance of God.

9   Ibid., pp. 75–8.

10   Ibid., pp. 79–80.

11   Ernst and Lawrence, *Sufi Martyrs of Love*, pp. 28–33.

12   For details see Arthur F. Buehler, *Sufi Heirs of the Prophet: The Indian Naqshbandiyya and the Rise of the Mediating Shaykh* (Columbia, SC: University of South Carolina Press), 1998.

13   Lest anyone think that Naqshbandis or other sufis have a monopoly on the system of subtle centres, Chinese Taoists have known for thousands of years about subtle centres (*dantiens*), the connection between the heart and the point between the middle of the eyes (the *yintang*) and much, much more.

14   Personal communication (2 March 2014).

15   There is a video of the turning ritual available at http://mevlanafoundation.com/

mevlevi_order_en.html that shows this line and the centre pivot place for the shaykh (accessed 2 September 2013).

16 Metin And, 'The Mevlana ceremony [Turkey]', *The Drama Review* 21/3 (1977), p. 84 [83–94].

17 His website is a useful resource for Rumi's *Mathnawi*, *Diwan*, and a variety of Mevlevi topics. Available at www.dar-al-masnavi.org (accessed 3 November 2015). I have relied on his personal communications and website for this section.

18 Available at http://mevlanafoundation.com/mevlevi_order_en.html, at the end of the page (accessed 2 September 2013).

7 Two Contemporary Women Sufi Teachers

1 See Shakina Reinhertz, *Women Called to the Path of Rumi: The Way of the Whirling Dervish* (Prescott, AZ: Hohm Press, 2001). Women's participation in the Mevlevi rituals seems to have waned in nineteenth-century Turkey.

Afterword: Future Scenarios for Sufi Practice – Guesses for the Twenty-first Century

1 See Nicholas Carr, *The Shallows: What the Internet Is Doing to Our Brains* (New York: W. W. Norton & Company, 2011), p. 220.

2 One exception is Otto Scharmer and Katrin Kaufer, *Leading from the Emerging Future: From Ego-System to Eco-System Economies* (San Francisco, CA: Berrett-Koehler Publishers, 2013), pp. 18, 67–9. They make it appear, however, that increasing awareness is almost as easy as changing clothes!

3 See the section entitled, 'Bringing awareness to contemplative studies' at the end of the chapter in Arthur F. Buehler, 'Sufi contemplation: 'Abdullah Shah's *Suluk-i Mujaddidiyya*', in Louis Komjathy (ed.), *Contemplative Literature: A Comparative Sourcebook on Meditation and Contemplative Prayer* (Albany, NY: State University of New York Press, 2015), pp. 324–27, for a brief summary of the study of transformative practice in the academy.

4 At least one exception is John Welwood, *Toward a Psychology of Awakening: Buddhism, Psychotherapy, and the Path of Personal and Spiritual Transformation* (Boston, MA: Shambhala, 2002). It is rare to find a scholar of sufism who uses the term 'transpersonal'. Transpersonal psychology as a concept has not yet arrived in the wider area of sufi studies.

5 For a discussion of how the study of sufism could be brought from its present cognocentric focus to something significantly more meaningful, see Arthur F. Buehler, 'Researching sufism in the 21st century: Expanding the context of inquiry', in Clinton Bennett (ed.), *The Continuum Companion Volume on Islam* (London: Continuum, 2013), pp. 93–118.

SUGGESTED READING

If you are reading this section, then you are not the typical sufi-book purchaser. Of the top 20 best-selling Amazon books on sufism at the time of writing (29 August 2015), only two are on this list. Therein lies a lesson. That does not mean, however, that *you* will like all the books below, so check before purchasing.

Introductory texts

The classic introductory text is Annemarie Schimmel's *Mystical Dimensions of Islam*. Those who like poetry will appreciate her treatment of the subject. A poetic follow up is her *A Two-Colored Brocade: The Imagery of Persian Poetry*. Carl Ernst's *Sufism: An Introduction to the Mystical Tradition of Islam* (formerly, *The Shambhala Guide to Sufism*) provides many new perspectives. The diversity of sufism around the world has been well covered by Nile Green in his *Sufism: A Global History*. For history buffs there is Ahmet Karamustafa's *Sufism: The Formative Period* and Alexander Knysh's ironically entitled *Islamic Mysticism: A Short History* (of 358 pages). Jack Renard's *Tales of God's Friends*, shares a wide variety of stories about the holy people of Islam, most of whom are pious sufis. Kabir Helminski's *The Knowing Heart* is a non-academic introduction written by a sufi teacher.

SUGGESTED READING

Translations of original sufi texts

There is a lot to choose from here and these are some starting points. Michael Sells's *Early Islamic Mysticism* gives the reader a taste of a wide variety of texts. The best Rumi translation is probably the *Spiritual Verses* by Alan Williams. If you do not mind Victorian English, then Reynold Nicholson's accurate but wooden translations are fine. If you are willing to sacrifice a lot for rhymed poetry, then Jawid Mojaddedi is your translator of choice for Rumi. *Me and Rumi: The Autobiography of Shams-i Tabrizi,* Rumi's teacher, is recommended for Rumi fans.

For the hardcore, Ibn al-'Arabi (only mentioned in passing in this book), and his *magum opus*, the *Meccan Revelations*, is partially translated into English by William C. Chittick in *The Sufi Path of Knowledge* and *The Self-Disclosure of God*. Probably the best translation of Ibn al-'Arabi's *Ringstones of Wisdom* (usually translated as *Bezels of Wisdom*) is by Caner Dagli. Peter Avery has translated 'Attar's *The Speech of the Birds*, a long poetic metaphor of the sufi path. Nahid Angha's *Stations of the Sufi Path* is a classic text that is now accessible to English readers. The late Muhtar Holland has translated many books by 'Abdulqadir al-Jilani, the founder figure of the Qadiriyya. Bruce Lawrence's translation of Nizamuddin Auliya's discourses, *Nizamuddin Auliya: Morals for the Heart,* gives you a chance to listen in on sufi conversations almost as if you were actually at the feet of the shaykh in fourteenth-century Delhi.

On specific sufi lineages and people

Carl Ernst and Bruce Lawrence's *Sufi Martyrs of Love* is quite accessible and is the best starting point for learning more about the Chishtiyya. More technical, but worth the effort, are Erik Ohlander's *Sufism in an Age of Transition* and John Curry's *The Transformation of Muslim Mystical Thought in the Ottoman Empire,* which deal with the Suhrawardiyya and Helvetiyya respectively. Itzchak Weismann's *The Naqshbandiyya* is for history buffs. These last three books are expensive, but should be available in any university library. Dina Le Gall's *A Culture of Sufism* provides a fascinating window on the Ottoman Naqshbandis. For the Muridiyya, Anta Babou's *Fighting the Greater Jihad* gives the reader a feel for Amadu Bamba and Senegal. Allen Roberts et al., *A Saint in the City: Sufi Arts of Urban Senegal* takes the reader to Senegal with colour visuals (as you have seen in black and white) and a text to match. Louis Massignon's four-volume work on al-Hallaj is a masterpiece. *Hallaj: Mystic and Martyr*, an abridged version, is a place to begin. For information on Ibn al-'Arabi, highly recommended is Michel Chodkiewicz's *An Ocean Without Shore* and Claude Addas's biography of Ibn al-'Arabi, *Quest for the Red Sulphur*. Frank Lewis's *Rumi: Past and Present* is the most comprehensive authority on Rumi in English.

Other books on sufism

A travel diary written while visiting blissed out people at sufi shrines, Jürgen Frembgen's *At the Shrine of the Red Sufi* is a genre unto itself. Nicolaas Biegman travels in a more sober crowd and takes lots of pictures in his *Living Sufism: Sufi Rituals in the Middle East and the Balkans*. Michaela Özelsel has written about her sufi-retreat experiences in *Forty Days*. For sufi transformative theory among the Jerrahis, see Robert Frager, *Heart, Self, and Soul*. Inayat Khan's *Mysticism of Sound and Music* shows how music can be transformational. For the sufi Islamization of Bengal, Richard Eaton's *The Rise of Islam and the Bengal Frontier* is still the best on the subject. Devin DeWeese's coverage of sufis facilitating conversion to Islam in Central Asia, *Islamization and Native Religion in the Golden Horde: Baba Tükles and Conversion to Islam*, is another classic. Sufi poetry does not come out very well in English unless one is a gifted translator so I am hesitant to recommend anything. One gem is the bilingual Sultan Bahu's *Death Before Dying*, translated by Jamal Elias. For the names of God as sufi medicine to address contemporary psycho-spiritual concerns, see *Physicians of the Heart: A Sufi View of the Ninety-nine Names of Allah*.

BIBLIOGRAPHY

Abou El Fadl, Khalid M., *The Great Theft: Wrestling Islam from the Extremists*. San Francisco: HarperCollins, 2005.

Abu-Manneh, Butrus, 'Khalwa and Râbita in the Khâlidî suborder', in Marc Gaborieau, Alexandre Popovic and Thierry Zarcone (eds), *Naqshbandis: cheminements et situation actuelle d'un ordre mystique musulman*. Istanbul/Paris: Éditions Isis, 1990.

Addas, Claude, *Quest for the Red Sulphur*, translated from the French by Peter Kingsley. Cambridge: The Islamic Texts Society, 1993.

Algar, Hamid, 'Devotional practices of the Khâlidî Naqshbandîs of Ottoman Turkey', in Raymond Lifchez and Ayla Esen Algar (eds), *The Dervish Lodge: Architecture, Art, and Sufism in Ottoman Turkey*. Berkeley: University of California Press, 1992, pp. 209–27.

Amuli, Haydar, *Jilwah-i dildar: tarjamah-i Jami' al-asrar wa-manba' al-anwar*, translated from the Arabic by Yusuf Ibrahimian Amuli. Tehran: Nashr-i Risanish, 2009.

And, Metin, 'The Mevlana ceremony [Turkey]', *The Drama Review* 21/3 (1977), pp. 83–94.

Angha, Nahid, *Stations of the Sufi Path: The 'One Hundred Fields' (Sad Maydan) of Abdullah Ansari of Herat*. London: Archetype, 2010.

Anon., *'Ilm at-tasawwuf*. Nasrollah Pourjavady and Mohammed Soori (eds). Tehran: Iranian Institute of Philosophy, 2012.

Arberry, A. J. (trans.), *The Discourses of Rumi*. London: Curzon Press, 1993.

Atacan, Fulya, 'Explaining religious politics at the crossroad: AKP-SP', *Turkish Studies* 6/2 (2005), pp. 187–99.

Atasoy, Nurhan, *Derviş Çeyizi*. Istanbul: T. C. Kültür Baklanliği, 2000.

Avery, Peter (trans.), *The Speech of the Birds*. Cambridge: The Islamic Texts Society, 1998.

Babou, Cheikh Anta, *Fighting the Greater Jihad: Amadu Bamba and the Founding of the Muridiyya of Senegal, 1853–1913*. Athens, OH: Ohio University Press, 2007.

Baig, Ubaidullah and A. A. K. Brohi, *Journey into Light: An Instant Guide to Devotional Tours*. Islamabad: Pakistan Tourism Development Corporation, 1985.

Biegman, Nicolaas, *Living Sufism: Sufi Rituals in the Middle East and the Balkans*. Cairo: American University in Cairo Press, 2009.

Böwering, Gerhard, *The Mystical Vision of Existence in Classical Islam: The Qur'ānic*

Hermeneutics of the Ṣūfī Sahl At-Tustarī (d. 283/896). New York: Walter de Gruyter, 1980.

Buehler, Arthur F., *Sufi Heirs of the Prophet: The Indian Naqshbandiyya and the Rise of the Mediating Shaykh*. Columbia, SC: University of South Carolina Press, 1998.

——— *Revealed Grace: The Juristic Sufism of Ahmad Sirhindi (1564–1624)*. Louisville, KY: Fons Vitae, 2011.

——— 'Researching sufism in the 21st century: Expanding the context of inquiry', in Clinton Bennett (ed.), *The Continuum Companion Volume on Islam*. London: Continuum, 2013, pp. 93–118.

——— 'Sufi contemplation: 'Abdullah Shah's *Suluk-i Mujaddidiyya*', in Louis Komjathy (ed.), *Contemplative Literature: A Comparative Sourcebook on Meditation and Contemplative Prayer*. Albany, NY: State University of New York Press, 2015, pp. 307–57.

Bulliet, Richard W., *Conversion to Islam in the Medieval Period: An Essay in Quantitative History*. Cambridge, MA: Harvard University Press, 1979.

Carr, Nicholas G., *The Shallows: What the Internet Is Doing to Our Brains*. New York: W. W. Norton & Company, 2011.

Chabbi, Jacqueline, 'Remarques sur le développement historique des mouvements ascétiques et mystiques au Khurasan: IIIe/IXe siècle –IVe/Xe siècle', *Studia Islamica*, 46 (1977), pp. 5–72.

Chelhod, Joseph, 'La *baraka* chez les Arabes ou l'infuence bienfaisante du sacré'. *Revue de l'Histoire des Religions* 148/1 (1955), pp. 68–88.

Chih, Rashida, 'What is a sufi order? Revisiting the concept through the case study of the Khalwatiyya in contemporary Egypt', in Martin van Bruinessen and Julia Day Howell (eds), *Sufism and the 'Modern' in Islam*. London: I.B.Tauris, 2007, pp. 21–38.

Chittick, William C., *The Sufi Path of Knowledge: Ibn al-'Arabi's Metaphysics of Imagination*. Albany, NY: State University of New York Press, 1989.

——— *The Self-Disclosure of God: Principles of Ibn al-'Arabi's Cosmology*. London: I.B.Tauris, 2006.

Chodkiewicz, Michel, *An Ocean Without Shore*, translated from the French by David Streight. Albany, NY: State University of New York Press, 1993.

Cornell, Rkia E. (trans.), *Early Sufi Women: Dhikr an-niswa al-muta 'abbidat as-sufiyyat*. Louisville, KY: Fons Vitae, 1999.

Crapanzano, Vincent, *The Hamadsha: A Study in Moroccan Ethnopsychiatry*. Berkeley, CA: University of California Press, 1981.

Curry, John J., *The Transformation of Muslim Mystical Thought in the Ottoman Empire: The Rise of the Halveti Order, 1350–1650*. Edinburgh: Edinburgh University Press, 2010.

Demirci, Emin Yaşar, *Modernisation, Religion and Politics in Turkey: The Case of the Iskenderpaşa Community*. Istanbul: Insan Publications, 2008.

Devre, Gülsen, 'The roots of political activism and modernity within the Naqshbandi sufi order and its enduring ideological influence on contemporary political Islamists in Turkey'. MA Thesis, University of Amsterdam, 2012.

DeWeese, Devin, *Islamization and Native Religion in the Golden Horde: Baba Tükles and Conversion to Islam in Historical and Epic Tradition*. Pennsylvania: The Pennsylvania State University Press, 1994.

——— 'The legitimization of Bahā ad-Dīn Naqshband', *Asiatische Studien* 50/2 (2006), pp. 261–305.

——— 'Succession protocols and the Early Khwajagani Schism in the *Maslak al-'ārifīn*', *Journal of Islamic Studies* 22/1 (2011), pp. 1–35.

—— 'Spiritual practice and corporate identity in medieval sufi communities of Iran, Central Asia, and India: The Khalvatī/'Ishqī/Shaṭṭārī continuum', in Steven E. Lindquist (ed.), *Religion and Identity in South Asia and Beyond: Essays in Honor of Patrick Olivelle*. London: Anthem Press, 2011, pp. 251–300.

Eaton, Richard, *The Rise of Islam and the Bengal Frontier, 1204–1760*. Berkeley, CA: University of California Press, 1993.

Elias, Jamal J., *On Wings of Diesel: Trucks, Identity and Culture in Pakistan*. London: Oneworld Publications, 2011.

Ernst, Carl W., *The Shambhala Guide to Sufism*. Boston: Shambhala Publications Inc., 1997.

—— *Sufism: An Introduction to the Mystical Tradition of Islam* (formerly entitled *The Shambhala Guide to Sufism*). Boston: Shambhala, 2011.

—— 'Sufism: History, Politics and Culture', *Sufi: Journal of Mystical Philosophy and Practice* (Winter 2014), pp. 28–35.

—— 'The theory and practice of Sama' (listening to music) in the sufi circle of Burhan al-Din Gharib', in Proceedings of the 1987 Conference on Amir Khusrau. Available at www.http://aksa.us/akconference.html (accessed 22 October 2015).

Ernst, Carl W. and Bruce B. Lawrence, *Sufi Martyrs of Love*. New York: Palgrave, 2002.

Fox, James J., 'Wali: the first preachers of Islam in Java', in James J. Fox (ed.), *Indonesian Heritage*. 10 vols. Singapore: Archipelago Press, 1996–8.

Frager, Robert, *Heart, Self, and Soul*. Wheaton, IL: Quest Books, 1999.

Frembgen, Jürgen Wasim, *At the Shrine of the Red Sufi: Five Days and Nights on Pilgrimage in Pakistan*. Oxford: Oxford University Press, 2012.

Furuzanfar, Badi' uz-Zaman, *Ahadith-i Mathnawi*, 3rd edn. Tehran: Amir Kabir, 1983.

Green, Nile, *Sufism: A Global History*. New York: Wiley-Blackwell, 2012.

Halman, Talat Sait and Metin And, *Mevlana Celaleddin Rumi and the Whirling Dervishes*. Istanbul: Dost, 1992.

Helminski, Kabir, *The Knowing Heart: A Sufi Path of Transformation*. Boston, MA: Shambhala Publications Inc., 1999.

Hoffman, Valerie J., *Sufism, Mystics, and Saints in Modern Egypt*. Columbia, SC: University of South Carolina Press, 1995.

Honerkamp, Kenneth Lee, 'Sufi foundations of the ethics of social life in Islam' in Virginia Gray Henry-Blakemore (ed.), *Voices of Islam*. 5 vols. Westport, CT: Praeger Publishers, 2007, 3:180–96.

Hongrie, Georges de, *Des Turcs: Traité sur les moeurs, les coutumes et la perfidie des Turcs*, translated from Latin by Joël Schnapp. Toulouse, France: Anarcharsis Éditions, 2007.

Howell, Julia Day, 'Sufism and the Indonesian Islamic revival', *The Journal of Asian Studies*, 60/3 (2001), pp. 701–29.

—— 'Urban heirs of Ibn al-'Arabi and the defence of religious pluralism in Indonesia', *Australian Religious Studies Review* 18/2 (2005), pp. 197–209.

—— 'Sufism and Neo-Sufism in Indonesia today', *Review of Indonesian and Malaysian Affairs* 46/2 (2012), pp. 1–24.

Hujwiri, 'Ali b. 'Uthman, *The Kashf al-mahjub: The Oldest Persian Treatise on Sufism*, translated by Reynold A. Nicholson. London: Luzac, 1911.

Ibn al-'Arabi, *The Ringstones of Wisdom (Fusus al-Hikam)*, translated by Caner K. Dagli. Chicago, IL: Kazi Publications, 2004.

Işın, Ekrem (ed.), *The Dervishes of Sovereignty, The Sovereignty of Dervishes: The Mevlevi Order in Istanbul*. Istanbul: Istanbul Research Institute, 2007.

James, William, *A Pluralistic Universe*, Fredson Bowers (ed.), Cambridge, MA: Harvard University Press, 1977.

Jamhari, 'In the center of meaning: *Ziarah* tradition in Java', *Studia Islamika* 7/1 (2000), pp. 54–90.

—— 'The meaning interpreted: The concept of *Barakah* in *Ziarah*', *Studia Islamika* 8/1 (2001), pp. 87–128.

Jami, 'Abd ur-Rahman, *Lawa'ih, A Treatise on Sufism*, translated by E. H. Whinfield and M. M. Kazvini. London: Royal Asiatic Society, 1914.

Jilani, 'Abdulqadir al-, *Secrets of Secrets*. Translated by Muhtar Holland. Fort Lauderdale, FL: Al-Baz Publshing, 2000.

Jonge, Huub de, 'Pilgrimages and local Islam on Java', *Studia Islamika* 5/2 (1998), pp. 1–25.

Karamustafa, Ahmet T., *God's Unruly Friends: Dervish Groups in the Islamic Later Middle Period, 1200–1550*. London: Oneworld, 2006.

—— *Sufism: The Formative Period*. Edinburgh: Edinburgh University Press, 2007.

Kemper, Michael, 'The changing images of Jihad Leaders: Shamil and Abd al-Qadir in Daghistani and Algerian historical writing', *Nova Religio: The Journal of Alternative and Emergent Religions* 11/2, 34 (2007), pp. 28–58.

—— 'The North Caucasian Khâlidiyya: Historiographical problems', *Journal of the History of Sufism* 5 (2008), pp. 151–68.

—— *Studying Islam in the Soviet Union*. Amsterdam: Amsterdam University Press, 2009, pp. 1–27.

Khan, Inayat, *The Mysticism of Sound and Music*. Boston, MA: Shambhala Publications Inc., 1991.

Kinberg, Leah, 'What is meant by *Zuhd*?', *Studia Islamica* 61 (1985), pp. 27–44.

Knysh, Alexander D., *Islamic Mysticism: A Short History*. Leiden: Brill, 2000.

Kornfield, Jack, *Buddha's Little Instruction Book*. New York: Bantam Books, 1994.

Kuhn, Thomas S., *The Structure of Scientific Revolutions*. Chicago: University of Chicago Press, 1996.

Lawrence, Bruce B., 'The early Chishti approach to Sama', in M. Israel and N. K. Wagle (eds), *Islamic Society and Culture: Essays in Honour of Professor Aziz Ahmad*. Delhi: Manohar, 1983.

—— (trans.), *Nizamuddin Auliya: Morals for the Heart*. Mahwah, NJ: Paulist Press, 1992.

Le Gall, Dina, *A Culture of Sufism*. Albany, NY: State University of New York Press, 2004.

Lewis, Franklin D., *Rumi: Past and Present, East and West: The Life, Teachings, and Poetry of Jalal al-Din Rumi*. Oxford: Oneworld Publications, 2000.

Lewis, Philip, *Pirs, Shrines and Pakistani Islam*. Rawalpindi: Christian Study Centre, 1985.

Massignon, Louis, *The Passion of al-Hallaj: Mystic and Martyr of Islam*, translated by Herbert Masorf. 4 vols. Princeton: Princeton University Press, 1982.

—— *Hallaj: Mystic and Martyr*. Translated by Herbert Mason. Princeton: Princeton University Press, 1994.

—— *Essay on the Origins of the Technical Language of Islamic Mysticism*, translated by Benjamin Clark. Notre Dame, IN: University of Notre Dame Press, 1997.

Mayer, Farhana (trans.), *Spiritual Gems: The Mystical Qur'an Commentary Ascribed to Ja'far al-Sadiq (d. 148/765) as Contained in Sulami's Haqaiq al-Tafsir from the Text of Paul Nwyia*. Louisville, KY: Fons Vitae, 2011.

Mayne, Peter, *Saints of Sind*. London: J. Murray, 1956.

Meyer, Wali Ali, Bilal Hyde, Faisal Muqaddam, Shabda Kahn, *Physicians of the Heart: A Sufi View of the Ninety-nine Names of Allah*. San Francisco: Sufi Ruhaniat International, 2011.

Mille, Richard de, *Castaneda's Journey: The Power and the Allegory*. Santa Barbara, CA: Capra Press, 1976.

Mittermaier, Amira, '(Re)imagining space, dreams and saint shrines in Egypt', in Georg Stauth and Samuli Schielke (eds), *Dimensions of Locality: Muslim Saints, Their Place and Space*. London: Transaction Publishers, 2008, pp. 47–66.

Mourad, Suleiman, *Early Islam between Myth and History: Al-Hasan al-Basri (d. 110H/728CE) and the Formation of his Legacy in Classical Islamic Scholarship*. Leiden: Brill, 2006.

Muhammad Ibn-i Munawwar, *The Secrets of God's Mystical Oneness*, translated from the Persian by John O'Kane. Costa Mesa, CA: Mazda Publishers, 1992.

Mujeeb, M., *The Indian Muslims*. London: George Allen and Unwin, 1967.

Murata, Sachiko, *Chinese Gleams of Sufi Light: Wang Tai-Yu's Great Learning of the Pure and Real*. Albany, NY: State University of New York Press, 2000.

Muslim ibn al-Hajjaj, *Sahih Muslim*, translated by Nasiruddin al-Khattab. 7 vols. Riyadh: Dar al-Salam, 2007.

Nasr Hamid Abu Zayd, 'Towards understanding the Qur'an's worldview: An autobiographical reflection', in Gabriel Said Reynolds (ed.), *New Perspectives on the Qur'ān: The Qur'ān in its Historical Context 2*. Oxford: Routledge, 2011, pp. 47–87.

Nguyen, Martin, *Sufi Master and Qur'an Scholar: Abu'l-Qasim al-Qushayri and the Lata'if al-Isharat*. Oxford: Oxford University Press, 2012.

Nicholson, Reynold (ed. and trans.), *The Mathnawi of Jalalu'ddin Rumi*. 3 vols. Cambridge: Cambridge University Press, 1971.

Nwyia, Paul, *Exégèse coranique et langage mystique. Nouvel essai sur le lexique technique des mystiques musulmans*. Beirut: Dar al-Machreq, 1970.

Ohlander, Erik S., *Sufism in an Age of Transition: 'Umar al-Suhrawardi and the Rise of the Islamic Mystical Brotherhoods*. Leiden: Brill, 2008.

Ömür, E. Melek Cevahiroğlu, 'The sufi orders in a modernizing empire: 1808–1876', *Tarih* 1/1 (2009), pp. 70–93.

Özelsel, Michaela M., *Forty Days*. Berkeley, CA: Shambhala, 2002.

Percy, Walter, *Lost in the Cosmos*. New York: Farrar, Straus and Giroux, 1983.

Picken, Gavin, *Spiritual Purification in Islam: The Life and Works of al-Muhāsibī*. New York: Routledge, 2011.

Reinhertz, Shakina, *Women Called to the Path of Rumi: The Way of the Whirling Dervish*. Prescott, AZ: Hohm Press, 2001.

Renard, Jack (ed.), *Tales of God's Friends: Islamic Hagiography in Translation*. Berkeley, CA: University of California Press, 2009.

Roberts, Allen F., Mary Nooter Roberts, Gassa Armenian and Osmane Gueye, *A Saint in the City: Sufi Arts of Urban Senegal*. Los Angeles: UCLA Fowler Museum, 2003.

Rumi, Jalaluddin, *The Masnavi: Book One*. Translated by Javid Mojaddedi. Oxford: Oxford University Press, 2008.

Scharmer, C. Otto and Katrin Kaufer, *Leading from the Emerging Future: From Ego-System to Eco-System Economies*. San Francisco, CA: Berrett-Koehler Publishers, 2013.

Schimmel, Annemarie, *Mystical Dimensions of Islam*. Chapel Hill, NC: University of North Carolina Press, 1975.

—— 'A Life of Learning', ACLS Occasional Paper no. 21, 1993. www.acls.org/Publications/OP/Haskins/1993_AnnemarieSchimmel.pdf (accessed 26 October 2015).

Sells, Michael, *Early Islamic Mysticism*. Mahwah, NJ: Paulist Press, 1996.

Sheldrake, Rupert, *The Sense of Being Stared At: And Other Unexplained Powers of Human Minds*. Rochester, VT: Park Street Press, 2013.

Sidky, M. Homayun, 'Malang, Sufis, and Mystics: An ethnographic and historical study of Shamanism in Afghanistan', *Asian Folklore Studies* 49/2 (1990), pp. 275–301.

Srivastava, Kumkum, *The Wandering Sufis: Qalandars and Their Path*. New Delhi: Aryan Books International, 2009.

Sulami, Abu 'Abd al-Rahman al-, *A Collection of Sufi Rules of Conduct*, translated by Elena Biagi. Cambridge, UK: Islamic Texts Society, 2010.

Tabrizi, Shams-i, *Me and Rumi: The Autobiography of Shams-i Tabrizi*, translated by William Chittick. Louisville, KY: Fons Vitae, 2004.

Toussulis, Yannis, *Sufism and the Way of Blame: Hidden Sources of a Sacred Psychology*. Wheaton, IL: Quest Books, 2011.

Turner, Victor, *The Ritual Process: Structure and Anti-Structure*. Ithaca, NY: Cornell University Press, 1977.

Tustari, Sahl b. 'Abd Allāh al-, *Tafsīr al-Tustarī*, translated by Annabel and Ali Keeler. Louisville, KY: Fons Vitae, 2011.

Tweedie, Irina, *Daughter of Fire: A Diary of a Spiritual Training with a Sufi Master*. Point Reyes, CA: Golden Sufi Center, 1995.

Venkataramiah, Sri Mungala, *Talks with Sri Ramana Maharshi*. 7th edn. Tiruvannamalai: Sri Ramanasramam, 1984.

Villalón, Leonardo A., *Islamic Society and State Power in Senegal: Disciples and Citizens in Fatick*. Cambridge: Cambridge University Press, 1995.

Watts, Alan, *The Book: On the Taboo Against Knowing Who You Are*. New York: Vintage Books, 1989.

Weismann, Itzchak, *Taste of Modernity: Sufism, Salafiyya, and Arabism in Late Ottoman Damascus*. Leiden: Brill, 2001.

────── *The Naqshbandiyya: Orthodoxy and Activism in a Worldwide Sufi Tradition*. London: Routledge, 2007.

Welwood, John, *Toward a Psychology of Awakening: Buddhism, Psychotherapy, and the Path of Personal and Spiritual Transformation*. Boston, MA: Shambhala, 2002.

Williams, Alan (trans. and ed.), *Spiritual Verses: The Jalaluddin Rumi*. London: Penguin Classics, 2006.

Windsor-Smith, Barry, *Opus, Volume Two*. Seattle, WA: Fantagraphics Books Inc., 2000.

Yavuz, M. Hakan, *Toward an Islamic Enlightenment: The Gülen Movement*. New York: Oxford University Press, 2013.

Zamhari, Arif, *Rituals of Islamic Spirituality: A Study of Majlis Dhikr Groups in East Java*. Canberra, Australia: ANU E Press, 2000.

Zayed, Ahmed A., 'Saints (*awliya*'), public places and modernity in Egypt', in Georg Stauth and Samuli Schielke (eds.), *Dimensions of Locality: Muslim Saints, their Place and Space*. London: Transaction Publishers, 2008, pp. 103–23.

INDEX